Injury and Asthma Among Youth Less Than 20 Years of Age on Minority Farm Operations in the United States, 2000

Volume I: Racial Minority National Data

John R. Myers, Kitty J. Hendricks,
E. Michael Goldcamp, and Larry A. Layne

DEPARTMENT OF HEALTH AND HUMAN SERVICES
Centers for Disease Control and Prevention
National Institute for Occupational Safety and Health

July, 2005

DISCLAIMER

Mention of the name of any company or product does not constitute endorsement by the National Institute for Occupational Safety and Health. In addition, citations to Web sites do not constitute NIOSH endorsement of the sponsoring organizations or their programs or products. Furthermore, NIOSH is not responsible for the content of these Web sites.

This document is in the public domain and may be freely copied or reprinted.

To receive documents or other information about occupational safety and health topics, contact NIOSH at

Publications Dissemination, EID
National Institute for Occupational Safety and Health
4676 Columbia Parkway
Cincinnati, OH 45226-1998

Telephone: 1-800-35-NIOSH (1-800-356-4674)
Fax: 1-513-533-8573
E-mail: pubstaft@cdc.gov

or visit the NIOSH Web site at **www.cdc.gov/niosh**

DHHS (NIOSH) Publication No. 2005-147

FOREWORD

In 1996, NIOSH began the Childhood Agricultural Injury Prevention Initiative to prevent farm-related injuries to the millions of youth less than 20 years of age who are exposed to agricultural hazards each year. Youth on farms may be exposed to a wide range of work and non-work-related hazards, including falls, all-terrain vehicles (ATVs), and animals. As a place of work and a place of residence, the farm presents unique challenges for injury prevention.

The NIOSH initiative is based on a comprehensive program of surveillance, research, and partnerships. In keeping with the breadth of the Initiative, the following document presents national data for non-fatal youth injuries on racial minority farms for 2000. These data, drawn from a special survey of minority farm operators across the U.S., indicate that 531 youth were injured on racial minority farms during 2000. The causes of these injuries included falls, animals, and vehicles such as ATVs. This document, which is the first in a series of four documents, fills a current data need by providing national demographic information on youth exposed to these hazards on minority farm operations.

This document is an important step in understanding the magnitude of youth injuries occurring on racial minority-operated farms in the U.S. We hope this information will serve as a valuable resource to federal, state and local agencies; health and safety professionals; and farm safety advocates in their efforts to develop focused and coordinated strategies to prevent youth injuries on farms.

John Howard, M.D.
Director
National Institute for Occupational
   Safety and Health
Centers for Disease Control and
   Prevention

Injury and Asthma Among Youth Less Than 20 Years of Age on Minority Farm Operations in the United States, 2000
Volume I: Racial Minority National Data

Contents

Foreword iii

Acknowledgments xiii

Public Health Summary xv

Section I: The Minority Farm Operator Childhood Agricultural Injury Survey 1

    Introduction 1
    Methods 2
    Layout and use of the data tables 7
    National highlights for racial minority farms 10
    References 13

Section II: National Demographic, Injury, and Asthma Estimates for Youth Less Than 20 Years of Age on Racial Minority Farm Operations 15

Demographic estimates of:
    Racial minority farms (Table 2.1) 17
    All youth (Table 2.2) 17
    All working youth (Table 2.3) 18
    Household youth by sex and age (Table 2.4) 19
    Household youth by type of farm (Tables 2.5 - 2.7) 19
    Household youth by work status (Tables 2.8 - 2.10) 22
    Household youth exposed to riding a horse (Tables 2.11 - 2.13) 24
    Household youth exposed to operating an all-terrain vehicle (Tables 2.14 - 2.16) 25
    Household youth exposed to operating a tractor (Tables 2.17 - 2.19) 27

Estimates of injuries to:
    All youth by relationship to the farm (Tables 2.20 - 2.22) 28
    All youth by race (Tables 2.23 - 2.25) 30
    All youth by sex and age (Table 2.26) 31
    All youth by work status (Tables 2.27 - 2.28) 31
    All youth by type of farm (Tables 2.29 - 2.31) 32

All youth by type of injury (Tables 2.32 - 2.34) 34
All youth by body part injured (Tables 2.35 - 2.38) 35
All youth by source of injury (Tables 2.39 - 2.41) 38
All youth by type of injury event (Tables 2.42 - 2.44) 41
Household youth by sex and age (Table 2.45) 44
Household youth by work status (Tables 2.46 - 2.47) 44
Household youth by type of farm (Tables 2.48 - 2.50) 45
Household youth by type of injury (Tables 2.51 - 2.53) 47
Household youth by body part injured (Tables 2.54 - 2.57) 48
Household youth by source of injury (Tables 2.58 - 2.60) 51
Household youth by type of injury event (Tables 2.61 - 2.63) 54

Estimates of injury rates for:

All youth by work status (Tables 2.64 - 2.69) 57
Household youth by sex and age (Table 2.70) 61
Household youth by work status (Tables 2.71 - 2.72) 61
Household youth by type of farm (Tables 2.73 - 2.75) 62
Household youth by type of injury (Tables 2.76 - 2.78) 63
Household youth by body part injured (Tables 2.79 - 2.81) 65
Household youth by source of injury (Tables 2.82 - 2.84) 66
Household youth by type of injury event (Tables 2.85 - 2.87) 69

Estimates of asthma among household youth:

By sex (Table 2.88) 72
By age (Tables 2.89 - 2.90) 72
By type of farm (Tables 2.91 - 2.92) 73
With 1 or more asthma attacks while doing farm work (Tables 2.93 - 2.95) 74
With 1 or more asthma attacks requiring professional medical attention
(Tables 2.96 - 2.98) 76

Estimates of asthma prevalence rates for household youth:

By sex and age (Table 2.99) 77
By type of farm (Tables 2.100 - 2.101) 78
With 1 or more asthma attacks while doing farm work (Tables 2.102 - 2.104) 79
With 1 or more asthma attacks requiring professional medical attention
(Tables 2.105 - 2.107) 80

Section III: National Demographic, Injury, and Asthma Estimates for Youth Less Than 20 Years of Age on Black Farm Operations 81

Demographic estimates of:

Black farms (Table 3.1) 83

All youth (Table 3.2)..83
All working youth (Table 3.3) 84
Household youth by sex and age (Table 3.4)...85
Household youth by type of farm (Tables 3.5 - 3.7)..85
Household youth by work status (Tables 3.8 - 3.10) 88
Household youth exposed to riding a horse (Tables 3.11 - 3.13)............................90
Household youth exposed to operating an all-terrain vehicle (Tables 3.14 - 3.16) 91
Household youth exposed to operating a tractor (Table 3.17 - 3.19).......................93

Estimates of injuries to:

All youth by relationship to the farm (Tables 3.20 - 3.22) 94
All youth by race (Tables 3.23 - 3.25) 95
All youth by sex and age (Table 3.26) 96
All youth by work status and age (Table 3.27) 97
All youth by type of farm (Tables 3.28 - 3.30) 97
All youth by type of injury (Tables 3.31 - 3.33) 98
All youth by body part injured (Tables 3.34 - 3.36) 100
All youth by source of injury (Tables 3.37 - 3.39)..101
All youth by type of injury event (Tables 3.40 - 3.42) 103
Household youth by sex and age (Table 3.43)...106
Household youth by work status and age (Table 3.44)...106
Household youth by sex and type of farm (Table 3.45)...106
Household youth by type of injury (Tables 3.46 - 3.47)..107
Household youth by body part injured (Tables 3.48 - 3.50) 108
Household youth by source of injury (Tables 3.51 - 3.53) 109
Household youth by type of injury event (Tables 3.54 - 3.55) 111

Estimates of injury rates for:

All youth by work status (Tables 3.56 - 3.61)...112
Household youth by sex and age (Table 3.62)...115
Household youth by work status and age (Table 3.63)...115
Household youth by sex and type of farm (Table 3.64)...115
Household youth by type of injury (Tables 3.65 - 3.66).......................................116
Household youth by body part injured (Tables 3.67 - 3.69) 116
Household youth by source of injury (Tables 3.70 - 3.72) 118
Household youth by type of injury event (Tables 3.73 - 3.74) 119

Estimates of asthma among household youth:

By sex (Table 3.75)...120
By age (Tables 3.76 - 3.77)..120
By type of farm (Tables 3.78 - 3.79)..121
With 1 or more asthma attacks while doing farm work (Tables 3.80 - 3.82) 122

With 1 or more asthma attacks requiring professional medical attention
(Tables 3.83 - 3.85) 124

Estimates of asthma prevalence rates for household youth:
By sex and age (Table 3.86)..125
By type of farm (Tables 3.87 - 3.88)..126
With 1 or more asthma attacks while doing farm work (Tables 3.89 - 3.91).........................127
With 1 or more asthma attacks requiring professional medical attention
(Tables 3.92 - 3.94) 128

Section IV: National Demographic, Injury, and Asthma Estimates for Youth Less Than 20 Years of Age on Native American Farm Operations **129**

Demographic estimates of:
Native American farms (Table 4.1) 131
All youth (Table 4.2)..131
All working youth (Table 4.3) 132
Household youth by sex and age (Table 4.4)...133
Household youth by type of farm (Tables 4.5 - 4.7)...133
Household youth by work status (Tables 4.8 - 4.10) 136
Household youth exposed to riding a horse (Tables 4.11 - 4.13).....................................137
Household youth exposed to operating an all-terrain vehicle (Tables 4.14 - 4.16) 139
Household youth exposed to operating a tractor (Tables 4.17 - 4.19) 140

Estimates of injuries to:
All youth by relationship to the farm (Tables 4.20 - 4.22) 142
All youth by race (Tables 4.23 - 4.25) 143
All youth by sex and age (Table 4.26) 144
All youth by work status and age (Table 4.27) 144
All youth by type of farm (Tables 4.28 - 4.30) 145
All youth by type of injury (Tables 4.31 - 4.33) 146
All youth by body part injured (Tables 4.34 - 4.36) 148
All youth by source of injury (Tables 4.37 - 4.39)...150
All youth by type of injury event (Tables 4.40 - 4.42) 153
Household youth by sex and age (Table 4.43)...156
Household youth by work status and age (Table 4.44)..156
Household youth by type of farm (Tables 4.45 - 4.46)..157
Household youth by type of injury (Tables 4.47 - 4.49)...158
Household youth by body part injured (Tables 4.50 - 4.52) 159
Household youth by source of injury (Tables 4.53 - 4.55) 161
Household youth by type of injury event (Table 4.56 - 4.58)..164

Estimates of injury rates for:

All youth by work status (Tables 4.59 - 4.64)..167

Household youth by sex and age (Table 4.65)...171

Household youth by work status and age (Table 4.66)..171

Household youth by type of farm (Tables 4.67 - 4.68)...172

Household youth by type of injury (Tables 4.69 - 4.71)...173

Household youth by body part injured (Tables 4.72 - 4.74)......................................174

Household youth by source of injury (Tables 4.75 - 4.77) 176

Household youth by type of injury event (Tables 4.78 - 4.80) 179

Estimates of asthma among household youth:

By sex (Table 4.81)..182

By age (Tables 4.82 - 4.83)..182

By type of farm (Tables 4.84 - 4.85)...183

With 1 or more asthma attacks while doing farm work (Tables 4.86 - 4.88) 184

With 1 or more asthma attacks requiring professional medical attention

(Tables 4.89 - 4.91)..185

Estimates of asthma prevalence rates for household youth:

By sex and age (Table 4.92)...187

By type of farm (Tables 4.93 - 4.94)...187

With 1 or more asthma attacks while doing farm work (Tables 4.95 - 4.97) 188

With 1 or more asthma attacks requiring professional medical attention

(Tables 4.98 - 4.100)..189

Section V: National Demographic, Injury, and Asthma Estimates for Youth Less Than 20 Years of Age on Asian Farm Operations **191**

Demographic estimates of:

Asian farms (Table 5.1)..193

All youth (Table 5.2)..193

All working youth (Table 5.3) 194

Household youth by sex and age (Table 5.4)...195

Household youth by type of farm (Tables 5.5 - 5.7)...195

Household youth by work status (Tables 5.8 - 5.10) 198

Household youth exposed to riding a horse (Tables 5.11 - 5.13)..............................199

Household youth exposed to operating an all-terrain vehicle (Tables 5.14 - 5.16) 201

Household youth exposed to operating a tractor (Tables 5.17 - 5.19) 202

Estimates of injuries to:

All youth by relationship to the farm (Table 5.20) 204

All youth by race (Table 5.21) 204

All youth by age (Table 5.22) 204
All youth by work status (Tables 5.23 - 5.27) 205

Estimates of injury rates for:
All youth by relationship to the farm (Table 5.28) 207
All youth by work status (Table 5.29 - 5.33) 207

Estimates of asthma among household youth:
By sex (Table 5.34) 209
By age (Tables 5.35 - 5.36) 210
By type of farm (Tables 5.37 - 5.38) 211
With 1 or more asthma attacks while doing farm work (Tables 5.39 - 5.41) 212
With 1 or more asthma attacks requiring professional medical attention
(Tables 5.42 - 5.44) 213

Estimates of asthma prevalence rates for household youth:
By sex and age (Table 5.45) 215
By type of farm (Tables 5.46 - 5.47) 215
With 1 or more asthma attacks while doing farm work (Tables 5.48 - 5.50) 216
With 1 or more asthma attacks requiring professional medical attention
(Tables 5.51 - 5.52) 217

Section VI: National Demographic, Injury, and Asthma Estimates for Youth Less Than 20 Years of Age on "Other Race" Farm Operations **219**

Demographic estimates of:
"Other race" farms (Table 6.1) 221
All youth (Table 6.2) 221
All working youth (Table 6.3) 221
Household youth by sex and age (Table 6.4) 222
Household youth by type of farm (Tables 6.5 - 6.7) 222
Household youth by work status (Tables 6.8 - 6.10) 223
Household youth exposed to riding a horse (Tables 6.11 - 6.13) 225
Household youth exposed to operating an all-terrain vehicle (Tables 6.14 - 6.16) 226
Household youth exposed to operating a tractor (Tables 6.17 - 6.19) 228

Estimates of injuries to:
All youth by relationship to the farm (Table 6.20) 229
All youth by race (Table 6.21) 229
All youth by age (Table 6.22) 229
All youth by work status (Tables 6.23 - 6.27) 230

Estimates of injury rates for:

    All youth by relationship to the farm (Table 6.28) 232

    All youth by work status (Tables 6.29 - 6.33)...232

Estimates of asthma among household youth:

    By sex (Table 6.34)..234

    By age (Tables 6.35 - 6.36)..234

    By type of farm (Tables 6.37 - 6.38)..235

    With 1 or more asthma attacks while doing farm work (Tables 6.39 - 6.41) 236

    With 1 or more asthma attacks requiring professional medical attention

    (Tables 6.42 - 6.43) 237

Estimates of asthma prevalence rates for household youth:

    By sex and age (Table 6.44)..237

    By type of farm (Tables 6.45 - 6.46)...238

    With 1 or more asthma attacks while doing farm work (Tables 6.47 - 6.49) 238

    With 1 or more asthma attacks requiring professional medical attention

    (Tables 6.50 - 6.51) 239

Appendix A: Bibliography of NIOSH Childhood Agricultural Injury Articles and Documents **241**

Appendix B: Minority Farm Operator Childhood Agricultural Injury Survey Questionnaire **249**

Appendix C: Definitions Used for the Racial Minority Farm Operator Childhood Agricultural Injury Survey..**265**

Appendix D: Sampling Estimators Used for the Racial Minority Farm Operator Childhood Agricultural Injury Survey..**269**

Acknowledgments

The authors are indebted to Doug Kleweno, Kevin Barnes, Montie Tesky, Joe Samson, and Gail Gregory of the U.S. Department of Agriculture (USDA), National Agricultural Statistics Service (NASS) for their invaluable assistance in the survey design, data collection, data entry, and review of this work; all of the NASS State cooperators who collected these data; Cheryl Paul of the Constella Group for her efforts in completing the layout of the document; and Patricia Ulakovic of NIOSH for her assistance in printing this document.

Public Health Summary

What is the purpose of this document?

This document provides previously unavailable youth demographic, injury and asthma estimates at the national level for youth on racial minority operated farms in the U.S. A racial minority is defined as any person who is Black, Native American, Asian, or who are of "other" races. These data represent the initial step in developing research and prevention programs to reduce the burden of injury and asthma on racial minority farms in the U.S.

What are the hazards?

According to data from the National Institute for Occupational Safety and Health and the U.S. Department of Agriculture, there were an estimated 531 youth less than 20 years of age injured on racial minority farm operations in the U.S. in 2000. Major causes of these injuries included contact with objects and falls. In addition, there were an estimated 2,506 youth with asthma living on these farms. The injury and asthma estimates reported here should be considered conservative because of the potential for recall and other reporting biases in the survey.

How are youth exposed or put at risk?

Exposures to farm hazards are not limited to youth who work on farms. In addition to injuries sustained during work activities, youth may be injured while living on farms, while visiting farms, or when they accompany their working parents or adults into the fields. The farm environment also contains many known triggers for asthma. The injury and asthma hazards these youth encounter may be work or non-work in nature, and make the farm a unique environment for developing prevention strategies.

What recommendations have the federal government made to protect the health of farm youth?

The Fair Labor Standards Act of 1938 (FLSA) and its amendments set standards for child labor in agriculture. However, the FLSA covers only employees whose work involves production of agricultural goods which will leave the state through interstate commerce. In addition, FLSA regulations do not apply to youth working for their parents or guardian(s) on the family's farm. Youth who work on farms are often not protected by workplace safety and health regulations from the Occupational Safety and Health Administration (OSHA) because these youth frequently work for small operations that are not inspected by OSHA, or because OSHA regulations do not apply to the farm household members. For all youth on farms, there are no protections for injuries from hazards associated with non-work activities, which often expose them to the same hazards as work activities. Given the limited protections for youth on farms, there is a need for states and communities to develop and implement programs to reduce childhood agricultural injuries.

Where can more information be found?

Additional NIOSH documents and information on childhood agricultural injuries or other related topics may be obtained by calling the NIOSH toll-free number (1-800-35-NIOSH; 1-800-356-4674) or visiting the NIOSH homepage http://www.cdc.gov/niosh.

Section I: The Minority Farm Operator Childhood Agricultural Injury Survey

INTRODUCTION

Youth who live on, work on, or visit farms in the United States (U.S.) have been identified as a special population at high risk for non-fatal and fatal injuries [Adekoya and Pratt, 2001; Myers and Hendricks, 2001; Castillo et al., 1999; Rivara, 1997; NCCAIP, 1996]. Since 1996, the National Institute for Occupational Safety and Health (NIOSH) has conducted the Childhood Agricultural Injury Prevention Initiative to promote the reduction of injuries and fatalities to youth on farms in the U.S. [Castillo et al., 1998]. A major component of this initiative is the development of an ongoing surveillance program to track the frequency and incidence of non-fatal injuries and fatalities occurring to the various types of youth exposed to farm hazards.

An initial step in the development of the surveillance program was the completion of a farm operator survey in 1999. NIOSH collaborated with the U.S. Department of Agriculture (USDA), National Agricultural Statistics Service (NASS) to conduct the Childhood Agricultural Injury Survey (CAIS). The results of this survey were released in 2001, and contained both injury and youth demographic estimates for farms in the U.S. [Myers and Hendricks, 2001]. While the CAIS provided a statistically representative picture of the injury experience of youth on farms in the U.S., it did have some limitations. One major limitation of the CAIS was that it did not adequately cover minority operated farms (i.e., farms operated by racial minorities or operators of Hispanic ethnicity). This is due in large part to the small number of minority farms in operation in the U.S. Based on the 1997 Census of Agriculture, minorities accounted for just 3.3% of the nearly 1.91 million farms in the U.S. that year [USDA, 1999].

To address this limitation, NIOSH, through an Interagency Agreement, again collaborated with USDA, NASS to administer the Minority Farm Operator Childhood Agricultural Injury Survey (M-CAIS) in 2001 by using the 1997 Census of Agriculture sampling frame to identify minority farms. Like the CAIS before it, the M-CAIS provides injury and youth demographic estimates at the national and regional level, but the estimates are specific to minority operated farms in the U.S. In addition to injury information, the M-CAIS provides prevalence information on asthma among youth living on minority farms, which should provide unique information for health professionals working in the area of childhood asthma.

This document presents the national M-CAIS results for racial minority farm operations in an easily accessible statistical abstract format. A racial minority farm operation includes farms operated by Blacks, Native Americans, Asians, or operators of "other" races. "Other races" includes operators native to or of ancestry from Mexico, the Caribbean, and Central or South America [USDA, 1999]. This document includes injuries to all youth on racial minority operated

1

farms regardless of the race or ethnicity of the injured youth (i.e., a white youth who worked and was injured on a racial minority farm would be included in these statistics). Future documents, in a similar format, will provide national data for Hispanic farm operations, regional data for racial minority farm operations, and regional data for Hispanic farm operations. Due to the quantity of data, no attempt was made to interpret the results presented. A list of NIOSH documents and publications that do provide interpretation of these and other childhood farm injury data is provided in Appendix A. It is hoped that the data presented here will be used by public health and safety professionals, engineers, and other groups working in the area of childhood farm safety and health to help in their intervention programs and injury control research.

The estimates, prevalence rates, and incidence rates presented in this statistical abstract were calculated by NIOSH and are presented with the approval of USDA, NASS. Access to all M-CAIS data files, or additional estimates from the M-CAIS data, are subject to the approval of USDA, NASS.

METHODS

General Survey Design: The M-CAIS was conducted for NIOSH by USDA, NASS through an Interagency Agreement. The survey was defined as a census of the 49,270 minority farm operations identified in the NASS 1997 Census of Agriculture list. A farm was considered to be eligible for M-CAIS regardless of whether youth were on the farm in 2000. This was necessary to allow for meaningful estimates of both injuries and the number of youth on farms for the various youth populations covered in the survey. Because of confidentiality concerns, racial minority farm operators and Hispanic operators were handled independently. This resulted in a certain number of farms being used to calculate both the racial minority estimates and the Hispanic estimates. In other words, individual operators who reported being a racial minority and of Hispanic ethnicity are represented in both sets of estimates. However, farm operators who are white and of Hispanic ethnicity are excluded from the racial minority estimates. Because of this overlap, it is not possible to add racial and Hispanic estimates together.

The survey used a Computer Assisted Telephone Interview (CATI) survey instrument. The interviews were conducted by 10 NASS calling centers between February and March of 2001. The M-CAIS was conducted in these winter months to increase the response rate of the survey. Participation in the survey was strictly voluntary. The survey instrument (Appendix B) used for the M-CAIS was designed to not exceed one-half hour, with an average response time of seven minutes. Definitions used in the questionnaire and throughout this document are provided in Appendix C.

In addition to the main CATI data collection effort, 5 NASS state offices conducted personal interviews with a sample of 2,088 minority operators that were not contacted during the CATI survey period. The two main reasons that these farm operators were not contacted during this period were that the operator was not available even upon repeated contact attempts, or that

NASS did not have a working telephone number on file. The 5 states that conducted the personal interviews were Alabama, Arizona, California, New Mexico, and Texas. These states were selected because they had the largest number of minority farm operations. The personal interviews were conducted during April and May of 2001 with the same survey instrument used in the CATI process.

The data collected for M-CAIS were self-reported by either the female or male head of household. If an injury occurred to a household youth 16-years of age or older, and the youth was available to talk to the NASS enumerator, he or she was asked to answer the injury section of the survey. Information such as youth demographics, the occurrence of an injury, and the characteristics of an injury event were subject to the interpretation of the respondent.

For the survey, a farm was defined as any operation with $1,000 or more of gross agricultural production within a calendar year, and included both crop and livestock operations. A youth was defined as any person under the age of 20 years. Household youth were defined as all youth who resided on the farm. Hired youth were defined as youth who were hired directly by the farm operator, excluding contract laborers, to work on the farm, but were not household members. Visitors were defined as all other youth who were on the farm, but were not household members or hired workers.

An injury was defined as any condition that resulted in 4 hours or more of restricted activity (e.g., the individual could not perform work or other normal duties, missed work, and/or missed school), or a condition that required professional medical treatment. While the total number of childhood agricultural injuries was requested for the calendar year 2000, descriptive information was collected only for the four most recent injury events. An agricultural work-related injury was defined as any injury meeting the above definition that occurred while performing work on the farm associated with the farm business, including chores. Non-work injuries were defined as injuries occurring on the farm that were not due to farm work. The survey excluded injuries to contractors working for the farm operation, or injuries that occurred to youth off the farm property. The categorical injury variables of "source of injury" and "event or exposure" were coded from narrative injury descriptions using the Bureau of Labor Statistics Occupational Injury and Illness Classification Manual [USDOL, 1992].

Asthma was assessed for household youth only. A household youth was defined as being an asthmatic if the asthma had been diagnosed by a health professional. An asthma attack at work was defined as any attack that occurred while the youth was doing farm work, and required the use of an inhaler or other medical treatment. A professionally treated asthma attack was defined as any attack that required an emergency room visit, hospitalization, or other professional medical attention, beyond the use of an inhaler. A positive response to either the asthma attack at work or the professionally treated asthma attack question indicated that at least one such attack occurred to the youth during 2000. The actual number of either type of attack was not collected. Therefore, these asthma statistics are measures of prevalence only. Finally, the two types of asthma attacks are not mutually exclusive. It is possible that an asthma attack incident occurred while the youth was doing farm work and that the youth received professional medical treatment for the same attack.

To facilitate the correct matching of injury estimates to youth at risk, specific demographic terms were used for the various combinations of youth populations in the survey (Table 1.1). In this document, "All youth" refers to the sum of all youth categories covered in the survey (i.e., "Household youth," "Hired youth," "Relatives," and "Non-relatives"). "Visiting youth" refers to the combination of "Relatives" and "Non-relatives" that were on the farm in the year 2000. "All working youth" refers to "Working household youth," combined with "Hired youth" and "Working relatives." Finally, "Non-household working youth" refers to the combination of "Hired youth" and "Working relatives."

The racial and Hispanic origin classification for the farm operator and all household youth were set to the racial and Hispanic classification provided on the 1997 Census of Agriculture sampling frame. In addition, "Asians" and "Native Hawaiian or Other Pacific Islanders" were combined into a single Asian category for all analyses. "Other races" was defined in the 1997 Census of Agriculture as persons native to or of ancestry from Mexico, the Caribbean, and Central and South America [USDA, 1999].

Table 1.1 Demographic terms and the specific youth populations they represent for all statistical tables presented in Sections I through VI

		Terms					
	Youth Population	All youth	Household youth	Visiting youth	Relatives	All working youth	Non-household working youth
Household	Non-working household youth	X	X				
	Working household youth	X	X			X	
Non-household	Hired youth	X				X	X
	Non-working relatives	X		X	X		
	Working relatives	X		X	X	X	X
	Non-relatives	X		X			

Estimation Procedures: The estimation procedure for the M-CAIS was developed as a two step process. The first step involved post-stratifying the CATI and personal interview results to account for farm operators who refused to participate in the survey, or were inaccessible. For the racial minority data, the results were post-stratified by the four farm operator racial categories (Black, Native American, Asian, and "Other") within the nine U.S. geographic regions defined by the U.S. Bureau of the Census (Table 1.2) [US Department of Commerce, 1975]. For the Hispanic data, post-stratification was for the nine geographic regions only. Variance estimates for the survey were derived by applying the unbiased estimators for a stratified simple random sample to these post-stratified data [Cochran, 1977]. The estimators for racial minority

Table 1.2 U.S. Bureau of the Census Geographic Regions of the U.S.

4 Regions	9 Regions
Northeast	**New England:** Connecticut, Maine, Massachusetts, New Hampshire Rhode Island, Vermont **Mid-Atlantic:** New Jersey, New York, Pennsylvania
Mid-West	**East North Central:** Illinois, Indiana, Michigan, Ohio, Wisconsin **West North Central:** Iowa, Kansas, Minnesota, Missouri, Nebraska North Dakota, South Dakota
South	**South Atlantic:** Delaware, Florida, Georgia, Maryland, North Carolina, South Carolina, Virginia, West Virginia **East South Central:** Alabama, Kentucky, Mississippi, Tennessee **West South Central:** Arkansas, Louisiana, Oklahoma, Texas
West	**Mountain:** Arizona, Colorado, Idaho, Montana, Nevada, New Mexico, Utah, Wyoming **Pacific:** Alaska, California, Hawaii, Oregon, Washington

population totals and their corresponding variances are presented in Appendix D. The estimators for Hispanic totals and variances are provided in Volume II.

The second step in the estimation process was benchmarking the post-stratified survey results to the published counts for minority-operated farms released in the 1997 Census of Agriculture. The 1997 Census of Agriculture reported 47,658 racial minority farms. This number includes imputed values for racial minority farm operations (i.e., some farm operations without racial data for the operator were classified as racial minority operations based on characteristics of the farm operation or other factors). Since these imputed values caused the published racial minority farm count (47,658) to be higher than the sampling frame racial minority farm count (35,084), the benchmarking process was necessary.

Benchmarking was applied by race within the nine geographic regions. Because benchmarking changed each post-stratified population total by a constant, it did not change the relative variance of any post-stratified population estimate. Therefore, the relative variances from the non-benchmarked post-stratified estimates were used to derive the standard errors for all benchmarked population estimates. The equations used to derive benchmarked racial minority population estimates and variances are provided in Appendix D. The benchmark equations for Hispanic population estimates and variances are provided in Volume II.

Incidence and Prevalence Rate Estimates: The injury incidence rates were calculated as the estimated number of injuries at the national level, divided by the estimated appropriate youth estimate at the national level. For work-related injury rates, only working household and working non-household youth were included in the denominator. For non-work-related injury rates, all youth were included in the denominator because it was assumed that all youth could sustain a non-work injury. The overall household youth asthma prevalence rate and the prevalence rate for professionally treated asthma attacks used all household youth as the denominator. The prevalence rate for asthma attacks while doing farm work used only working household youth in the denominator. All rates are expressed in terms of 1,000 youth potentially exposed.

The variance calculations for the population-based incidence or prevalence rates were estimated using the linear combination of variances for the injury or asthma estimate and the youth estimate as described by Cochran [1977] (Appendix D).

Categorical Frequency Estimates: The frequency estimates for categorical variables from the M-CAIS were based on three types of information: demographic, injury, and asthma. Demographic data included an estimate of household youth, the number of hired youth, and the number of visiting youth for the calendar year 2000. For household youth, estimates by sex, age, and various types of exposure information (e.g., working on the farm, riding a horse) were also calculated. Injury data included information such as whether an injury was work-related or not, the nature of the injury, the source of the injury, the event or exposure leading to the injury, and the body part injured. This information was only collected for the four most recent injuries that occurred on a farm. Asthma data were collected for household youth only, and included prevalence estimates for youth with asthma, asthmatic youth with at least one asthma attack while doing farm work in 2000, and asthmatic youth who required professional medical treatment for an asthma attack in 2000.

Frequency tables for the various racial categories are presented at differing levels of detail because of differing levels of sampling error and minimum case requirements between the various estimates. In all instances, an estimate was required to have 3 or more farms with a non-zero value to be reportable. This was the only restriction placed on injury or asthma estimates from the M-CAIS. Youth estimates were further restricted if the relative standard error of an estimate exceeded 34%. For some tables, youth estimates are reported with relative standard errors above 34% because they were deemed critical to the interpretation of the frequency table. However, no youth estimate is reported with a relative standard error greater than 50%. If an injury or youth estimate was censored because of either of these two criteria, a series of other cells within the table were also censored to prevent obtaining restricted data through subtraction. Where possible, these secondary censored values were targeted at broader categories within a table.

Survey Limitations: There are several limitations to the results presented in this report. The first limitation is the NASS census sampling frame used for the survey. The 1997 Census of Agriculture list does not account for new minority farming operations that were established after 1997. In addition, some minority farm operators may have been left out of the sample because the operator self-selected themselves into non-minority categories for race or ethnicity in the 1997 Census of Agriculture. The extent of self-misclassification in the 1997 Census of Agriculture is unknown. A second limitation is that the recall period for an injury or asthma attack in this survey was up to 15 months. While the definition of an injury or asthma attack was for more severe cases, which may be easier to recall, there is still the possibility that a reportable injury or asthma attack was not remembered by a respondent. A third limitation is that most surveys were conducted with the female head of household, which may have resulted in an under-reporting of hired youth injuries, especially for larger farming operations with many employees. Fourth, there was no way to verify the accuracy or completeness of the responses given in this survey, which could impart some response bias into the overall results. Fifth, this survey did not include injuries which occurred to youth contract farm workers. Injuries to contract farm workers are being assessed through a separate NIOSH study, and will be provided in a separate report.

A final limitation is the possibility of a bias because of non-response to the telephone survey. Due to the survey design, it was not possible to make a second contact to farm operators who refused to participate in the survey. This did not allow for a follow-back questionnaire to assess these refusals. For non-response due to inaccessibility, the inclusion of 2,088 personal interviews did improve the coverage, but did not eliminate all bias. The post-stratification of the M-CAIS results by race and geographic region greatly reduced the impact of the non-response bias.

LAYOUT AND USE OF THE DATA TABLES

The data tables contained within this document are designed to provide the user as much information as possible. However, as with all such documents, the tables are subject to the usual limitations of 2-way or 3-way classification tables, as well as the limitations imposed by printing space. Because of this, no percentages are provided in any of the frequency tables. Rather, the reader is provided the grand total and marginal totals in each table, except for values that are suppressed for reasons of confidentiality.

Frequency Table Layout: Frequency tables generally follow the same layout (Table 1.3). The grand total, A, is displayed as the bottom left data cell. Marginal totals, B, are displayed in the far left data column, and in the bottom row. The grand total and marginal totals are typically shaded in gray. The 2-way variable estimates, C, are presented in the non-highlighted body of the table. The standard errors a, b, and c are provided immediately next to each corresponding estimate.

In addition to the typical row or column marginal values, certain tables may also contain major group, subgroup, and detailed values. Major group and subgroup values occur on most tables involving "Age" and "Type of farming operation." Detailed values are associated with most tables involving "Relationship to the farm," "Source of injury," and "Type of injury event." A major group represents a broad grouping of values for a particular variable, while the subgroup represents either individual values for the variable, or smaller groupings of values for the variable. Detailed values represent the most detailed estimate possible for the specific variable. Major groups are shown in bolded text, while subgroups are shown as indented, non-bolded text beneath major group entries. Detailed entries are provided in indented, italicized text beneath subgroup entries.

Table 1.3 General layout of data tables in Sections II through VI. "A" represents the grand table total, "B" the marginal totals, and "C" the 2-way variable estimates within the table. The values "a," "b," and "c" are the corresponding standard error estimates of "A," "B," and "C." Bold table entries denote major group estimates for variables, non-bolded entries denote subgroup estimates for variables, and italicized entries denote a detailed estimate for a variable.

Variable 2	Total † Estimate	se	Variable 1 major group Estimate	se	Variable 1 major group Estimate	se	Unknown Estimate
Variable 2 major group	**B**	**b**	**C**	**c**	**C**	**c**	**C**
Variable 2 subgroup	B	b	C	c	C	c	C
Variable 2 detailed	*B*	*b*	*C*	*c*	*C*	*c*	*C*
Variable 2 major group	**B**	**b**	**C**	**c**	**C**	**c**	**C**
Variable 2 subgroup	B	b	C	c	C	c	C
Variable 2 detailed	*B*	*b*	*C*	*c*	*C*	*c*	*C*
Unknown	**B**	**b**	**C**	**c**	**C**	**c**	**C**
Total †	**A**	**a**	**B**	**b**	**B**	**b**	**B**

† Estimates may not add to the total because of rounding.

The following is an example of this layout for the variable "Age," using Table 2.4 on page 19. The major groups for age in the document are "**<10 years**," "**10-15 years**," "**16-19 years**," and "**Unknown**." In addition to these 4 major age groups, there are 5 age subgroups. Under the major group "**10-15 years**," there are three subgroups: "10-11 years," "12-13 years," and "14-15 years." For the major group "**16-19 years**," there are two subgroups: "16-17 years" and "18-19 years." The major groups "**<10 years**" and "**Unknown**" have no subgroups.

Collapsed categories: Because of reporting restrictions, not all values may be reported in a table (see discussion of reporting requirements under "Categorical Frequency Estimates" in the Methods section, page 6). In this document, a non-reportable cell is denoted in a table as "***." In some circumstances, values for a variable may be collapsed into a broader category. For example, in Table 3.43, page 106, the major age groups of "10-15" and "16-19" are collapsed into a single broad age group, "10-19." A second example can be seen in Table 2.29 on page 32. Here, the subgroup farm types of "Tobacco," "Cotton," "Nursery and floriculture," and "Other crop" farms are collapsed into a single broad category, "All other crop" farms. In the same table, "Dairy," "Aquaculture," and "Other livestock" farms are collapsed into the single group, "All other livestock" farms. Collapsed categories for most variables are footnoted in individual tables. Standard error estimates for these collapsed categories are not provided in the document.

Calculating Percentages within Frequency Tables: Percentage distributions from these tables may be calculated at the table level, row marginal level, column marginal level, and for subgroups within major groups. Using the notation from Table 1.3, table level percentages (T%) can be obtained by dividing any table entry B or C, by the grand table total A. Using Table 2.4 as an example, the table level percentage for household youth less than 10 years of age is:

$$T\%_{\text{household youth <10 years}} = (9{,}339/28{,}577)*100 = 32.7\%,$$

meaning 32.7 percent of all household youth are less than 10 years of age. Similarly, the table level percentage for household males less than 10 years of age is:

$$T\%_{\text{household males <10 years}} = (4{,}799/28{,}577)*100 = 16.8\%,$$

meaning 16.8 percent of all household youth are males below the age of 10 years.

The row marginal percentages (RM%) involve dividing values of C by the corresponding row marginal total, B. Using Table 2.4 again, the row marginal percentage for household males less than 10 years of age is:

$$RM\%_{\text{household males <10 years}} = (4{,}799/9{,}339)*100 = 51.4\%,$$

meaning 51.4 percent of all household youth less than 10 years of age are male.

Using the same approach, the column marginal percentage (CM%) for males less than 10 years of age from Table 2.4 is:

$$CM\%_{\text{household males <10 years}} = (4{,}799/14{,}643)*100 = 32.8\%,$$

meaning 32.8 percent of all household males are less than 10 years of age.

When looking at tables with major groups and subgroups, the T% values of the row or column major group marginal cells will add to 100%, except for rounding. The T% values for the row or column subgroup marginal cells will add to the corresponding major group percentage they are beneath, except where subgroup values are suppressed. Using a similar logic, percentages may also be derived for subgroup values within major groups. For example, from Table 2.4, the percentage of household youth 10-11 years of age out of all household youth 10-15 years of age is (3,219/10,577)*100, or 30.4 percent.

Rate Table Layout: The layout for rate tables in this document is similar to that for frequency tables. Rates are provided for the grand total, row marginal values, column marginal values, and where appropriate, the 2-way table values (see "Incidence and Prevalence Rate Estimates" on page 5 of the Methods section for a discussion of how rates were derived). As with frequency tables, standard errors are not provided for rates involving collapsed cells.

Comparison to Other Public Health Data: Readers are asked to use care in comparing the results provided in this document to those reported from other public health data sets. Readers should review carefully the definitions, methods, and limitations presented in this document before making comparisons to other published reports, or studies.

The data provided in this document are derived using statistical weights, and are reported with standard errors. Confidence intervals can be calculated for any level of confidence by multiplying the standard error by the appropriate value of "t" from the Students-t distribution (e.g., 1.96 for a 95% confidence interval). It is important that comparisons to other published reports or data take these standard errors or confidence intervals into account.

NATIONAL HIGHLIGHTS FOR RACIAL MINORITY FARMS

The following is an overview of the national results of the M-CAIS for racial minority farm operations. Detailed results with standard errors (se) are presented in Sections II through VI. Section II presents results for all racial minority operated farms combined. Sections III through VI provide results by specific racial categories (i.e., Black, Native American, Asian, and "Other").

Survey Response: A total of 49,270 minority farm operations were identified in the 1997 Census of Agriculture sampling list. The number of racial minority farms identified by the list was 35,084. Of all eligible farms, 36,424 were contacted either by telephone or by a NASS field enumerator. The remaining 12,846 eligible farms were inaccessible. Of the 36,424 farms who were contacted, 9,254 refused to participate, for a responding farm count of 27,170. This resulted in an overall adjusted M-CAIS response rate of 74.6%. The number of racial minority farms among these respondents was 19,083. These 19,083 were weighted to the 35,084 racial minority farms on the NASS sampling list and then benchmarked to the 47,658 racial minority farms published in the 1997 Census of Agriculture (see Estimation Procedures on page 4 for more information).

Youth Demographics: There were an estimated 416,088 (±5,473) youth under the age of 20 years who lived on, worked on, or visited a racial minority operated farm in 2000. Youth living in the farm household accounted for an estimated 28,577 (±254) youth. Youth hired directly by the farm accounted for 7,435 (±533) youth and an estimated 380,076 (±5,404) youth were visitors to the farm. Relatives accounted for 191,848 (±1,653) of these visitors. Livestock operations had the greatest number of youth on the farm in 2000 (253,330 ±3,951) with crop operations having an estimated 152,222 (±3,979) youth on their operations. There were 147,573 (±2,597) youth under the age of 20 years present on farms with Black operators. Farms with a Native American operator had 127,947 (±2,765) youth, while Asian-operated farms had 46,465 (±2,919) youth. The remaining 94,103 (±2,792) youth were on farms operated by some "other" racial minority.

There were an estimated 34,525 (±682) youth under the age of 20 years who did work on racial minority operated farms in 2000. These included household youth who performed work on the farm, youth hired directly by the farm, and any non-household relatives who worked on the farm. Livestock operations accounted for the most working youth (20,863±393). Crop operations accounted for an additional 13,208 (±573) working youth.

Of the 28,577 youth less than 20 years living on racial minority operated farms, 14,643 (±160) were males and 13,042 (±151) were females. There were 9,339 (±136) household youth under the age of 10 years, 10,577 (±134) between the ages of 10 and 15 years, and 7,648 (±105) between the ages of 16 and 19 years. There were 7,688 (±116) household youth on farms with a Black operator. Farms with a Native American operator had 7,381 (±123) household youth, Asian-operated farms had 5,700 (±127) household youth, and an estimated 7,808 (±142) youth were living on farms operated by some "other" racial minority. A total of 11,753 (±159) household youth on all racial minority farms did farm work during 2000. Also during that year, 7,459 (±130) household youth were reported to have ridden a horse for either work or recreation, 6,514 (±117) operated an ATV for work or recreation, and 6,452 (±106) youth were said to have operated a tractor on the farm.

Injuries to All Youth: There were an estimated 531 (±30) youth injuries on racial minority operated farms in 2000. Of these injuries, 200 (±18) were work-related and 326 (±23) were non-work-related. The work-related injury rate for all youth was 5.8 per 1,000 working youth (±0.5), while the non-work-related injury rate was 0.8 injuries per 1,000 youth (±0.1). Household youth accounted for the highest number of injuries (348 ±25), followed by relatives (124 ±13), visitors that were not relatives (37 ±8), and hired workers (20 ±6). Most injuries occurred to males (382 ±25). Youth less than 10 years of age had the highest number of injuries (166 ±17), followed by youth 14 and 15 years of age (112 ±12). For work-related injuries, the highest number occurred to youth 16 and 17 years of age (54 ±9), followed by youth 14 and 15 years of age (47 ±8).

Native American youth experienced the highest number of injuries (206±18). Black youth experienced 78 injuries (±11), white youth had 92 (±12) injuries, Asian youth experienced 40 (±8) injuries, and youth of some "other" minority race accounted for 108 (±15) of the injuries on racial minority farms. White youth injured on these farms were identified as relatives, hired workers, or visitors.

The most common source of injury for all youth on these farms was structures/surfaces. This source, which includes the ground, floors, and fences, accounted for 164 (±15) of the injuries. The most common type of injury event was contact with an object (163 ±15), while 147 (±14) injuries were the result of a fall. The parts of the body most commonly injured were the arm (91 ±11); hand, wrist, and finger (79 ±11); or the leg (77 ±11). Injuries most frequently resulted in cuts (130 ±14) or fractures (121 ±13).

Livestock operations accounted for 362 (±24) of all injuries to youth on these farms, while crop farms reported 163 (±17) injuries to youth. Beef operations had the highest number of youth injuries (244 ±20), followed by grain and oil seed farms (61 ±12), and equine operations (46 ±9). Although livestock operations experienced the majority of injuries, the difference in injury rates for livestock and crop operations was small: livestock operations had an injury rate of 1.4 per 1,000 youth (±0.1) compared to 1.1 per 1,000 youth (±0.1) on crop operations.

Injuries to Household Youth: There were 348 (±25) household youth injuries on racial minority farms in 2000. The injury rate for household youth on racial minority operated farms was 12.2/ 1,000 household youth (±0.9). Males accounted for 245 (±20) of these injuries while 103 (±13) were to females. The rate of injury for males was 16.7 per 1,000 household youth (±1.4), which was more than twice the injury rate for females (7.9 per 1,000 household youth ±1.0). Household youth less than 10 years of age were estimated to have the highest number of injuries (112 ±15), followed by household youth age 14 and 15 years (74 ±10), and household youth 16 and 17 years of age (52 ±9).

There were 138 (±15) work-related injuries to household youth on racial minority farms, for a corresponding work-related injury rate of 11.8 per 1,000 working household youth (±1.3). Males accounted for 114 (±13) of these injuries. The highest number of these work-related injuries were found for household youth 14 and 15 years of age (40 ±7) and youth 16 and 17 years of age (39 ±8). Youth 14 and 15 years of age had the highest work-related injury rate among household youth (19.3/1,000 working household youth ±2.6), followed by youth 10 and 11 years of age (14.0/1,000 working household youth ±2.4).

Youth living on a farm operated by a Native American had the highest injury rate for household youth (24.0 injuries/1,000 Native American household youth ±2.2), followed by household youth living on "other" race farms (12.3 injuries/1,000 "other" race household youth ±1.9). Household youth on Black farms had an injury rate of 6.4 per 1,000 Black household youth (±1.2). Household youth on Asian farms had the lowest rate of 4.5 per 1,000 Asian household youth (±1.1).

As was seen for all youth, household youth on livestock operations reported the most injuries (247 ±20), followed by crop operations (101±14). By specific type of farm, beef operations had the highest number of youth injuries (162 ±17) followed by grain and oil seed operations (42 ±11). Unlike the injury rates seen for all youth where the injury rates for livestock and crop operations were similar, livestock operations had a household injury rate twice that of crop operations (16.8 per 1,000 household youth ±1.4 and 8.2 per 1,000 household youth ±1.1, respectively). Sheep and goat operations had the highest injury rate (46.7 per 1,000 household youth ±13.7). This rate was nearly four times the overall rate for household youth. Other types of farms that had an injury rate higher than 20 injuries per 1,000 household youth were: equine operations (33.4 ±8.5), poultry and egg operations (20.9 ±9.0), and grain and oil seed operations (20.6 ±5.2).

The most common source of injury for youth living on racial minority operated farms was structures and surfaces (117 ±13). Falls were the most common injury event (109 ±13), followed by contact with objects (108 ±12). The parts of the body most commonly injured were the arm (58 ±9); the leg (54 ±9); or the hand, wrist, and finger (48 ±8). Injuries most frequently resulted in cuts (95 ±12) or fractures (78 ±10).

Asthma Among Household Youth: An estimated 2,506 (±63) household youth living on racial minority farm operations were reported as having been diagnosed with asthma. Of these asthmatic youth, 813 (±36) reportedly experienced at least one asthma attack while doing farm work during 2000, while 530 (±26) experienced at least one asthma attack serious enough to require professional medical attention. The overall asthma prevalence rate for these household youth was 87.7 asthmatics per 1,000 household youth (±2.3). Males had a higher prevalence rate at 108.1 asthmatics per 1,000 household youth (±3.5), while females had a prevalence rate of 70.5 asthmatics per 1,000 household youth (±2.8).

The number of household youth reported to have asthma was somewhat higher on livestock operations (1,324 asthmatics ±45) than on crop farms (1,111 asthmatics ±43). The prevalence rates, however, were statistically identical for livestock and crop operations (90.0 asthmatics/ 1,000 household youth ± 3.3 and 90.6 asthmatics/1,000 household youth ±3.8, respectively). The number of household youth who reportedly experienced one or more asthma attacks while doing farm work during 2000 was also higher on livestock operations (422 working asthmatics ±25) than on crop farms (367 working asthmatics ±25). However, crop farms had the highest rate of household youth with one or more asthma attacks while doing farm work (88.7 working asthmatics/1,000 working household youth ±6.5) when compared to livestock operations (57.3 working asthmatics/1,000 household youth ±3.5).

Household youth living on Black farm operations had the highest number and rate of reported asthma in this survey (745 asthmatics ±30 and 96.9 ±4.2 asthmatics/1,000 Black household youth, respectively). Native Americans had the second highest number of household youth with asthma (660 asthmatics ±33), followed by household youth on "other" race farms (632 asthmatics ±34), and household youth on Asian farms (469 asthmatics ±28). Household youth on Native American farms had the second highest rate of asthma (89 asthmatics ±5), followed by Asian household youth (82 ±5), and "Other" race household youth (81 ±5).

REFERENCES

Adekoya N, Pratt SG [2001]. Fatal unintentional farm injuries among persons less than 20 years of age in the United States: geographic profiles. Cincinnati, OH: U.S. Department of Health and Human Services, Public Health Service, Centers for Disease Control and Prevention, National Institute for Occupational Safety and Health, DHHS (NIOSH) Publication No. 2001-131.

Castillo DN, Hard DL, Myers JR, Pizatella T, Stout NA [1998]. A national childhood agricultural injury prevention initiative. J Agric Saf Health, Special Issue (1):183-191.

Castillo DN, Adekoya N, Myers JR [1999]. Fatal work-related injuries in the agricultural production and services sectors among youth in the United States. J Agromedicine, 6(3):27-42.

Cochran WG [1977]. Sampling techniques, 3rd ed. New York, NY: J Wiley and Sons.

Myers JR, Hendricks KJ [2001]. Injuries among youth on farms in the United States, 1998. Cincinnati, OH: U.S. Department of Health and Human Services, Public Health Service, Centers for Disease Control and Prevention, National Institute for Occupational Safety and Health, DHHS (NIOSH) Publication No. 2001-154.

NCCAIP [1996]. Children and agriculture: opportunities for safety and health–a national action plan. Marshfield, WI: National Committee for Childhood Agricultural Injury Prevention.

Rivara F [1997]. Fatal and nonfatal farm injuries to children and adolescents in the United States, 1990-1993. Inj Prev 3:190-194.

USDA [1999]. 1997 Census of agriculture United States summary and state data, volume 1, geographic area series, part 51. Washington, DC: U.S. Department of Agriculture, National Agricultural Statistics Service.

USDOL [1992]. Occupational injury and illness classification manual. Washington, DC: U.S. Department of Labor, Bureau of Labor Statistics.

US Department of Commerce [1975]. The methods and materials of demography: vol. I. Washington, DC: Shryock, Siegal, and Associates.

Section II: National Demographic, Injury, and Asthma Estimates for Youth Less Than 20 Years of Age on Racial Minority Farm Operations

Table 2.1   National estimates of racial minority farms from the 1997 Census of Agriculture by business status, 2000

Status	Total† Estimate	se
In business	41,072	80
Out of business	6,587	81
Total†	47,658	

† Estimates may not add to the total because of rounding.

Table 2.2   National estimates of **all youth** less than 20 years of age on racial minority farms by relationship to the farm and type of farm, 2000

Type of Farm	Total†		Household Youth		Hired Youth		Visiting Youth		Relatives		Non-Relatives	
	Estimate	se	Estimate	se	Estimate	se	Estimate	se	Estimate	se	Estimate	se
All crop	**152,222**	**3,979**	**12,265**	**183**	**4,653**	**528**	**135,305**	**3,897**	**66,250**	**1,062**	**69,055**	**3,555**
Grain and oil seed	33,804	1,734	2,063	77	340	36	31,401	1,705	15,091	535	16,310	1,499
Tobacco	8,478	469	452	31	357	38	7,669	451	4,943	294	2,726	249
Cotton	5,387	875	388	35	55	11	4,944	868	2,365	216	2,579	719
Vegetable and melon	22,124	1,391	2,173	90	905	82	19,046	1,362	9,227	401	9,819	1,224
Fruit, nut, and berry	33,736	1,669	3,508	99	1,682	440	28,547	1,573	14,345	487	14,202	1,421
Nursery and floriculture	13,814	2,432	1,274	66	413	86	12,127	2,419	3,478	222	8,649	2,373
Other crop	34,879	1,360	2,407	85	901	277	31,571	1,299	16,801	587	14,770	956
All livestock	**253,330**	**3,951**	**14,711**	**189**	**2,742**	**113**	**235,876**	**3,893**	**120,704**	**1,393**	**115,172**	**3,325**
Beef	195,143	3,223	11,547	165	2,079	99	181,517	3,170	99,103	1,269	82,414	2,590
Dairy	6,843	1,121	323	40	88	19	6,432	1,102	2,064	262	4,368	1,002
Hog	7,092	514	497	40	63	15	6,533	490	3,924	284	2,609	292
Sheep and goat	8,242	883	478	38	76	17	7,689	866	2,980	242	4,709	759
Equine	21,367	1,461	927	50	246	35	20,193	1,467	7,758	407	12,436	1,301
Poultry and egg	6,484	925	522	50	114	25	5,848	911	2,359	188	3,490	866
Aquaculture	1,659	451	94	18	***		***		461	93		
Other livestock	6,500	698	324	34	***		***		2,057	206	***	
Unknown	**10,536**		**1,601**		**40**		**8,895**		**4,894**		**4,001**	
Total†	**416,088**	**5,473**	**28,577**	**254**	**7,435**	**533**	**380,076**	**5,404**	**191,848**	**1,653**	**188,228**	**4,869**

† Estimates may not add to the total because of rounding.
*** Estimate is not reportable or is suppressed because of a non-reportable cell.

17

Table 2.3 National estimates of **all working youth** less than 20 years of age on racial minority farms by relationship to the farm and type of farm, 2000

Type of Farm	Total †		Working Household Youth		Non-Household Working Youth		Hired Youth		Working Relatives	
	Estimate	se	Estimate	se	Estimate	se	Estimate	se	Estimate	se
All crop	**13,208**	**573**	**4,140**	**99**	**9,068**	**555**	**4,653**	**528**	**4,415**	**176**
Grain and oil seed	1,946	103	804	46	1,141	81	340	36	801	68
Tobacco	983	72	188	18	795	66	357	38	438	49
Cotton	307	32	142	17	165	22	55	11	110	18
Vegetable and melon	2,503	146	714	43	1,789	128	905	82	885	88
Fruit, nut, and berry	3,733	456	998	48	2,735	448	1,682	440	1,053	94
Nursery and floriculture	930	98	293	29	637	91	413	86	224	31
Other crop	2,806	290	1,001	49	1,805	283	901	277	904	82
All livestock	**20,863**	**393**	**7,369**	**129**	**13,494**	**354**	**2,742**	**113**	**10,751**	**328**
Beef	16,592	349	5,729	112	10,863	314	2,079	99	8,784	291
Dairy	515	66	176	26	339	55	88	19	251	49
Hog	452	47	229	27	223	32	63	15	160	28
Sheep and goat	558	58	299	29	259	43	76	17	183	38
Equine	1,574	122	485	35	1,090	112	246	35	843	104
Poultry and egg	536	53	265	31	271	38	114	25	157	27
Aquaculture	77	19	45	13	31	13	***		***	
Other livestock	559	103	141	19	418	96	***		***	
Unknown	**455**		**244**		**211**		**40**		**171**	
Total †	**34,525**	**682**	**11,753**	**159**	**22,773**	**651**	**7,435**	**533**	**15,338**	**371**

† Estimates may not add to the total because of rounding.
*** Estimate is not reportable or is suppressed because of a non-reportable cell.

Table 2.4   National estimates of **household youth** less than 20 years of age on racial minority farms by sex and age, 2000

Age	Total † Estimate	se	Male Estimate	se	Female Estimate	se	Unknown Estimate
<10 years	**9,339**	**136**	**4,799**	**87**	**4,537**	**87**	**3**
10-15 years	**10,577**	**134**	**5,621**	**91**	**4,954**	**85**	**2**
10-11 years	3,219	64	1,821	48	1,396	42	2
12-13 years	3,514	67	1,815	48	1,699	47	0
14-15 years	3,844	69	1,985	50	1,859	48	0
16-19 years	**7,648**	**105**	**4,148**	**76**	**3,501**	**68**	**0**
16-17 years	4,222	74	2,232	54	1,990	50	0
18-19 years	3,426	66	1,916	49	1,511	44	0
Unknown	**1,012**		**75**		**50**		**887**
Total †	**28,577**	**254**	**14,643**	**160**	**13,042**	**151**	**892**

† Estimates may not add to the total because of rounding.

Table 2.5   National estimates of **household youth** less than 20 years of age on racial minority farms by sex and type of farm, 2000

	Total † Estimate	se	Male Estimate	se	Female Estimate	se	Unknown Estimate
All crop	**12,265**	**183**	**6,460**	**114**	**5,698**	**107**	**106**
Grain and oil seed	2,063	77	1,091	48	964	46	8
Tobacco	452	31	227	19	225	19	0
Cotton	388	35	217	22	171	19	0
Vegetable and melon	2,173	90	1,134	52	974	48	65
Fruit, nut, and berry	3,508	99	1,876	61	1,616	57	16
Nursery and floriculture	1,274	66	669	42	590	36	15
Other crop	2,407	85	1,246	52	1,159	51	2
All livestock	**14,711**	**189**	**7,725**	**120**	**6,935**	**112**	**51**
Beef	11,547	165	6,114	105	5,392	98	42
Dairy	323	40	176	25	146	21	0
Hog	497	40	259	25	233	23	4
Sheep and goat	478	38	239	21	236	23	3
Equine	927	50	436	31	489	32	2
Poultry and egg	522	50	279	29	243	28	0
Aquaculture	94	18	59	14	36	8	0
Other livestock	324	34	163	20	161	19	0
Unknown	**1,601**		**457**		**409**		**734**
Total †	**28,577**	**254**	**14,643**	**160**	**13,042**	**151**	**892**

† Estimates may not add to the total because of rounding.

Table 2.6 National estimates of **household youth** less than 20 years of age on racial minority farms by age and type of farm, 2000

Type of Farm	Total[†] Estimate	se	<10 years Estimate	se	10-11 years Estimate	se	12-13 years Estimate	se
All crop	**12,265**	**183**	**4,241**	**96**	**1,441**	**44**	**1,503**	**45**
Grain and oil seed	2,063	77	676	39	234	18	232	19
Tobacco	452	31	163	17	44	6	69	9
Cotton	388	35	146	18	48	8	51	9
Vegetable and melon	2,173	90	710	43	247	18	275	20
Fruit, nut, and berry	3,508	99	1,179	50	446	25	431	24
Nursery and floriculture	1,274	66	493	35	137	14	181	18
Other crop	2,407	85	874	45	286	20	264	19
All livestock	**14,711**	**189**	**4,849**	**99**	**1,668**	**46**	**1,882**	**49**
Beef	11,547	165	3,800	86	1,326	40	1,471	43
Dairy	323	40	122	22	30	6	42	9
Hog	497	40	186	20	72	12	75	10
Sheep and goat	478	38	117	17	41	7	75	10
Equine	927	50	310	26	110	12	98	12
Poultry and egg	522	50	171	21	51	11	70	11
Aquaculture	94	18	36	10	***		***	
Other livestock	324	34	106	16	***		***	
Unknown	**1,601**		**249**		**111**		**129**	
Total[†]	**28,577**	**254**	**9,339**	**136**	**3,219**	**64**	**3,514**	**67**

Type of Farm	14-15 years Estimate	se	16-17 years Estimate	se	18-19 years Estimate	se	Unknown Estimate
All crop	**1,642**	**46**	**1,888**	**50**	**1,422**	**44**	**128**
Grain and oil seed	288	19	333	21	285	19	15
Tobacco	69	8	63	8	43	8	0
Cotton	49	9	58	9	33	6	4
Vegetable and melon	288	20	373	23	214	18	68
Fruit, nut, and berry	471	25	504	25	454	25	22
Nursery and floriculture	159	15	195	18	95	12	15
Other crop	317	22	363	22	298	21	5
All livestock	**2,099**	**52**	**2,207**	**54**	**1,901**	**49**	**105**
Beef	1,699	46	1,666	47	1,495	43	90
Dairy	44	9	39	8	45	8	0
Hog	41	7	63	9	53	8	7
Sheep and goat	73	10	90	12	79	11	3
Equine	114	13	193	17	99	13	2
Poultry and egg	72	11	85	11	69	10	4
Aquaculture	***		19	5	9	3	0
Other livestock	***		52	9	51	9	0
Unknown	**103**		**127**		**104**		**778**
Total[†]	**3,844**	**69**	**4,222**	**74**	**3,426**	**66**	**1,012**

† Estimates may not add to the total because of rounding.
*** Estimate is not reportable or is suppressed because of a non-reportable cell.

Table 2.7   National estimates of **household youth** less than 20 years of age on racial minority farms by age, sex, and type of farm, 2000

	<10 years						
	Total [†]		Male		Female		Unknown
Type of Farm	Estimate	se	Estimate	se	Estimate	se	Estimate
All crop	**4,241**	**96**	**2,179**	**60**	**2,059**	**61**	**3**
Grain and oil seed	676	39	352	24	321	24	3
Tobacco	163	17	87	12	76	10	0
Cotton	146	18	86	12	59	10	0
Vegetable and melon	710	43	370	27	340	25	0
Fruit, nut, and berry	1,179	50	602	31	577	33	0
Nursery and floriculture	493	35	255	23	238	21	0
Other crop	874	45	427	27	447	30	0
All livestock	**4,849**	**99**	**2,509**	**64**	**2,340**	**62**	**0**
Beef	3,800	86	1,951	56	1,850	54	0
Dairy	122	22	74	14	48	11	0
Hog	186	20	96	13	90	13	0
Sheep and goat	117	17	65	11	52	10	0
Equine	310	26	145	15	165	18	0
Poultry and egg	171	21	88	12	84	14	0
Aquaculture	36	10	20	6	16	6	0
Other livestock	106	16	71	12	35	7	0
Unknown	**249**		**111**		**139**		**0**
Total [†]	**9,339**	**136**	**4,799**	**87**	**4,537**	**87**	**3**

	10-15 years						
	Total [†]		Male		Female		Unknown
Type of Farm	Estimate	se	Estimate	se	Estimate	se	Estimate
All crop	**4,586**	**92**	**2,521**	**63**	**2,065**	**56**	**0**
Grain and oil seed	754	39	425	26	330	24	0
Tobacco	182	16	99	11	84	10	0
Cotton	147	17	75	10	72	10	0
Vegetable and melon	810	43	437	27	373	25	0
Fruit, nut, and berry	1,348	51	786	36	562	29	0
Nursery and floriculture	477	32	249	21	228	20	0
Other crop	867	41	450	27	417	25	0
All livestock	**5,649**	**100**	**2,921**	**66**	**2,727**	**64**	**2**
Beef	4,496	88	2,370	59	2,125	56	2
Dairy	116	18	58	11	58	10	0
Hog	188	21	100	13	88	13	0
Sheep and goat	189	19	89	11	100	13	0
Equine	323	25	144	16	178	18	0
Poultry and egg	192	25	94	15	98	15	0
Aquaculture	30	9	***		***		0
Other livestock	115	15	***		***		0
Unknown	**343**		**180**		**163**		**0**
Total [†]	**10,577**	**134**	**5,621**	**91**	**4,954**	**85**	**2**

Continued

Table 2.7 National estimates of **household youth** less than 20 years of age on racial minority farms by age, sex, and type of farm, 2000 (Continued)

	16-19 years						
	Total [†]		Male		Female		Unknown
Type of Farm	Estimate	se	Estimate	se	Estimate	se	Estimate
All crop	**3,310**	**72**	**1,744**	**50**	**1,566**	**46**	**0**
Grain and oil seed	618	31	305	21	313	21	0
Tobacco	106	11	41	6	65	8	0
Cotton	91	12	54	9	38	8	0
Vegetable and melon	586	31	325	22	261	19	0
Fruit, nut, and berry	958	39	488	26	470	25	0
Nursery and floriculture	289	25	164	18	125	13	0
Other crop	661	34	366	24	295	22	0
All livestock	**4,108**	**79**	**2,266**	**57**	**1,842**	**50**	**0**
Beef	3,161	69	1,770	50	1,391	43	0
Dairy	84	15	44	8	41	9	0
Hog	116	13	62	9	54	8	0
Sheep and goat	169	18	86	11	84	12	0
Equine	292	23	147	16	145	15	0
Poultry and egg	155	17	94	13	61	10	0
Aquaculture	28	7	19	5	9	3	0
Other livestock	103	15	46	9	57	10	0
Unknown	**231**		**137**		**93**		**0**
Total [†]	**7,648**	**105**	**4,148**	**76**	**3,501**	**68**	**0**

† Estimates may not add to the total because of rounding.
*** Estimate is not reportable or is suppressed because of a non-reportable cell.

Table 2.8 National estimates of **household youth** less than 20 years of age on racial minority farms by work status and sex, 2000

	Total [†]		Working		Non-Working		Unknown
Sex	Estimate	se	Estimate	se	Estimate	se	Estimate
Male	14,643	160	7,303	112	7,293	112	47
Female	13,042	151	4,441	89	8,571	121	30
Unknown	892		9		60		823
Total [†]	28,577	254	11,753	159	15,924	186	900

† Estimates may not add to the total because of rounding.

Table 2.9 National estimates of **household youth** less than 20 years of age on racial minority farms by work status and age, 2000

Age	Total [†] Estimate	se	Working Estimate	se	Non-Working Estimate	se	Unknown Estimate
<10 years	**9,339**	**136**	**1,626**	**53**	**7,702**	**123**	**12**
10-15 years	**10,577**	**134**	**5,614**	**98**	**4,949**	**91**	**15**
10-11 years	3,219	64	1,453	43	1,763	48	3
12-13 years	3,514	67	1,862	49	1,642	47	10
14-15 years	3,844	69	2,299	54	1,543	44	2
16-19 years	**7,648**	**105**	**4,459**	**81**	**3,163**	**66**	**26**
16-17 years	4,222	74	2,501	57	1,710	47	11
18-19 years	3,426	66	1,959	50	1,453	43	15
Unknown	**1,012**		**54**		**110**		**847**
Total [†]	**28,577**	**254**	**11,753**	**159**	**15,924**	**186**	**900**

† Estimates may not add to the total because of rounding.

Table 2.10 National estimates of **household youth** less than 20 years of age on racial minority farms by age, work status, and sex, 2000

	<10 years						
Sex	Total [†] Estimate	se	Working Estimate	se	Non-Working Estimate	se	Unknown Estimate
Male	4,799	87	924	37	3,866	78	9
Female	4,537	87	701	33	3,833	79	3
Unknown	3		0		3		0
Total [†]	9,339	136	1,626	53	7,702	123	12

	10-15 years						
Sex	Total [†] Estimate	se	Working Estimate	se	Non-Working Estimate	se	Unknown Estimate
Male	5,621	91	3,428	71	2,185	57	8
Female	4,954	85	2,186	58	2,761	63	7
Unknown	2		0		2		0
Total [†]	10,577	134	5,614	98	4,949	91	15

	16-19 years						
Sex	Total [†] Estimate	se	Working Estimate	se	Non-Working Estimate	se	Unknown Estimate
Male	4,148	76	2,930	64	1,214	40	14
Female	3,501	68	1,540	46	1,949	51	13
Total [†]	7,648	105	4,459	81	3,163	66	26

† Estimates may not add to the total because of rounding.

Table 2.11   National estimates of **household youth** less than 20 years of age on racial minority farms by whether they rode a horse and sex, 2000

Sex	Total [†] Estimate	se	Rode a Horse: Yes Estimate	se	Rode a Horse: No Estimate	se	Unknown Estimate
Male	14,643	160	3,966	85	10,614	139	63
Female	13,042	151	3,491	79	9,518	131	33
Unknown	892		2		48		842
Total [†]	28,577	254	7,459	130	20,181	218	937

† Estimates may not add to the total because of rounding.

Table 2.12   National estimates of **household youth** less than 20 years of age on racial minority farms by whether they rode a horse and age, 2000

Age	Total [†] Estimate	se	Rode a Horse: Yes Estimate	se	Rode a Horse: No Estimate	se	Unknown Estimate
<10 years	**9,339**	**136**	**2,042**	**63**	**7,281**	**120**	**17**
10-15 years	**10,577**	**134**	**3,247**	**75**	**7,308**	**113**	**22**
10-11 years	3,219	64	979	36	2,234	53	6
12-13 years	3,514	67	1,048	37	2,454	57	12
14-15 years	3,844	69	1,221	40	2,619	57	5
16-19 years	**7,648**	**105**	**2,153**	**57**	**5,465**	**90**	**31**
16-17 years	4,222	74	1,201	40	3,009	63	13
18-19 years	3,426	66	952	35	2,456	56	19
Unknown	**1,012**		**18**		**128**		**866**
Total [†]	**28,577**	**254**	**7,459**	**130**	**20,181**	**218**	**937**

† Estimates may not add to the total because of rounding.

Table 2.13 National estimates of **household youth** less than 20 years of age on racial minority farms by age, whether they rode a horse, and sex, 2000

	<10 years						
	Total [†]		Rode a Horse: Yes		Rode a Horse: No		Unknown
Sex	Estimate	se	Estimate	se	Estimate	se	Estimate
Male	4,799	87	1,051	41	3,734	78	14
Female	4,537	87	991	40	3,543	77	3
Unknown	3		0		3		0
Total [†]	9,339	136	2,042	63	7,281	120	17

	10-15 years						
	Total [†]		Rode a Horse: Yes		Rode a Horse: No		Unknown
Sex	Estimate	se	Estimate	se	Estimate	se	Estimate
Male	5,621	91	1,667	50	3,941	77	13
Female	4,954	85	1,581	50	3,364	70	10
Unknown	2		0		2		0
Total [†]	10,577	134	3,247	75	7,308	113	22

	16-19 years						
	Total [†]		Rode a Horse: Yes		Rode a Horse: No		Unknown
Sex	Estimate	se	Estimate	se	Estimate	se	Estimate
Male	4,148	76	1,246	42	2,886	634	16
Female	3,501	68	907	35	2,579	59	15
Total [†]	7,648	105	2,153	57	5,465	90	31

† Estimates may not add to the total because of rounding.

Table 2.14 National estimates of **household youth** less than 20 years of age on racial minority farms by whether they drove an all-terrain vehicle (ATV) and sex, 2000

	Total [†]		Drove an ATV: Yes		Drove an ATV: No		Unknown
Sex	Estimate	se	Estimate	se	Estimate	se	Estimate
Male	14,643	160	4,047	83	9,140	128	1,455
Female	13,042	151	2,467	63	9,200	127	1,375
Unknown	892		0		5		887
Total [†]	28,577	254	6,514	117	18,345	203	3,717

† Estimates may not add to the total because of rounding.

Table 2.15 National estimates of **household youth** less than 20 years of age on racial minority farms by whether they drove an all-terrain vehicle (ATV) and age, 2000

Age	Total [†] Estimate	se	Drove an ATV: Yes Estimate	se	Drove an ATV: No Estimate	se	Unknown Estimate
<10 years	**9,339**	**136**	**807**	**37**	**5,887**	**100**	**2,646**
10-15 years	**10,577**	**134**	**3,151**	**73**	**7,406**	**114**	**21**
10-11 years	3,219	64	818	32	2,395	55	6
12-13 years	3,514	67	933	35	2,568	58	13
14-15 years	3,844	69	1,399	42	2,443	56	2
16-19 years	**7,648**	**105**	**2,557**	**62**	**5,053**	**87**	**38**
16-17 years	4,222	74	1,358	42	2,847	61	17
18-19 years	3,426	66	1,199	40	2,206	54	21
Unknown	**1,012**		**0**		**0**		**1,012**
Total [†]	**28,577**	**254**	**6,514**	**117**	**18,345**	**203**	**3,714**

† Estimates may not add to the total because of rounding.

Table 2.16 National estimates of **household youth** less than 20 years of age on racial minority farms by age, whether they drove an all-terrain vehicle (ATV), and sex, 2000

< 10 years							
Sex	Total [†] Estimate	se	Drove an ATV: Yes Estimate	se	Drove an ATV: No Estimate	se	Unknown Estimate
Male	4,799	87	468	26	2,983	66	1,348
Female	4,537	87	338	22	2,901	66	1,298
Unknown	3		0		3		0
Total [†]	9,339	136	807	37	5,887	100	2,646

10-15 years							
Sex	Total [†] Estimate	se	Drove an ATV: Yes Estimate	se	Drove an ATV: No Estimate	se	Unknown Estimate
Male	5,621	91	1,909	53	3,701	75	11
Female	4,954	85	1,241	43	3,703	74	10
Unknown	2		0		2		0
Total [†]	10,577	134	3,151	73	7,406	114	21

16-19 years							
Sex	Total [†] Estimate	se	Drove an ATV: Yes Estimate	se	Drove an ATV: No Estimate	se	Unknown Estimate
Male	4,148	76	1,670	49	2,456	59	21
Female	3,501	68	887	34	2,596	59	17
Total [†]	7,648	105	2,557	62	5,053	87	38

† Estimates may not add to the total because of rounding.

Table 2.17 National estimates of **household youth** less than 20 years of age on racial minority farms by whether they drove a tractor and sex, 2000

Sex	Total [†] Estimate	se	Drove a Tractor: Yes Estimate	se	Drove a Tractor: No Estimate	se	Unknown Estimate
Male	14,643	160	4,675	85	8,516	122	1,452
Female	13,042	151	1,777	53	9,888	129	1,377
Unknown	892		0		5		887
Total [†]	28,577	254	6,452	106	18,408	198	3,716

† Estimates may not add to the total because of rounding.

Table 2.18 National estimates of **household youth** less than 20 years of age on racial minority farms by whether they drove a tractor and age, 2000

Age	Total [†] Estimate	se	Drove a Tractor: Yes Estimate	se	Drove a Tractor: No Estimate	se	Unknown Estimate
<10 years	**9,339**	**136**	**321**	**21**	**6,375**	**104**	**2,644**
10-15 years	**10,577**	**134**	**2,860**	**64**	**7,694**	**114**	**23**
10-11 years	3,219	64	543	26	2,270	58	6
12-13 years	3,514	67	873	33	2,628	59	13
14-15 years	3,844	69	1,444	42	2,396	55	4
16-19 years	**7,648**	**105**	**3,271**	**69**	**4,340**	**79**	**38**
16-17 years	4,222	74	1,703	47	2,504	57	15
18-19 years	3,426	66	1,568	45	1,836	48	23
Unknown	**1,012**		**0**		**0**		**1,012**
Total [†]	**28,577**	**254**	**6,452**	**106**	**18,408**	**198**	**3,716**

† Estimates may not add to the total because of rounding.

Table 2.19   National estimates of **household youth** less than 20 years of age on racial minority farms by age, whether they drove a tractor, and sex, 2000

	<10 years						
	Total [†]		Drove a Tractor: Yes		Drove a Tractor: No		Unknown
Sex	Estimate	se	Estimate	se	Estimate	se	Estimate
Male	4,799	87	215	17	3,239	69	1,345
Female	4,537	87	106	11	3,133	69	1,298
Unknown	3		0		3		0
Total [†]	9,339	136	321	21	6,375	104	2,644

	10-15 years						
	Total [†]		Drove a Tractor: Yes		Drove a Tractor: No		Unknown
Sex	Estimate	se	Estimate	se	Estimate	se	Estimate
Male	5,621	91	2,047	52	3,561	73	13
Female	4,954	85	814	33	4,131	78	10
Unknown	2		0		2		0
Total [†]	10,577	134	2,860	64	7,694	114	23

	16-19 years						
	Total [†]		Drove a Tractor: Yes		Drove a Tractor: No		Unknown
Sex	Estimate	se	Estimate	se	Estimate	se	Estimate
Male	4,148	76	2,414	58	1,715	49	19
Female	3,501	68	858	34	2,624	59	19
Total [†]	7,648	105	3,271	69	4,340	79	38

[†] Estimates may not add to the total because of rounding.

Table 2.20   National estimates of **injuries to all youth** less than 20 years of age on racial minority farms by sex and relationship to the farm, 2000

Relationship to Farm	Total [†]		Male		Female		Unknown
	Estimate	se	Estimate	se	Estimate	se	Estimate
Household youth	348	25	245	20	103	13	0
Hired youth	20	6	20	6	0		0
Visiting youth	161	15	117	13	43	7	0
Relatives	124	13	95	12	28	6	0
Non-relatives	37	8	22	6	15	4	0
Unknown	2		0		0		2
Total [†]	531	30	382	25	147	15	2

[†] Estimates may not add to the total because of rounding.

Table 2.21   National estimates of **injuries to all youth** less than 20 years of age on racial minority farms by age and relationship to farm, 2000

Relationship to Farm	Total [†] Estimate	se	<10 years Estimate	se	10-15 years Estimate	se	16-19 years Estimate	se	Unknown Estimate
Household youth	348	25	112	15	161	15	73	10	3
Hired youth	20	6	***		***		18	5	0
Visiting youth	161	15	***		***		37	7	0
Relatives	124	13	46	8	52	8	26	6	0
Non-relatives	37	8	***		***		11	4	0
Unknown	2		0		0		0		2
Total [†]	531	30	166	17	233	18	128	14	5

† Estimates may not add to the total because of rounding.
*** Estimate is not reportable or is suppressed because of a non-reportable cell.

Table 2.22   National estimates of **injuries to all youth** less than 20 years of age on racial minority farms by work status and relationship to the farm, 2000

Relationship to Farm	Total [†] Estimate	se	Working Estimate	se	Non-Working Estimate	se	Unknown Estimate
Household youth	348	25	138	15	210	19	0
Hired youth	20	6	20	6	0		0
Visiting youth	161	15	42	8	117	13	3
Relatives	124	13	42	8	79	10	3
Non-relatives	37	8	0		37	8	0
Unknown	2		0		0		2
Total [†]	531	30	200	18	326	23	5

† Estimates may not add to the total because of rounding.

Table 2.23   National estimates of **injuries to all youth** less than 20 years of age on racial minority farms by sex and race, 2000

Race	Total [†]		Male		Female		Unknown
	Estimate	se	Estimate	se	Estimate	se	Estimate
White	92	12	75	10	17	5	0
Black	78	11	53	8	25	7	0
Native American	206	18	132	14	74	10	0
Asian	40	8	***		***		0
Other races	108	15	***		***		0
Unknown	8		3		3		2
Total [†]	531	30	382	25	147	15	2

† Estimates may not add to the total because of rounding.

*** Estimate is not reportable or is suppressed because of a non-reportable cell.

Table 2.24   National estimates of **injuries to all youth** less than 20 years of age on racial minority farms by age and race, 2000

Race	Total [†]		<10 years		10-15 years		16-19 years		Unknown
	Estimate	se	Estimate	se	Estimate	se	Estimate	se	Estimate
White	92	12	20	6	32	7	40	8	0
Black	78	11	31	7	38	7	9	3	0
Native American	206	18	59	9	106	12	41	7	0
Asian	40	8	10	5	13	4	17	5	0
Other races	108	15	43	11	41	8	21	6	3
Unknown	8		3		3		0		2
Total [†]	531	30	166	17	233	18	128	14	5

† Estimates may not add to the total because of rounding

Table 2.25   National estimates of **injuries to all youth** less than 20 years of age on racial minority farms by work status and race, 2000

Race	Total [†]		Working		Non-Working		Unknown
	Estimate	se	Estimate	se	Estimate	se	Estimate
White	92	12	38	8	54	9	0
Black	78	11	27	6	51	9	0
Native American	206	18	85	11	121	13	0
Asian	40	8	***		***		3
Other races	108	15	***		***		0
Unknown	8		0		5		2
Total [†]	531	30	200	18	326	23	5

† Estimates may not add to the total because of rounding.

*** Estimate is not reportable or is suppressed because of a non-reportable cell.

Table 2.26 National estimates of **injuries to all youth** less than 20 years of age on racial minority farms by sex and age, 2000

Age	Total [†] Estimate	se	Male Estimate	se	Female Estimate	se	Unknown Estimate
<10 years	**166**	**17**	**102**	**13**	**63**	**10**	**0**
10-15 years	**233**	**18**	**177**	**16**	**56**	**9**	**0**
10-11 years	59	9	41	7	18	5	0
12-13 years	62	9	47	8	15	4	0
14-15 years	112	12	89	11	23	5	0
16-19 years	**128**	**14**	**101**	**12**	**27**	**6**	**0**
16-17 years	77	11	***		***		0
18-19 years	51	8	***		***		0
Unknown	**5**		**3**		**0**		**2**
Total [†]	**531**	**30**	**382**	**25**	**147**	**15**	**2**

† Estimates may not add to the total because of rounding.
*** Estimate is not reportable or suppressed because of a non-reportable cell.

Table 2.27 National estimates of **injuries to all youth** less than 20 years of age on racial minority farms by work status and sex, 2000

Sex	Total [†] Estimate	se	Working Estimate	se	Non-Working Estimate	se	Unknown Estimate
Male	382	25	173	17	206	17	3
Female	147	15	27	6	120	13	0
Unknown	2		0		0		2
Total [†]	531	30	200	18	326	23	5

† Estimates may not add to the total because of rounding.

Table 2.28 National estimates of **injuries to all youth** less than 20 years of age on racial minority farms by work status and age, 2000

Age	Total [†] Estimate	se	Working Estimate	se	Non-Working Estimate	se	Unknown Estimate
<10 years	**166**	**17**	**26**	**7**	**139**	**16**	**0**
10-15 years	**233**	**18**	**89**	**11**	**144**	**14**	**0**
10-11 years	59	9	12	4	47	8	0
12-13 years	62	9	29	6	33	7	0
14-15 years	112	12	47	8	64	9	0
16-19 years	**128**	**14**	**85**	**11**	**40**	**7**	**3**
16-17 years	77	11	54	9	21	5	3
18-19 years	51	8	32	7	19	5	0
Unknown	**5**		**0**		**3**		**2**
Total [†]	**531**	**30**	**200**	**18**	**326**	**23**	**5**

† Estimates may not add to the total because of rounding.

Table 2.29 National estimates of **injuries to all youth** less than 20 years of age on racial minority farms by sex and type of farm, 2000

Type of Farm	Total [†] Estimate	se	Male Estimate	se	Female Estimate	se	Unknown Estimate
All crop	**163**	**17**	**125**	**14**	**38**	**9**	**0**
Grain and oil seed	61	12	44	10	17	7	0
Vegetable and melon	21	6	21	6	0		0
Fruit, nut, and berry	30	7	***		***		0
All other crop*	51		***		***		0
All livestock	**362**	**24**	**251**	**20**	**109**	**12**	**2**
Beef	244	20	171	16	71	10	2
Hog	11	4	***		***		0
Sheep and goat	33	8	***		***		0
Equine	46	9	28	7	18	5	0
Poultry and egg	13	5	13	5	0		0
All other livestock**	15		***		***		0
Unknown	**6**		**6**		**0**		**0**
Total [†]	**531**	**30**	**382**	**25**	**147**	**15**	**2**

† Estimates may not add to the total because of rounding.
* All other crop includes "Tobacco," "Cotton," "Nursery and floriculture," and "Other crop" farms.
** All other livestock includes "Dairy," "Aquaculture," and "Other livestock" farms.
*** Estimate is not reportable or is suppressed because of a non-reportable cell.

Table 2.30 National estimates of **injuries to all youth** less than 20 years of age on racial minority farms by age and type of farm, 2000

Type of Farm	Total[†] Estimate	se	<10 years Estimate	se	10-15 years Estimate	se	16-19 years Estimate	se	Unknown Estimate
All crop	**163**	**17**	**47**	**10**	**67**	**10**	**46**	**8**	**3**
Grain and oil seed	61	12	25	8	21	7	12	4	3
Vegetable and melon	21	6	***		***		10	4	0
Fruit, nut, and berry	30	7	***		***		14	4	0
All other crop*	51		7		33		11		0
All livestock	**362**	**24**	**118**	**14**	**163**	**15**	**79**	**11**	**2**
Beef	244	20	71	11	122	12	50	8	2
Hog	11	4	***		***		***		0
Sheep and goat	33	8	12	5	8	3	13	5	0
Equine	46	9	25	7	13	5	8	4	0
Poultry and egg	13	5	***		***		***		0
All other livestock**	15		***		***		***		0
Unknown	**6**		**0**		**3**		**2**		**0**
Total[†]	**531**	**30**	**166**	**17**	**233**	**18**	**128**	**14**	**5**

† Estimates may not add to the total because of rounding.
* All other crop includes "Tobacco," "Cotton," "Nursery and floriculture," and "Other crop" farms.
** All other livestock includes "Dairy," "Aquaculture," and "Other livestock" farms.
*** Estimate is not reportable or is suppressed because of a non-reportable cell.

Table 2.31 National estimates of **injuries to all youth** less than 20 years of age on racial minority farms by work status and type of farm, 2000

Type of Farm	Total[†] Estimate	se	Working Estimate	se	Non-Working Estimate	se	Unknown Estimate
All crop	**163**	**17**	**49**	**9**	**112**	**14**	**3**
Grain and oil seed	61	12	22	6	40	10	0
Vegetable and melon	21	6	***		***		0
Fruit, nut, and berry	30	7	11	4	19	6	0
All other crop*	51		***		***		0
All livestock	**362**	**24**	**151**	**16**	**209**	**17**	**2**
Beef	244	20	101	13	141	14	2
Hog	11	4	***		***		0
Sheep and goat	33	8	***		***		0
Equine	46	9	16	5	30	4	0
Poultry and egg	13	5	***		***		0
All other livestock**	39		***		***		0
Unknown	**6**		**0**		**6**		**0**
Total[†]	**531**	**30**	**200**	**18**	**326**	**23**	**5**

† Estimates may not add to the total because of rounding.
* All other crop includes "Tobacco," "Cotton," "Nursery and floriculture," and "Other crop" farms.
** All other livestock includes "Dairy," "Aquaculture," and "Other livestock" farms.
*** Estimate is not reportable or is suppressed because of a non-reportable cell.

Table 2.32   National estimates of **injuries to all youth** less than 20 years of age on racial minority farms by sex and type of injury, 2000

Type of Injury	Total [†] Estimate	se	Male Estimate	se	Female Estimate	se	Unknown Estimate
Scrape, abrasion	34	7	24	6	11	4	0
Bruise, contusion	61	9	45	8	17	4	0
Sprain, strain	31	7	9	4	22	5	0
Broken bone, fracture	121	13	94	11	27	6	0
Cut, laceration	130	14	101	12	29	8	0
Puncture, stab, jab	53	9	45	8	7	3	0
Burn, blister, scald	12	4	10	3	2	1	0
Multiple injuries	31	6	13	4	17	5	0
All other injuries*	51		39		13		0
Unknown	8		2		3		2
Total [†]	531	30	382	25	147	15	2

† Estimates may not add to the total because of rounding.
* All other injuries includes "Dislocation," "Traumatic rupture," "Crushed," "Amputation," "Nerve injury," and "Other injury."

Table 2.33   National estimates of **injuries to all youth** less than 20 years of age on racial minority farms by age and type of injury, 2000

Type of Injury	Total [†] Estimate	se	<10 years Estimate	se	10-15 years Estimate	se	16-19 years Estimate	se	Unknown Estimate
Scrape, abrasion	34	7	***		19	5	***		0
Bruise, contusion	61	9	14	4	33	6	15	5	0
Sprain, strain	31	7	***		***		19	5	0
Broken bone, fracture	121	13	40	8	52	8	30	7	0
Cut, laceration	130	14	63	11	38	7	26	6	3
Puncture, stab, jab	53	9	7	3	32	7	14	5	0
Burn, blister, scald	12	4	***		***		***		0
Multiple injuries	31	6	***		22	5	***		0
All other injuries*	51		18		22		11		0
Unknown	8		0		5		0		2
Total [†]	531	30	166	17	233	18	128	14	5

† Estimates may not add to the total because of rounding.
* All other injuries includes "Dislocation," "Traumatic rupture," "Crushed," "Amputation," "Nerve injury," and "Other injury."
*** Estimate is not reportable or is suppressed because of a non-reportable cell.

Table 2.34   National estimates of **injuries to all youth** less than 20 years of age on racial minority farms by work status and type of injury, 2000

Type of Injury	Total[†] Estimate	se	Working Estimate	se	Non-Working Estimate	se	Unknown Estimate
Scrape, abrasion	34	7	***		***		0
Bruise, contusion	61	9	20	6	41	7	0
Sprain, strain	31	7	11	4	20	5	0
Broken bone, fracture	121	13	40	8	81	10	0
Cut, laceration	130	14	56	9	74	11	0
Puncture, stab, jab	53	9	20	6	32	7	0
Burn, blister, scald	12	4	***		***		0
Multiple injuries	31	6	19	5	12	4	0
All other injuries*	51		20		28		3
Unknown	8		3		2		2
Total[†]	531	30	200	18	326	23	5

† Estimates may not add to the total because of rounding.
* All other injuries includes "Dislocation," "Traumatic rupture," "Crushed," "Amputation," "Nerve injury," and "Other injury."
*** Estimate is not reportable or is suppressed because of a non-reportable cell.

Table 2.35   National estimates of **injuries to all youth** less than 20 years of age on racial minority farms by sex and body part injured, 2000

Body Part Injured	Total[†] Estimate	se	Male Estimate	se	Female Estimate	se	Unknown Estimate
Head, skull	57	9	50	8	7	3	0
Face	50	9	39	8	11	4	0
Shoulder, chest, back	38	7	27	6	11	4	0
Arm	91	11	61	9	30	6	0
Hand, wrist, fingers	79	11	70	10	9	4	0
Leg	77	11	43	9	34	7	0
Foot, ankle, toes	68	10	50	8	18	5	0
Multiple body parts	30	6	20	5	9	3	0
All other body parts*	36		18		18		0
Unknown	5		3		0		2
Total[†]	531	30	382	25	147	15	2

† Estimates may not add to the total because of rounding.
* All other body parts includes "Neck," "Abdomen," "Pelvic region," "Internal injury," and "Other body parts."

Table 2.36   National estimates of **injuries to all youth** less than 20 years of age on racial minority farms by age and body part injured, 2000

Body Part Injured	Total [†] Estimate	se	<10 years Estimate	se	10-15 years Estimate	se	16-19 years Estimate	se	Unknown Estimate
Head, skull	57	9	25	5	23	6	10	3	0
Face	50	9	28	6	12	4	11	4	0
Shoulder, chest, back	38	7	8	3	13	4	17	5	0
Arm	91	11	41	8	40	7	10	4	0
Hand, wrist, fingers	79	11	17	5	42	8	21	6	0
Leg	77	11	19	6	38	7	21	5	0
Foot, ankle, toes	68	10	11	4	29	6	29	7	0
Multiple body parts	30	6	***		17	4	***		0
All other body parts*	36		***		21		***		0
Unknown	5		0		0		0		5
Total [†]	531	30	166	17	233	18	128	14	5

† Estimates may not add to the total because of rounding.
* All other body parts includes "Neck," "Abdomen," "Pelvic region," "Internal injury," and "Other body parts."
*** Estimate is not reportable or is suppressed because of a non-reportable cell.

Table 2.37   National estimates of **injuries to all youth** less than 20 years of age on racial minority farms by work status and body part injured, 2000

Body Part Injured	Total [†] Estimate	se	Working Estimate	se	Non-Working Estimate	se	Unknown Estimate
Head, skull	57	9	22	5	35	7	0
Face	50	9	8	3	40	8	3
Shoulder, chest, back	38	7	12	5	26	6	0
Arm	91	11	25	6	66	10	0
Hand, wrist, fingers	79	11	39	7	40	8	0
Leg	77	11	34	8	43	8	0
Foot, ankle, toes	68	10	33	7	35	7	0
Multiple body parts	30	6	14	4	15	4	0
All other body parts*	36		14		23		0
Unknown	5		0		3		2
Total [†]	531	30	200	18	326	23	5

† Estimates may not add to the total because of rounding.
* All other body parts includes "Neck," "Abdomen," "Pelvic region," "Internal injury," and "Other body parts."

Table 2.38   National estimates of **injuries to all youth** less than 20 years of age on racial minority farms by body part injured and type of injury, 2000

Body Part Injured	Type of Injury	Total [†] Estimate	se
Head, skull	**All injury types**	**57**	**9**
	Bruise, contusion	9	3
	Cut, laceration	28	6
Face	**All injury types**	**50**	**9**
	Cut, laceration	28	6
	Puncture, stab, jab	8	3
Shoulder, chest, back	**All injury types**	**38**	**7**
	Bruise, contusion	10	4
	Fracture	8	3
Arm	**All injury types**	**90**	**11**
	Scrape, abrasion	7	3
	Fracture	61	9
	Cut, laceration	15	4
Hand, wrist, fingers	**All injury types**	**79**	**11**
	Fracture	26	6
	Cut, laceration	24	6
	Puncture, stab, jab	10	5
Leg	**All injury types**	**77**	**11**
	Bruise, contusion	22	6
	Fracture	8	3
	Cut, laceration	15	5
	Multiple injuries	8	3
Foot, ankle, toes	**All injury types**	**68**	**10**
	Sprain, strain	16	5
	Fracture	13	4
	Cut, laceration	9	4
	Puncture, stab, jab	22	6
Multiple body parts	**All injury types**	**30**	**6**
	Multiple injuries	10	3
All other body parts*	**All injury types**	**36**	
	Sprain, strain	8	
Unknown	**All injury types**	**5**	
Total [†]	**All injury types**	**531**	**30**

† Estimates may not add to the total because of rounding.
* All other body parts includes "Neck," "Abdomen," "Pelvic region," "Internal injury," and "Other body parts."

Table 2.39   National estimates of **injuries to all youth** less than 20 years of age on racial minority farms by sex and source of injury, 2000

Source of Injury ‡	Total †		Male		Female		Unknown
	Estimate	se	Estimate	se	Estimate	se	Estimate
Chemicals (0)	10	4	***		***		0
Containers (1)	11	4	***		***		0
Machinery (3)	7	3	7	3	0		0
Parts/Materials (4)	46	9	***		***		0
Fasteners (42)	18	5	***		***		0
Nails (4212)	*11*	*4*	***		***		*0*
Vehicle Parts (48)	23	6	***		***		0
Trailers (483)	*17*	*5*	***		***		*0*
Persons/Animals/Plants/Minerals (5)	83	11	52	8	31	6	0
Animals (51)	68	10	37	7	31	6	0
Insects (514)	*8*	*5*	***		***		*0*
Cattle (5152)	*11*	*4*	***		***		*0*
Dogs (5153)	*20*	*5*	***		***		*0*
Horses (5154)	*20*	*5*	***		***		*0*
Plants/Trees (58)	8	3	8	3	0		0
Structures and Surfaces (6)	164	15	119	13	46	7	0
Floors/Walkways/Ground (62)	132	14	94	12	38	7	0
Building Floor (6221)	*13*	*4*	***		***		*0*
Ground (623)	*114*	*13*	*79*	*11*	*36*	*6*	*0*
Other Structural Elements (63)	27	6	19	5	8	3	0
Fences (632)	*15*	*4*	***		***		*0*
Tools/Instruments/Equipment (7)	51	8	41	7	10	4	0
Nonpowered Hand Tools (71)	16	4	***		***		0
Knives (7124)	*11*	*4*	***		***		*0*
Recreation Equipment (78)	26	6	18	5	8	3	0
Gymnasium Equipment (782)	*7*	*2*	***		***		*0*
Water Sports Equipment (786)	*8*	*3*	***		***		*0*
Recreation Equipment n.e.c. (789)*	*8*	*3*	*8*	*3*	*0*		*0*
Vehicles (8)	62	9	48	7	14	5	0
Highway Vehicles (82)	12	4	***		***		0
Off-Road Vehicles (84)	35	7	***		***		0
All Terrain Vehicle (841)	*32*	*7*	***		***		*0*
Industrial Vehicles (85)	13	4	***		***		0
Tractors (853)	*13*	*4*	***		***		*0*
Other and Unknown Sources**	97		63		32		2
Total †	531	30	382	25	147	15	2

† Estimates may not add to the total because of rounding.

‡ Categories based on the Bureau of Labor Statistics Occupational Injury and Illness Coding Structure (OIICS). OIICS codes are provided in parentheses.

* "n.e.c." is an abbreviation for "not elsewhere classified."

** Other and Unknown Sources includes "Furniture and Fixtures," "Other Sources," and "Unknown Sources."

*** Estimate is not reportable or is suppressed because of a non-reportable cell.

Table 2.40   National estimates of **injuries to all youth** less than 20 years of age on racial minority farms by age and source of injury, 2000

Source of Injury ‡	Total † Estimate	se	<10 years Estimate	se	10-15 years Estimate	se	16-19 years Estimate	se	Unknown Estimate
Chemicals (0)	10	4	***		***		***		0
Containers (1)	11	4	***		***		***		0
Machinery (3)	7	3	***		***		***		0
Parts/Materials (4)	46	9	12	5	16	5	18	5	0
Fasteners (42)	18	5	***		***		9	4	0
Nails (4212)	*8*	*4*	***		***		***		*0*
Vehicle Parts (48)	23	6	***		11	4	***		0
Trailers (483)	*17*	*5*	***		*11*	*4*	***		*0*
Persons/Animals/Plants/Minerals (5)	83	11	33	8	30	6	21	5	0
Animals (51)	68	10	30	7	23	5	15	4	0
Insects (514)	*8*	*5*	***		***		***		*0*
Cattle (5152)	*11*	*4*	***		***		***		*0*
Dogs (5153)	*20*	*5*	*9*	*4*	***		***		*0*
Horses (5154)	*20*	*5*	*8*	*3*	***		***		*0*
Plants/Trees (58)	8	3	***		***		***		0
Structures and Surfaces (6)	164	15	59	10	77	10	29	7	0
Floors/Walkways/Ground (62)	132	14	54	9	58	9	20	5	0
Building Floor (6221)	*13*	*4*	*11*	*4*	***		***		*0*
Ground (623)	*114*	*13*	*41*	*8*	*56*	*8*	*18*	*5*	*0*
Other Structural Elements (63)	27	6	***		17	4	***		0
Fences (632)	*15*	*4*	***		*9*	*3*	***		*0*
Tools/Instruments/Equipment (7)	51	8	17	4	18	5	17	5	0
Nonpowered Hand Tools (71)	16	4	***		8	3	***		0
Knives (7124)	*11*	*4*	***		***		***		*0*
Recreation Equipment (78)	26	6	12	4	***		***		0
Gymnasium Equipment (782)	*7*	*2*	*7*	*2*	*0*		*0*		*0*
Water Sports Equipment (786)	*8*	*3*	***		***		***		*0*
Recreation Equipment n.e.c. (789)*	*8*	*3*	***		***		***		*0*
Vehicles (8)	62	9	***		41	7	***		0
Highway Vehicles (82)	12	4	***		***		***		0
Off-Road Vehicles (84)	35	7	***		26	6	***		0
All Terrain Vehicle (841)	*32*	*7*	***		*23*	*5*	***		*0*
Industrial Vehicles (85)	13	4	***		7	3	***		0
Tractors (853)	*13*	*4*	***		*7*	*3*	***		*0*
Other and Unknown Sources **	97		23		40		28		5
Total †	531	30	166	17	233	18	128	14	5

† Estimates may not add to the total because of rounding.

‡ Categories based on the Bureau of Labor Statistics Occupational Injury and Illness Coding Structure (OIICS). OIICS codes are provided in parentheses.

* "n.e.c." is an abbreviation for "not elsewhere classified."

** Other and Unknown Sources includes "Furniture and Fixtures," "Other Sources," and "Unknown Sources."

*** Estimate is not reportable or is suppressed because of a non-reportable cell.

Table 2.41   National estimates of **injuries to all youth** less than 20 years of age on racial minority farms by work status and source of injury, 2000

Source of Injury ‡	Total †		Working		Non-Working		Unknown
	Estimate	se	Estimate	se	Estimate	se	Estimate
Chemicals (0)	**10**	**4**	***		***		**0**
Containers (1)	**11**	**4**	***		***		**0**
Machinery (3)	**7**	**3**	***		***		**0**
Parts/Materials (4)	**46**	**9**	**34**	**7**	**12**	**5**	**0**
Fasteners (42)	18	5	***		***		0
Nails (4212)	*8*	*4*	***		***		*0*
Vehicle Parts (48)	23	6	14	5	9	4	0
Trailers (483)	*17*	*5*	***		***		*0*
Persons/Animals/Plants/Minerals (5)	**83**	**11**	**25**	**6**	**56**	**9**	**3**
Animals (51)	68	10	17	5	51	9	0
Insects (514)	*8*	*5*	***		***		*0*
Cattle (5152)	*11*	*4*	***		***		*0*
Dogs (5153)	*20*	*5*	*0*		*19*	*5*	*0*
Horses (5154)	*20*	*5*	***		***		*0*
Plants/Trees (58)	8	3	8	3	0		0
Structures and Surfaces (6)	**164**	**15**	**53**	**9**	**111**	**12**	**0**
Floors/Walkways/Ground (62)	132	14	35	7	96	12	0
Building Floor (6221)	*13*	*4*	*0*		*13*	*4*	*0*
Ground (623)	*114*	*13*	*35*	*7*	*79*	*11*	*0*
Other Structural Elements (63)	27	6	12	4	15	4	0
Fences (632)	*15*	*4*	***		***		*0*
Tools/Instruments/Equipment (7)	**51**	**8**	**19**	**5**	**33**	**6**	**0**
Nonpowered Hand Tools (71)	16	4	***		***		0
Knives (7124)	*11*	*4*	***		***		*0*
Recreation Equipment (78)	26	6	0		26	6	0
Gymnasium Equipment (782)	*7*	*2*	*0*		*7*	*2*	*0*
Water Sports Equipment (786)	*8*	*3*	*0*		*8*	*3*	*0*
Recreation Equipment n.e.c. (789)*	*8*	*3*	*0*		*8*	*3*	*0*
Vehicles (8)	**62**	**9**	**20**	**5**	**42**	**7**	**0**
Highway Vehicles (82)	12	4	***		***		0
Off-Road Vehicles (84)	35	7	12	4	23	5	0
All Terrain Vehicle (841)	*32*	*7*	*12*	*4*	*20*	*5*	*0*
Industrial Vehicles (85)	13	4	***		***		0
Tractors (853)	*13*	*4*	***		***		*0*
Other and Unknown Sources**	**97**		**34**		**60**		**2**
Total †	**531**	**30**	**200**	**18**	**326**	**23**	**5**

† Estimates may not add to the total because of rounding.

‡ Categories based on the Bureau of Labor Statistics Occupational Injury and Illness Coding Structure (OIICS). OIICS codes are provided in parentheses.

* "n.e.c." is an abbreviation for "not elsewhere classified."

** Other and Unknown Sources includes "Furniture and Fixtures," "Other Sources," and "Unknown Sources."

*** Estimate is not reportable or is suppressed because of a non-reportable cell.

Table 2.42   National estimates of **injuries to all youth** less than 20 years of age on racial minority farms by sex and type of injury event, 2000

Type of Injury Event [‡]	Total [†] Estimate	se	Male Estimate	se	Female Estimate	se	Unknown Estimate
Contact With Objects (0)	**163**	**15**	**132**	**13**	**30**	**7**	**0**
Contact With Object Unspecified (00)	16	5	***		***		0
Struck Against Object (01)	53	8	39	7	14	5	0
Stepped on Object (011)	*11*	*4*	*11*	*4*	*0*		*0*
Against Stationary Object (012)	*40*	*7*	*28*	*6*	*12*	*4*	*0*
Struck by Object (02)	78	10	69	9	9	4	0
Struck by Falling Object (021)	*32*	*7*	***		***		*0*
Struck by Slipping Handheld Object (0232)	*18*	*5*	*18*	*5*	*0*		*0*
Struck by Object n.e.c. (029)*	*7*	*3*	***		***		*0*
Caught in Objects (03)	17	4	***		***		0
Caught in Objects n.e.c. (039)*	*12*	*4*	***		***		*0*
Falls (1)	**147**	**14**	**106**	**13**	**41**	**7**	**0**
Fall to Lower Level (11)	91	11	68	10	23	5	0
Fall From Nonmoving Vehicle (118)	*9*	*4*	*9*	*4*	*0*		*0*
Fall to Lower Level n.e.c. (119)*	*82*	*11*	*59*	*9*	*23*	*5*	*0*
Fall on Same Level (13)	47	8	32	6	16	5	0
Fall to Floor/Walkway/Ground (131)	*29*	*6*	*19*	*5*	*9*	*3*	*0*
Fall Onto Objects (132)	*8*	*3*	***		***		*0*
Fall on Same Level n.e.c. (139)*	*11*	*4*	***		***		*0*
Bodily Reaction/Exertion (2)	**8**	**3**	***		***		**0**
Bodily Reaction (21)	8	3	***		***		0
Exposure to Substances/Environments (3)	**32**	**7**	**22**	**5**	**10**	**4**	**3**
Contact With Temperature Extremes (32)	7	3	***		***		0
Exposure Caustic/Allergenic Substance (34)	26	6	18	5	8	3	3
Contact With Skin/Tissues (342)	*10*	*3*	*10*	*3*	*0*		*3*
Bee Sting (3432)	*8*	*5*	***		***		*0*
Transportation Events (4)	**60**	**9**	**52**	**8**	**9**	**5**	**0**
Non-highway Events (42)	55	9	46	8	9	5	0
Vehicle Struck Stationary Object (422)	*9*	*5*	*0*		*9*	*5*	*0*
Fall From Moving Vehicle (4231)	*13*	*4*	*13*	*4*	*0*		*0*
Overturn (4233)	*18*	*5*	*18*	*5*	*0*		*0*
Loss of Control (4234)	*7*	*3*	*7*	*3*	*0*		*0*
Assaults and Violent Acts (6)	**49**	**8**	**24**	**6**	**26**	**6**	**0**
Assault by Animal (63)	49	8	24	6	26	6	0
Nonvenomous Bites (631)	*20*	*5*	***		***		*0*
Assault by Animal n.e.c. (639)*	*30*	*6*	***		***		*0*
Other and Unknown Events**	**72**		**43**		**26**		**2**
Total [†]	**531**	**30**	**382**	**25**	**147**	**15**	**2**

† Estimates may not add to the total because of rounding.

‡ Categories based on the Bureau of Labor Statistics Occupational Injury and Illness Coding Structure (OIICS). OIICS codes are provided in parentheses.

* "n.e.c." is an abbreviation for "not elsewhere classified."

** Other and Unknown Events includes "Fires and Explosions," "Other Events," and "Unknown Events."

*** Estimate is not reportable or is suppressed because of a non-reportable cell.

Table 2.43   National estimates of **injuries to all youth** less than 20 years of age on racial minority farms by age and type of injury event, 2000

Type of Injury Event ‡	Total † Estimate	se	<10 years Estimate	se	10-15 years Estimate	se	16-19 years Estimate	se	Unknown Estimate
Contact With Objects (0)	163	15	34	7	74	9	55	9	0
Contact With Object Unspecified (00)	16	5	***		10	4	***		0
Struck Against Object (01)	53	8	18	5	19	4	16	5	0
Stepped on Object (011)	11	4	***		***		***		0
Against Stationary Object (012)	40	7	15	5	14	4	10	4	0
Struck by Object (02)	78	10	13	4	34	6	31	7	0
Struck by Falling Object (021)	32	7	***		14	4	17	5	0
Struck by Slipping Handheld Object (0232)	18	5	***		10	4	***		0
Struck by Object n.e.c. (029)*	7	3	***		***		***		0
Caught in Objects (03)	17	4	***		11	3	***		0
Caught in Objects n.e.c. (039)*	12	4	***		9	3	***		0
Falls (1)	147	14	68	10	59	9	20	5	0
Fall to Lower Level (11)	91	11	41	7	37	7	13	4	0
Fall From Nonmoving Vehicle (118)	9	4	***		***		***		0
Fall to Lower Level n.e.c. (119)*	82	11	35	7	34	7	13	4	0
Fall on Same Level (13)	47	8	27	6	***		***		0
Fall to Floor/Walkway/Ground (131)	29	6	16	5	***		***		0
Fall Onto Objects (132)	8	3	8	3	0		0		0
Fall on Same Level n.e.c. (139)*	11	4	***		***		***		0
Bodily Reaction/Exertion (2)	8	3	***		***		***		0
Bodily Reaction (21)	8	3	***		***		***		0
Exposure to Substances/Environments (3)	32	7	13	5	12	4	8	3	0
Contact With Temperature Extremes (32)	7	3	***		***		***		0
Exposure Caustic/Allergenic Substance (34)	26	6	11	5	***		***		0
Contact With Skin/Tissues (342)	10	3	***		***		***		0
Bee Sting (3432)	8	5	***		***		***		0
Transportation Events (4)	60	9	12	4	40	7	8	4	0
Non-highway Events (42)	55	9	***		37	7	***		0
Vehicle Struck Stationary Object (422)	9	5	***		***		***		0
Fall From Moving Vehicle (4231)	13	4	***		8	3	***		0
Overturn (4233)	18	5	***		16	4	***		0
Loss of Control (4234)	7	3	***		***		***		0
Assaults and Violent Acts (6)	49	8	21	5	18	5	10	3	0
Assault by Animal (63)	49	8	21	5	18	5	10	3	0
Nonvenomous Bites (631)	20	5	9	4	***		***		0
Assault by Animal n.e.c. (639)*	30	6	13	4	***		***		0
Other and Unknown Events**	72		15		28		24		5
Total †	531	30	166	17	233	18	128	14	5

† Estimates may not add to the total because of rounding.

‡ Categories based on the Bureau of Labor Statistics Occupational Injury and Illness Coding Structure (OIICS). OIICS codes are provided in parentheses.

* "n.e.c." is an abbreviation for "not elsewhere classified."

** Other and Unknown Events includes "Fires and Explosions," "Other Events," and "Unknown Events."

*** Estimate is not reportable or is suppressed because of a non-reportable cell.

Table 2.44   National estimates of **injuries to all youth** less than 20 years of age on racial minority farms by work status and type of injury event, 2000

Type of Injury Event [‡]	Total [†] Estimate	se	Working Estimate	se	Non-Working Estimate	se	Unknown Estimate
Contact With Objects (0)	**163**	**15**	**90**	**11**	**73**	**10**	**0**
Contact With Object Unspecified (00)	16	5	***		***		0
Struck Against Object (01)	53	8	37	7	17	5	0
Stepped on Object (011)	*11*	*4*	***		***		*0*
Against Stationary Object (012)	*40*	*7*	*28*	*6*	*12*	*4*	*0*
Struck by Object (02)	78	10	38	7	40	7	0
Struck by Falling Object (021)	*32*	*7*	*16*	*5*	*16*	*5*	*0*
Struck by Slipping Handheld Object (0232)	*18*	*5*	***		***		*0*
Struck by Object n.e.c.* (029)	*7*	*3*	*0*		*7*	*3*	*0*
Caught in Objects (03)	17	4	10	3	7	3	0
Caught in Objects n.e.c.* (039)	*12*	*4*	***		***		*0*
Falls (1)	**147**	**14**	**42**	**8**	**106**	**12**	**0**
Fall to Lower Level (11)	91	11	25	6	65	9	0
Fall From Nonmoving Vehicle (118)	*9*	*4*	***		***		*0*
Fall to Lower Level n.e.c.* (119)	*82*	*11*	*22*	*5*	*60*	*9*	*0*
Fall on Same Level (13)	47	8	16	5	31	6	0
Fall to Floor/Walkway/Ground (131)	*29*	*6*	*11*	*4*	*18*	*5*	*0*
Fall Onto Objects (132)	*8*	*3*	*0*		*8*	*3*	*0*
Fall on Same Level n.e.c.* (139)	*11*	*4*	***		***		*0*
Bodily Reaction/Exertion (2)	**8**	**3**	***		***		**0**
Bodily Reaction (21)	8	3	***		***		0
Exposure to Substances/Environments (3)	**32**	**7**	**14**	**4**	**16**	**6**	**3**
Contact With Temperature Extremes (32)	7	3	***		***		0
Exposure Caustic/Allergenic Substance (34)	26	6	10	3	13	5	3
Contact With Skin/Tissues (342)	*10*	*3*	***		***		*3*
Bee Sting (3432)	*8*	*5*	***		***		*0*
Transportation Events (4)	**60**	**9**	**21**	**5**	**39**	**7**	**0**
Non-highway Events (42)	55	9	21	5	34	6	0
Vehicle Struck Stationary Object (422)	*9*	*5*	***		***		*0*
Fall From Moving Vehicle (4231)	*13*	*4*	*0*		*13*	*4*	*0*
Overturn (4233)	*18*	*5*	*10*	*3*	*8*	*3*	*0*
Loss of Control (4234)	*7*	*3*	***		***		*0*
Assaults and Violent Acts (6)	**49**	**8**	***		***		**0**
Assault by Animal (63)	49	8	***		***		0
Nonvenomous Bites (631)	*20*	*5*	*0*		*20*	*5*	*0*
Assault by Animal n.e.c.* (639)	*30*	*6*	***		***		*0*
Other and Unknown Events**	**72**		**25**		**45**		**2**
Total [†]	**531**	**30**	**200**	**18**	**326**	**23**	**5**

† Estimates may not add to the total because of rounding.

‡ Categories based on the Bureau of Labor Statistics Occupational Injury and Illness Coding Structure (OIICS). OIICS codes are provided in parentheses.

* "n.e.c." is an abbreviation for "not elsewhere classified."

** Other and Unknown Events includes "Fires and Explosions," "Other Events," and "Unknown Events."

*** Estimate is not reportable or is suppressed because of a non-reportable cell.

Table 2.45   National estimates of **injuries to household youth** less than 20 years of age on racial minority farms by sex and age, 2000

Age	Total [†] Estimate	se	Male Estimate	se	Female Estimate	se
<10 years	**112**	**15**	**66**	**10**	**46**	**9**
10-15 years	**161**	**15**	**124**	**14**	**37**	**7**
10-11 years	45	8	34	7	11	4
12-13 years	42	8	29	7	13	4
14-15 years	74	10	61	9	13	4
16-19 years	**73**	**10**	**53**	**9**	**20**	**5**
16-17 years	52	9	***		***	
18-19 years	21	5	***		***	
Unknown	**3**		**3**		**0**	
Total [†]	**348**	**25**	**245**	**20**	**103**	**13**

† Estimates may not add to the total because of rounding.
*** Estimate is not reportable or is suppressed because of a non-reportable cell.

Table 2.46   National estimates of **injuries to household youth** less than 20 years of age on racial minority farms by work status and sex, 2000

Sex	Total [†] Estimate	se	Working Estimate	se	Non-Working Estimate	se
Male	245	20	114	13	131	14
Female	103	13	24	6	79	11
Total [†]	348	25	138	15	210	19

† Estimates may not add to the total because of rounding.

Table 2.47   National estimates of **injuries to household youth** less than 20 years of age on racial minority farms by work status and age, 2000

Age	Total [†]		Working		Non-Working	
	Estimate	se	Estimate	se	Estimate	se
<10 years	**112**	**15**	**15**	**5**	**96**	**14**
10-15 years	**161**	**15**	**72**	**10**	**89**	**11**
10-11 years	45	8	12	4	33	7
12-13 years	42	8	21	5	21	6
14-15 years	74	10	40	7	35	6
16-19 years	**73**	**10**	**51**	**9**	**22**	**5**
16-17 years	52	9	39	8	13	4
18-19 years	21	5	12	4	9	4
Unknown	**3**		**0**		**3**	
Total [†]	**348**	**25**	**138**	**15**	**210**	**19**

† Estimates may not add to the total because of rounding.

Table 2.48   National estimates of **injuries to household youth** less than 20 years of age on racial minority farms by sex and type of farm, 2000

Type of Farm	Total [†]		Male		Female	
	Estimate	se	Estimate	se	Estimate	se
All crop	**101**	**14**	**76**	**11**	**25**	**8**
Grain and oil seed	42	11	28	8	15	7
Vegetable and melon	9	4	9	4	0	
Fruit, nut, and berry	17	5	17	5	0	
All other crop*	33		23		11	
All livestock	**247**	**20**	**169**	**17**	**78**	**11**
Beef	162	17	112	14	50	8
Hog	8	4	***		***	
Sheep and goat	22	6	***		***	
Equine	31	8	17	6	14	4
Poultry and egg	11	5	11	5	0	
All other livestock**	13		5		8	
Total [†]	**348**	**25**	**245**	**20**	**103**	**13**

† Estimates may not add to the total because of rounding.
* All other crop includes "Tobacco," "Cotton," "Nursery and floriculture," and "Other crop" farms.
** All other livestock includes "Dairy," "Aquaculture," and "Other livestock" farms.
*** Estimate is not reportable or is suppressed because of a non-reportable cell.

Table 2.49 National estimates of **injuries to household youth** less than 20 years of age on racial minority farms by age and type of farm, 2000

Type of Farm	Total [†] Estimate	se	<10 years Estimate	se	10-15 years Estimate	se	16-19 years Estimate	se	Unknown Estimate
All crop	101	14	31	9	47	8	17	5	3
Grain and oil seed	42	11	23	8	***		***		3
Vegetable and melon	9	4	***		***		***		0
Fruit, nut, and berry	17	5	***		***		8	3	0
All other crop*	33		5		26		3		0
All livestock	247	20	78	12	114	13	56	9	0
Beef	162	17	41	8	80	10	41	7	0
Hog	8	4	***		***		***		0
Sheep and goat	22	6	10	4	***		***		0
Equine	31	8	18	6	***		***		0
Poultry and egg	11	5	***		***		***		0
All other livestock**	13		2		8		2		0
Total [†]	348	25	112	15	161	15	73	10	3

† Estimates may not add to the total because of rounding.
* All other crop includes "Tobacco," "Cotton," "Nursery and floriculture," and "Other crop" farms.
** All other livestock includes "Dairy," "Aquaculture," and "Other livestock" farms.
*** Estimate is not reportable or is suppressed because of a non-reportable cell.

Table 2.50 National estimates of **injuries to household youth** less than 20 years of age on racial minority farms by work status and type of farm, 2000

Type of Farm	Total [†] Estimate	se	Working Estimate	se	Non-Working Estimate	se
All crop	101	14	19	5	82	12
Grain and oil seed	42	11	9	4	34	9
Vegetable and melon	9	4	0		9	4
Fruit, nut, and berry	17	5	***		***	
All other crop*	33		5		29	
All livestock	247	20	119	14	128	14
Beef	162	17	83	12	79	11
Hog	8	4	***		***	
Sheep and goat	22	6	11	4	11	5
Equine	31	8	10	4	21	6
Poultry and egg	11	5	***		***	
All other livestock**	13		8		5	
Total [†]	348	25	138	15	210	19

† Estimates may not add to the total because of rounding.
* All other crop includes "Tobacco," "Cotton," "Nursery and floriculture," and "Other crop" farms.
** All other livestock includes "Dairy," "Aquaculture," and "Other livestock" farms.
*** Estimate is not reportable or is suppressed because of a non-reportable cell.

Table 2.51   National estimates of **injuries to household youth** less than 20 years of age on racial minority farms by sex and type of injury, 2000

Type of Injury	Total [†] Estimate	se	Male Estimate	se	Female Estimate	se
Scrape, abrasion	27	6	19	5	8	3
Bruise, contusion	47	9	38	8	9	3
Sprain, strain	20	5	***		***	
Broken bone, fracture	78	10	59	9	20	5
Cut, laceration	95	12	69	10	26	7
Puncture, stab, jab	21	5	21	5	0	
Burn, blister, scald	7	3	7	3	0	
Multiple injuries	28	6	13	4	15	4
All other injuries*	21		***		***	
Unknown	3		0		3	
Total [†]	348	25	245	20	103	13

† Estimates may not add to the total because of rounding.

* All other injuries includes "Dislocation," "Traumatic rupture," "Crushed," "Amputation," "Nerve injury," and "Other injury."

*** Estimate is not reportable or is suppressed because of a non-reportable cell.

Table 2.52   National estimates of **injuries to household youth** less than 20 years of age on racial minority farms by age and type of injury, 2000

Type of Injury	Total [†] Estimate	se	<10 years Estimate	se	10-15 years Estimate	se	16-19 years Estimate	se	Unknown Estimate
Scrape, abrasion	27	6	***		15	4	***		0
Bruise, contusion	47	9	11	4	23	6	13	5	0
Sprain, strain	20	5	***		***		8	3	0
Broken bone, fracture	78	10	32	7	32	6	15	5	0
Cut, laceration	95	12	45	10	33	6	15	4	3
Puncture, stab, jab	21	5	***		13	4	***		0
Burn, blister, scald	7	3	***		***		***		0
Multiple injuries	28	6	***		20	5	***		0
All other injuries*	21	5	***		13		***		0
Unknown	3		0		3		0		0
Total [†]	348	25	112	15	161	15	73	10	3

† Estimates may not add to the total because of rounding.

* All other injuries includes "Dislocation," "Traumatic rupture," "Crushed," "Amputation," "Nerve injury," and "Other injury."

*** Estimate is not reportable or is suppressed because of a non-reportable cell.

Table 2.53   National estimates of **injuries to household youth** less than 20 years of age on racial minority farms by work status and type of injury, 2000

Type of Injury	Total [†] Estimate	se	Working Estimate	se	Non-Working Estimate	se
Scrape, abrasion	27	6	***		***	
Bruise, contusion	47	9	20	6	27	6
Sprain, strain	20	5	***		***	
Broken bone, fracture	78	10	25	7	53	8
Cut, laceration	95	12	36	6	59	11
Puncture, stab, jab	21	5	14	4	8	3
Burn, blister, scald	7	3	***		***	
Multiple injuries	28	6	19	5	10	3
All other injuries*	21		8		13	
Unknown	3		3		0	
Total [†]	348	25	138	15	210	19

† Estimates may not add to the total because of rounding.

* All other injuries includes "Dislocation," "Traumatic rupture," "Crushed," "Amputation," "Nerve injury," and "Other injury."

*** Estimate is not reportable or is suppressed because of a non-reportable cell.

Table 2.54   National estimates of **injuries to household youth** less than 20 years of age on racial minority farms by sex and body part injured, 2000

Body Part Injured	Total [†] Estimate	se	Male Estimate	se	Female Estimate	se
Head, skull	35	7	***		***	
Face	36	7	25	6	11	4
Shoulder, chest, back	27	6	19	5	8	3
Arm	58	9	39	7	20	5
Hand, wrist, fingers	48	8	***		***	
Leg	54	9	35	7	20	5
Foot, ankle, toes	41	8	27	6	14	4
Multiple body parts	21	8	15	4	7	3
All other body parts*	24		11		13	
Unknown	3		3		0	
Total [†]	348	25	245	20	103	13

† Estimates may not add to the total because of rounding.

* All other body parts includes "Neck," "Abdomen," "Pelvic region," "Internal injury," and "Other body parts."

*** Estimate is not reportable or is suppressed because of a non-reportable cell.

Table 2.55   National estimates of **injuries to household youth** less than 20 years of age on racial minority farms by age and body part injured, 2000

Body Part Injured	Total [†]	se	<10 years	se	10-15 years	se	16-19 years	se	Unknown
	Estimate		Estimate		Estimate		Estimate		Estimate
Head, skull	35	7	***		23	6	***		0
Face	36	7	23	6	***		***		0
Shoulder, chest, back	27	6	***		***		17	5	0
Arm	58	9	***		29	6	***		0
Hand, wrist, fingers	48	8	***		28	6	***		0
Leg	54	9	8	3	28	6	18	5	0
Foot, ankle, toes	41	8	11	4	15	4	14	5	0
Multiple body parts	21	8	***		14	4	***		0
All other body parts*	24		***		11		***		0
Unknown	3		0		0		0		3
Total [†]	348	25	112	15	161	15	73	10	3

† Estimates may not add to the total because of rounding.
* All other body parts includes "Neck," "Abdomen," "Pelvic region," "Internal injury," and "Other body parts."
*** Estimate is not reportable or is suppressed because of a non-reportable cell.

Table 2.56   National estimates of **injuries to household youth** less than 20 years of age on racial minority farms by work status and body part injured, 2000

Body Part Injured	Total [†]	se	Working	se	Non-Working	se
	Estimate		Estimate		Estimate	
Head, skull	35	7	14	4	21	5
Face	36	7	***		***	
Shoulder, chest, back	27	6	12	5	15	4
Arm	58	9	19	5	40	7
Hand, wrist, fingers	48	8	16	4	33	7
Leg	54	9	25	6	29	7
Foot, ankle, toes	41	8	24	6	16	5
Multiple body parts	21	8	14	4	7	3
All other body parts*	24		***		***	
Unknown	3		0		3	
Total [†]	348	25	138	15	210	19

† Estimates may not add to the total because of rounding.
* All other body parts includes "Neck," "Abdomen," "Pelvic region," "Internal injury," and "Other body parts."
*** Estimate is not reportable or is suppressed because of a non-reportable cell.

Table 2.57 National estimates of **injuries to household youth** less than 20 years of age on racial minority farms by body part injured and type of injury, 2000

Body Part Injured	Type of Injury	Total[†] Estimate	se
Head, skull	**All injury types**	**35**	**7**
	Bruise, contusion	7	3
	Cut, laceration	18	5
Face	**All injury types**	**36**	**7**
	Cut, laceration	28	6
Shoulder, chest, back	**All injury types**	**27**	**6**
Arm	**All injury types**	**58**	**9**
	Scrape, abrasion	7	3
	Fracture	42	8
	Cut, laceration	7	3
Hand, wrist, fingers	**All injury types**	**48**	**8**
	Fracture	15	4
	Cut, laceration	19	5
Leg	**All injury types**	**54**	**9**
	Bruise, contusion	22	6
	Fracture	8	3
	Cut, laceration	7	3
	Multiple injuries	8	3
Foot, ankle, toes	**All injury types**	**41**	**8**
	Sprain, strain	10	3
	Cut, laceration	9	4
	Puncture, stab, jab	11	4
Multiple body parts	**All injury types**	**21**	**8**
	Multiple injuries	10	3
All other body parts*	**All injury types**	**24**	
Unknown	**All injury types**	**3**	
Total[†]	**All injury types**	**348**	**25**

† Estimates may not add to the total because of rounding.
* All other body parts includes "Neck," "Abdomen," "Pelvic region," "Internal injury," and "Other body parts."

Table 2.58   National estimates of **injuries to household youth** less than 20 years of age on racial minority farms by sex and source of injury, 2000

Source of Injury ‡	Total [†]		Male		Female	
	Estimate	se	Estimate	se	Estimate	se
Containers (1)	11	4	***		***	
Parts/Materials (4)	28	7	***		***	
Fasteners (42)	9	4	***		***	
Vehicle Parts (48)	14	5	***		***	
Trailers (483)	14	5	***		***	
Persons/Animals/Plants/Minerals (5)	40	7	26	6	14	4
Animals (51)	35	7	22	6	14	4
Cattle (5152)	11	4	***		***	
Horses (5154)	15	4	***		***	
Structures and Surfaces (6)	117	13	77	11	41	7
Floors/Walkways/Ground (62)	92	12	59	10	33	6
Ground (623)	79	11	49	9	30	6
Other Structural Elements (63)	20	5	12	3	8	3
Fences (632)	7	3	***		***	
Tools/Instruments/Equipment (7)	34	7	***		***	
Nonpowered Hand Tools (71)	10	3	10	3	0	
Recreation Equipment (78)	16	5	***		***	
Gymnasium Equipment (782)	7	2	***		***	
Vehicles (8)	49	8	37	7	12	5
Off-Road Vehicles (84)	29	6	***		***	
All Terrain Vehicle (841)	27	6	***		***	
Other and Unknown Sources*	69		46		23	
Total [†]	348	25	245	20	103	13

† Estimates may not add to the total because of rounding.

‡ Categories based on the Bureau of Labor Statistics Occupational Injury and Illness Coding Structure (OIICS). OIICS codes are provided in parentheses.

* Other and Unknown Sources includes "Chemicals," "Furniture and Fixtures," "Machinery," "Other Sources," and "Unknown Sources."

*** Estimate is not reportable or is suppressed because of a non-reportable cell.

Table 2.59 National estimates of **injuries to household youth** less than 20 years of age on racial minority farms by age and source of injury, 2000

Source of Injury ‡	Total †		<10 years		10-15 years		16-19 years		Unknown
	Estimate	se	Estimate	se	Estimate	se	Estimate	se	Estimate
Containers (1)	**11**	**4**	***		***		***		**0**
Parts/Materials (4)	**28**	**7**	***	**5**	**14**	**5**	***		**0**
Fasteners (42)	9	4							0
Vehicle Parts (48)	14	5	***		8	4	***		0
Trailers (483)	14	5	***		8	4	***		0
Persons/Animals/Plants/Minerals (5)	**40**	**7**	**13**	**5**	**15**	**4**	**13**	**4**	**0**
Animals (51)	35	7	13	5	10	3	13	4	0
Cattle (5152)	11	4	***		***		***		0
Horses (5154)	15	4	***		***		7	3	0
Structures and Surfaces (6)	**117**	**13**	**43**	**8**	**60**	**9**	**15**	**5**	**0**
Floors/Walkways/Ground (62)	92	12	40	8	43	7	10	4	0
Ground (623)	79	11	30	7	40	7	10	4	0
Other Structural Elements (63)	20	5	***		15	4	***		0
Fences (632)	7	3	0		7	3	0		0
Tools/Instruments/Equipment (7)	**34**	**7**	**10**	**3**	**14**	**4**	**10**	**4**	**0**
Nonpowered Hand Tools (71)	10	3	***		***		***		0
Recreation Equipment (78)	16	5	10	3	***		***		0
Gymnasium Equipment (782)	7	2	7	2	0		0		0
Vehicles (8)	**49**	**8**	***		**31**	**6**	***		**0**
Off-Road Vehicles (84)	29	6	***		21	5	***		0
All Terrain Vehicle (841)	27	6	***		17	4	***		0
Other and Unknown Sources*	**69**		**22**		**23**		**21**		**3**
Total †	**348**	**25**	**112**	**15**	**161**	**15**	**73**	**10**	**3**

† Estimates may not add to the total because of rounding.

‡ Categories based on the Bureau of Labor Statistics Occupational Injury and Illness Coding Structure (OIICS). OIICS codes are provided in parentheses.

* Other and Unknown Sources includes "Chemicals," "Furniture and Fixtures," "Machinery," "Other Sources," and "Unknown Sources."

*** Estimate is not reportable or is suppressed because of a non-reportable cell.

Table 2.60 National estimates of **injuries to household youth** less than 20 years of age on racial minority farms by work status and source of injury, 2000

Source of Injury [‡]	Total [†]		Working		Non-Working	
	Estimate	se	Estimate	se	Estimate	se
Containers (1)	11	4	***		***	
Parts/Materials (4)	28	7	***		***	
Fasteners (42)	9	4	***		***	
Vehicle Parts (48)	14	5	***		***	
Trailers (483)	*14*	*5*	***		***	
Persons/Animals/Plants/Minerals (5)	40	7	19	5	21	5
Animals (51)	35	7	17	5	19	5
Cattle (5152)	*11*	*4*	***		***	
Horses (5154)	*15*	*4*	***		***	
Structures and Surfaces (6)	117	13	41	8	76	11
Floors/Walkways/Ground (62)	92	12	27	6	65	10
Ground (623)	*79*	*11*	*27*	*6*	*53*	*9*
Other Structural Elements (63)	20	5	9	4	11	4
Fences (632)	*7*	*3*	***		***	
Tools/Instruments/Equipment (7)	34	7	15	4	18	5
Nonpowered Hand Tools (71)	10	3	***		***	
Recreation Equipment (78)	16	5	0		16	5
Gymnasium Equipment (782)	*7*	*2*	*0*		*7*	*2*
Vehicles (8)	49	8	15	4	34	7
Off-Road Vehicles (84)	29	6	10	3	20	5
All Terrain Vehicle (841)	*27*	*6·*	*10*	*3*	*17*	*4*
Other and Unknown Sources*	69		18		51	
Total [†]	348	25	138	15	210	19

† Estimates may not add to the total because of rounding.

‡ Categories based on the Bureau of Labor Statistics Occupational Injury and Illness Coding Structure (OIICS). OIICS codes are provided in parentheses.

* Other and Unknown Sources includes "Chemicals," "Furniture and Fixtures," "Machinery," "Other Sources," and "Unknown Sources."

*** Estimate is not reportable or is suppressed because of a non-reportable cell.

Table 2.61   National estimates of **injuries to household youth** less than 20 years of age on racial minority farms by sex and type of injury event, 2000

Type of Injury Event ‡	Total † Estimate	se	Male Estimate	se	Female Estimate	se
Contact With Objects (0)	**108**	**12**	**82**	**10**	**26**	**6**
Contact With Object Unspecified (00)	11	4	***		***	
Struck Against Object (01)	39	7	25	6	14	5
Against Stationary Object (012)	*31*	*6*	*19*	*5*	*12*	*4*
Struck by Object (02)	50	8	***		***	
Struck by Falling Object (021)	*32*	*5*	***		***	
Struck by Slipping Handheld Object (0232)	*12*	*4*	*12*	*4*	*0*	
Caught in Objects (03)	7	3	***		***	
Caught in Objects n.e.c. (039)*	*7*	*3*	***		***	
Falls (1)	**109**	**13**	**73**	**11**	**36**	**7**
Fall to Lower Level (11)	61	9	43	8	18	5
Fall to Lower Level n.e.c. (119)*	*55*	*9*	*37*	*7*	*18*	*5*
Fall on Same Level (13)	41	7	25	6	16	5
Fall to Floor/Walkway/Ground (131)	*26*	*6*	*17*	*5*	*9*	*3*
Fall on Same Level n.e.c. (139)*	*8*	*4*	***		***	
Exposure to Substances/Environments (3)	**12**	**4**	***		***	
Exposure Caustic/Allergenic Substance (34)	10	3	***		***	
Transportation Events (4)	**49**	**8**	**41**	**7**	**9**	**5**
Non-highway Events (42)	44	8	35	6	9	5
Vehicle Struck Stationary Object (422)	*9*	*5*	*0*		*9*	*5*
Fall From Moving Vehicle (4231)	*10*	*4*	*10*	*4*	*0*	
Overturn (4233)	*12*	*4*	*12*	*4*	*0*	
Assaults and Violent Acts (6)	**22**	**6**	**11**	**4**	**12**	**4**
Assault by Animal (63)	22	6	11	4	12	4
Assault by Animal n.e.c. (639)*	*16*	*5*	***		***	
Other and Unknown Events**	**48**		**29**		**19**	
Total †	**348**	**25**	**245**	**20**	**103**	**13**

† Estimates may not add to the total because of rounding.

‡ Categories based on the Bureau of Labor Statistics Occupational Injury and Illness Coding Structure (OIICS). OIICS codes are provided in parentheses.

* "n.e.c." is an abbreviation for "not elsewhere classified."

** Other and Unknown Events includes "Bodily Reaction/Exertion," "Fires and Explosions," "Other Events," and "Unknown Events."

*** Estimate is not reportable or is suppressed because of a non-reportable cell.

Table 2.62 National estimates of **injuries to household youth** less than 20 years of age on racial minority farms by age and type of injury event, 2000

Type of Injury Event ‡	Total †		<10 years		10-15 years		16-19 years		Unknown
	Estimate	se	Estimate	se	Estimate	se	Estimate	se	Estimate
Contact With Objects (0)	**108**	**12**	**26**	**6**	**56**	**8**	**26**	**6**	**0**
Contact With Object Unspecified (00)	11	4	***		***		***		0
Struck Against Object (01)	39	7	15	5	17	4	8	3	0
Against Stationary Object (012)	31	6	***		14	4	***		0
Struck by Object (02)	50	8	8	4	29	6	13	4	0
Struck by Falling Object (021)	21	5	***		11	4	***		0
Struck by Slipping Handheld Object (0232)	12	4	***		10	4	***		0
Caught in Objects (03)	7	3	***		***		***		0
Caught in Objects n.e.c. (039)*	7	3	***		***		***		0
Falls (1)	**109**	**13**	**53**	**9**	**43**	**8**	**13**	**5**	**0**
Fall to Lower Level (11)	61	9	28	6	24	6	10	4	0
Fall to Lower Level n.e.c. (119)*	55	9	22	5	24	6	10	4	0
Fall on Same Level (13)	41	7	25	6	***		***		0
Fall to Floor/Walkway/Ground (131)	26	6	16	5	***		***		0
Fall on Same Level n.e.c. (139)*	8	4	***		***		***		0
Exposure to Substances/Environments (3)	**12**	**4**	***		**7**	**3**	***		**0**
Exposure Caustic/Allergenic Substance (34)	10	3	***		7	3	***		0
Transportation Events (4)	**49**	**8**	***		**34**	**7**	***		**0**
Non-highway Events (42)	44	8	***		32	6	***		0
Vehicle Struck Stationary Object (422)	9	5	***		***		***		0
Fall From Moving Vehicle (4231)	10	4	***		8	3	***		0
Overturn (4233)	12	4	***		10	3	***		0
Assaults and Violent Acts (6)	**22**	**6**	**9**	**4**	***		***		**0**
Assault by Animal (63)	22	6	9	4	***		***		0
Assault by Animal n.e.c. (639)*	16	5	***		***		***		0
Other and Unknown Events**	**48**		**12**		**15**		**19**		**3**
Total †	**348**	**25**	**112**	**15**	**161**	**15**	**73**	**10**	**3**

† Estimates may not add to the total because of rounding.

‡ Categories based on the Bureau of Labor Statistics Occupational Injury and Illness Coding Structure (OIICS). OIICS codes are provided in parentheses.

* "n.e.c." is an abbreviation for "not elsewhere classified."

** Other and Unknown Events includes "Bodily Reaction/Exertion," "Fires and Explosions," "Other Events," and "Unknown Events."

*** Estimate is not reportable or is suppressed because of a non-reportable cell.

Table 2.63 National estimates of **injuries to household youth** less than 20 years of age on racial minority farms by work status and type of injury event, 2000

Type of Injury Event ‡	Total †		Working		Non-Working	
	Estimate	se	Estimate	se	Estimate	se
Contact With Objects (0)	**108**	**12**	**61**	**9**	**47**	**8**
Contact With Object Unspecified (00)	11	4	***		***	
Struck Against Object (01)	39	7	25	5	14	5
Against Stationary Object (012)	*31*	*6*	*19*	*5*	*12*	*4*
Struck by Object (02)	50	8	26	6	24	6
Struck by Falling Object (021)	*21*	*5*	*11*	*4*	*10*	*4*
Struck by Slipping Handheld Object (0232)	*12*	*4*	***		***	
Caught in Objects (03)	7	3	***		***	
Caught in Objects n.e.c. (039)*	*7*	*3*	***		***	
Falls (1)	**109**	**13**	**33**	**7**	**76**	**10**
Fall to Lower Level (11)	61	9	17	5	44	8
Fall to Lower Level n.e.c. (119)*	*55*	*9*	*17*	*5*	*38*	*7*
Fall on Same Level (13)	41	7	16	5	24	6
Fall to Floor/Walkway/Ground (131)	*26*	*6*	*11*	*4*	*16*	*4*
Fall on Same Level n.e.c. (139)*	*8*	*4*	***		***	
Exposure to Substances/Environments (3)	**12**	**4**	***		***	
Exposure Caustic/Allergenic Substance (34)	10	3	***		***	
Transportation Events (4)	**49**	**8**	**19**	**5**	**31**	**6**
Non-highway Events (42)	44	8	19	5	25	5
Vehicle Struck Stationary Object (422)	*9*	*5*	***		***	
Fall From Moving Vehicle (4231)	*10*	*4*	*0*		*10*	*4*
Overturn (4233)	*12*	*4*	***		***	
Assaults and Violent Acts (6)	**22**	**6**	***		***	
Assault by Animal (63)	22	6	***		***	
Assault by Animal n.e.c. (639)*	*16*	*5*	***		***	
Other and Unknown Events**	**48**		**13**		**36**	
Total †	**348**	**25**	**138**	**15**	**210**	**19**

† Estimates may not add to the total because of rounding.

‡ Categories based on the Bureau of Labor Statistics Occupational Injury and Illness Coding Structure (OIICS). OIICS codes are provided in parentheses.

* "n.e.c." is an abbreviation for "not elsewhere classified."

** Other and Unknown Events includes "Bodily Reaction/Exertion," "Fires and Explosions," "Other Events," and "Unknown Events."

*** Estimate is not reportable or is suppressed because of a non-reportable cell.

Table 2.64   National estimates of **injury rates for all youth** less than 20 years of age on racial minority farms by work status and relationship to the farm, 2000

Relationship to Farm	Total Rate/1000	se	Working Rate/1000	se	Non-Working Rate/1000	se
Household youth	**12.18**	**0.87**	**11.74**	**1.29**	**7.34**	**0.67**
Hired youth	**2.69**	**0.76**	**2.69**	**0.83**	**0.00**	
Visiting youth	**0.42**	**0.04**	**2.71**	**0.53**	**0.31**	**0.03**
Relatives	0.64	0.07	2.74	0.53	0.41	0.05
Non-relatives	0.20	0.04	0.00		0.20	0.04
Total	**1.28**	**0.07**	**5.79**	**0.53**	**0.78**	**0.06**

Table 2.65   National estimates of **injury rates for all youth** less than 20 years of age on racial minority farms by work status and type of farm, 2000

Type of Farm	Total Rate/1000	se	Working Rate/1000	se	Non-Working Rate/1000	se
All crop	**1.07**	**0.12**	**3.68**	**0.67**	**0.74**	**0.09**
Grain and oil seed	1.82	0.37	11.26	3.24	1.17	0.29
Vegetable and melon	0.94	0.27	***		***	
Fruit, nut, and berry	0.90	0.22	11.94	4.38	0.57	0.18
All other crop*	0.81		***		***	
All livestock	**1.43**	**0.10**	**7.26**	**0.76**	**0.82**	**0.07**
Beef	1.25	0.10	6.08	0.80	0.72	0.07
Hog	1.54	0.57	***		***	
Sheep and goat	3.97	1.09	29.21	9.11	1.99	0.70
Equine	2.15	0.45	10.10	3.40	1.40	0.22
Poultry and egg	2.07	0.80	***		***	
All other livestock**	1.37		***		***	
Total	**1.28**	**0.07**	**5.79**	**0.53**	**0.78**	**0.06**

* All other crop includes "Tobacco," "Cotton," "Nursery and floriculture," and "Other crop" farms.

** All other livestock includes "Dairy," "Aquaculture," and "Other livestock" farms.

*** Estimate is not reportable or is suppressed because of a non-reportable cell.

Table 2.66   National estimates of **injury rates for all youth** less than 20 years of age on racial minority farms by work status and type of injury, 2000

Type of Injury	Total Rate/1000	se	Working Rate/1000	se	Non-Working Rate/1000	se
Scrape, abrasion	0.08	0.02	***		***	
Bruise, contusion	0.15	0.02	0.59	0.17	0.10	0.02
Sprain, strain	0.07	0.02	0.32	0.11	0.05	0.01
Broken bone, fracture	0.29	0.03	1.17	0.24	0.19	0.02
Cut, laceration	0.31	0.03	1.63	0.26	0.18	0.03
Puncture, stab, jab	0.13	0.02	0.58	0.17	0.08	0.02
Burn, blister, scald	0.03	0.01	***		***	
Multiple injuries	0.07	0.01	0.54	0.15	0.03	0.01
All other injuries*	0.12		0.59		0.07	
Total	1.28	0.07	5.79	0.53	0.78	0.06

* All other injuries includes "Dislocation," "Traumatic rupture," "Crushed," "Amputation," "Nerve injury," and "Other injury."

*** Estimate is not reportable or is suppressed because of a non-reportable cell.

Table 2.67   National estimates of **injury rates for all youth** less than 20 years of age on racial minority farms by work status and body part injured, 2000

Body Part Injured	Total Rate/1000	se	Working Rate/1000	se	Non-Working Rate/1000	se
Head, skull	0.14	0.02	0.64	0.15	0.08	0.02
Face	0.12	0.02	0.22	0.09	0.10	0.02
Shoulder, chest, back	0.09	0.02	0.35	0.13	0.06	0.01
Arm	0.22	0.03	0.73	0.17	0.16	0.02
Hand, wrist, fingers	0.19	0.03	1.12	0.22	0.10	0.02
Leg	0.19	0.03	0.98	0.22	0.10	0.02
Foot, ankle, toes	0.16	0.02	0.96	0.20	0.08	0.02
Multiple body parts	0.07	0.01	0.41	0.11	0.04	0.01
All other body parts*	0.09		0.39		0.05	
Total	1.28	0.07	5.79	0.53	0.78	0.06

* All other body parts includes "Neck," "Abdomen," "Pelvic region," "Internal injury," and "Other body parts."

Table 2.68   National estimates of **injury rates for all youth** less than 20 years of age on racial minority farms by work status and source of injury, 2000

Source of Injury [†]	Total		Working		Non-Working	
	Rate/1000	se	Rate/1000	se	Rate/1000	se
Chemicals (0)	**0.02**	**0.01**	***		***	
Containers (1)	**0.03**	**0.01**	***		***	
Machinery (3)	**0.02**	**0.01**	***		***	
Parts/Materials (4)	**0.11**	**0.02**	**0.98**	**0.21**	**0.03**	**0.01**
Fasteners (42)	0.04	0.01	***		***	
Nails (4212)	*0.02*	*0.01*	***		***	
Vehicle Parts (48)	0.05	0.01	0.40	0.13	0.02	0.01
Trailers (483)	*0.04*	*0.01*	***		***	
Persons/Animals/Plants/Minerals (5)	**0.20**	**0.03**	**0.71**	**0.17**	**0.13**	**0.02**
Animals (51)	0.16	0.02	0.48	0.14	0.12	0.02
Insects (514)	*0.02*	*0.01*	***		***	
Cattle (5152)	*0.03*	*0.01*	***		***	
Dogs (5153)	*0.05*	*0.01*	*0.00*		*0.05*	*0.01*
Horses (5154)	*0.05*	*0.01*	***		***	
Plants/Trees (58)	0.02	0.01	0.22	0.09	0.00	
Structures and Surfaces (6)	**0.40**	**0.04**	**1.54**	**0.26**	**0.27**	**0.03**
Floors/Walkways/Ground (62)	0.32	0.03	1.03	0.20	0.23	0.03
Building Floor (6221)	*0.03*	*0.01*	*0.00*		*0.03*	*0.01*
Ground (623)	*0.27*	*0.03*	*1.03*	*0.20*	*0.19*	*0.03*
Other Structural Elements (63)	0.06	0.01	0.35	0.12	0.04	0.01
Fences (632)	*0.04*	*0.01*	***		***	
Tools/Instruments/Equipment (7)	**0.12**	**0.02**	**0.54**	**0.14**	**0.08**	**0.02**
Nonpowered Hand Tools (71)	0.04	0.01	***		***	
Knives (7124)	*0.03*	*0.01*	***		***	
Recreation Equipment (78)	0.06	0.01	0.00		0.06	0.01
Gymnasium Equipment (782)	*0.02*	*0.01*	*0.00*		*0.02*	*0.01*
Water Sports Equipment (786)	*0.02*	*0.01*	*0.00*		*0.02*	*0.01*
Recreation Equipment n.e.c. (789)*	*0.02*	*0.01*	*0.00*		*0.02*	*0.01*
Vehicles (8)	**0.15**	**0.02**	**0.58**	**0.14**	**0.10**	**0.02**
Highway Vehicles (82)	0.03	0.01	***		***	
Off-Road Vehicles (84)	0.08	0.02	0.34	0.10	0.06	0.01
All Terrain Vehicle (841)	*0.08*	*0.02*	*0.34*	*0.10*	*0.05*	*0.01*
Industrial Vehicles (85)	0.03	0.01	***		***	
Tractors (853)	*0.03*	*0.01*	***		***	
Other and Unknown Sources**	**0.23**		**1.00**		**0.14**	
Total	**1.28**	**0.07**	**5.79**	**0.53**	**0.78**	**0.06**

† Categories based on the Bureau of Labor Statistics Occupational Injury and Illness Coding Structure (OIICS). OIICS codes are provided in parentheses.

* "n.e.c." is an abbreviation for "not elsewhere classified."

** Other and Unknown Sources includes "Furniture and Fixtures," "Other Sources," and "Unknown Sources."

*** Estimate is not reportable or is suppressed because of a non-reportable cell.

Table 2.69   National estimates of **injury rates for all youth** less than 20 years of age on racial minority farms by work status and type of injury event, 2000

Type of Injury Event [†]	Total Rate/1000	se	Working Rate/1000	se	Non-Working Rate/1000	se
Contact With Objects (0)	**0.39**	**0.04**	**2.59**	**0.33**	**0.18**	**0.02**
Contact With Object Unspecified (00)	0.04	0.01	***		***	
Struck Against Object (01)	0.13	0.02	1.06	0.20	0.04	0.01
Stepped on Object (011)	*0.03*	*0.01*	***		***	
Against Stationary Object (012)	*0.10*	*0.02*	*0.81*	*0.17*	*0.03*	*0.01*
Struck by Object (02)	0.19	0.02	1.10	0.21	0.10	0.02
Struck by Falling Object (021)	*0.08*	*0.02*	*0.48*	*0.14*	*0.04*	*0.01*
Struck by Slipping Handheld Object (0232)	*0.04*	*0.01*	***		***	
Struck by Object n.e.c.* (029)	*0.02*	*0.01*	*0.00*		*0.02*	*0.01*
Caught in Objects (03)	0.04	0.01	0.28	0.10	0.02	0.01
Caught in Objects n.e.c.* (039)	*0.03*	*0.01*	***		***	
Falls (1)	**0.35**	**0.03**	**1.20**	**0.22**	**0.25**	**0.03**
Fall to Lower Level (11)	0.22	0.03	0.74	0.17	0.16	0.02
Fall From Nonmoving Vehicle (118)	*0.02*	*0.01*	***		***	
Fall to Lower Level n.e.c.* (119)	*0.20*	*0.03*	*0.65*	*0.16*	*0.14*	*0.02*
Fall on Same Level (13)	0.11	0.02	0.47	0.14	0.07	0.02
Fall to Floor/Walkway/Ground (131)	*0.07*	*0.01*	*0.31*	*0.11*	*0.04*	*0.01*
Fall Onto Objects (132)	*0.02*	*0.01*	*0.00*		*0.02*	*0.01*
Fall on Same Level n.e.c.* (139)	*0.03*	*0.01*	***		***	
Bodily Reaction/Exertion (2)	**0.02**	**0.01**	***		***	
Bodily Reaction (21)	0.02	0.01	***		***	
Exposure to Substances/Environments (3)	**0.08**	**0.02**	**0.41**	**0.11**	**0.04**	**0.01**
Contact With Temperature Extremes (32)	0.02	0.01	***		***	
Exposure Caustic/Allergenic Substance (34)	0.06	0.02	0.28	0.09	0.03	0.01
Contact With Skin/Tissues (342)	*0.02*	*0.01*	***		***	
Bee Sting (3432)	*0.02*	*0.01*	***		***	
Transportation Events (4)	**0.14**	**0.02**	**0.61**	**0.15**	**0.09**	**0.02**
Non-highway Events (42)	0.13	0.02	0.61	0.15	0.08	0.02
Vehicle Struck Stationary Object (422)	*0.02*	*0.01*	***		***	
Fall From Moving Vehicle (4231)	*0.03*	*0.01*	*0.00*		*0.03*	*0.01*
Overturn (4233)	*0.04*	*0.01*	*0.28*	*0.10*	*0.02*	*0.01*
Loss of Control (4234)	*0.02*	*0.01*	***		***	
Assaults and Violent Acts (6)	**0.12**	**0.02**	***		***	
Assault by Animal (63)	0.12	0.02	***		***	
Nonvenomous Bites (631)	*0.05*	*0.01*	*0.00*		*0.05*	*0.01*
Assault by Animal n.e.c.* (639)	*0.07*	*0.01*	***		***	
Other and Unknown Events**	**0.17**		**0.71**		**0.11**	
Total	**1.28**	**0.07**	**5.79**	**0.53**	**0.78**	**0.06**

† Categories based on the Bureau of Labor Statistics Occupational Injury and Illness Coding Structure (OIICS). OIICS codes are provided in parentheses.

* "n.e.c." is an abbreviation for "not elsewhere classified."

** Other and Unknown Events includes "Fires and Explosions," "Other Events," and "Unknown Events."

*** Estimate is not reportable or is suppressed because of a non-reportable cell.

Table 2.70   National estimates of **injury rates for household youth** less than 20 years of age on racial minority farms by sex and age, 2000

Age	Total		Male		Female	
	Rate/1000	se	Rate/1000	se	Rate/1000	se
<10 years	**11.95**	**1.57**	**13.65**	**2.18**	**10.16**	**2.04**
10-15 years	**15.24**	**1.44**	**22.10**	**2.43**	**7.47**	**1.40**
10-11 years	14.01	2.38	18.78	3.60	7.81	2.80
12-13 years	11.92	2.20	16.03	3.66	7.53	2.42
14-15 years	19.27	2.55	30.68	4.55	7.15	2.16
16-19 years	**9.49**	**1.34**	**12.66**	**2.16**	**5.77**	**1.40**
16-17 years	12.27	2.10	***		***	
18-19 years	6.10	1.52	***		***	
Total	**12.18**	**0.87**	**16.72**	**1.37**	**7.92**	**1.00**

*** Estimate is not reportable or is suppressed because of a non-reportable cell.

Table 2.71   National estimates of **injury rates for household youth** less than 20 years of age on racial minority farms by work status and sex, 2000

Sex	Total		Working		Non-Working	
	Rate/1000	se	Rate/1000	se	Rate/1000	se
Male	16.73	1.37	15.61	1.84	8.93	0.96
Female	7.92	1.00	5.47	1.27	6.06	0.88
Total	12.18	0.87	11.78	1.27	7.34	0.65

Table 2.72   National estimates of **injury rates for household youth** less than 20 years of age on racial minority farms by work status and age, 2000

Age	Total		Working		Non-Working	
	Estimate	se	Rate/1000	se	Rate/1000	se
<10 years	**11.95**	**1.57**	**9.35**	**3.09**	**10.32**	**1.46**
10-15 years	**15.24**	**1.44**	**12.86**	**1.80**	**8.41**	**1.03**
10-11 years	14.01	2.38	8.33	2.49	10.25	2.06
12-13 years	11.92	2.20	11.07	2.75	6.09	1.65
14-15 years	19.27	2.55	17.18	3.12	9.00	1.65
16-19 years	**9.49**	**1.34**	**11.44**	**1.96**	**2.82**	**0.69**
16-17 years	12.27	2.10	***		***	
18-19 years	6.10	1.52	***		***	
Total	**12.18**	**0.87**	**11.78**	**1.27**	**7.34**	**0.65**

*** Estimate is not reportable or is suppressed because of a non-reportable cell.

Table 2.73   National estimates of **injury rates for household youth** less than 20 years of age on racial minority farms by sex and type of farm, 2000

Type of Farm	Total Rate/1000	se	Male Rate/1000	se	Female Rate/1000	se
All crop	**8.24**	**1.12**	**11.72**	**1.75**	**4.44**	**1.34**
Grain and oil seed	20.55	5.15	25.30	7.33	15.36	6.99
Vegetable and melon	4.05	1.80	7.76	3.46	0.00	
Fruit, nut, and berry	4.79	1.38	8.95	2.57	0.00	
All other crop*	7.32		9.58		4.94	
All livestock	**16.80**	**1.40**	**21.89**	**2.16**	**11.25**	**1.54**
Beef	14.03	1.44	18.32	2.23	9.26	1.57
Hog	16.72	7.18	***		***	
Sheep and goat	46.69	13.70	***		***	
Equine	33.44	8.50	39.90	12.92	27.62	9.18
Poultry and egg	20.88	9.04	39.07	16.96	0.00	
All other livestock**	17.14		11.56		23.90	
Total	**12.18**	**0.87**	**16.72**	**1.37**	**7.92**	**1.00**

* All other crop includes "Tobacco," "Cotton," "Nursery and floriculture," and "Other crop" farms.
** All other livestock includes "Dairy," "Aquaculture," and "Other livestock" farms.
*** Estimate is not reportable or is suppressed because of a non-reportable cell.

Table 2.74   National estimates of **injury rates for household youth** less than 20 years of age on racial minority farms by age and type of farm, 2000

Type of Farm	Total Rate/1000	se	<10 years Rate/1000	se	10-15 years Rate/1000	se	16-19 years Rate/1000	se
All crop	**8.24**	**1.12**	**7.33**	**2.08**	**10.31**	**1.82**	**5.11**	**1.45**
Grain and oil seed	20.55	5.15	33.86	11.55	***		***	
Vegetable and melon	4.05	1.80	***		***		***	
Fruit, nut, and berry	4.79	1.38	***		***		8.77	3.57
All other crop*	7.32		2.81		15.42		2.35	
All livestock	**16.80**	**1.40**	**15.98**	**2.43**	**20.14**	**2.28**	**13.56**	**2.18**
Beef	14.03	1.44	10.79	2.20	17.81	2.34	12.88	2.36
Hog	16.72	7.18	***		***		***	
Sheep and goat	46.69	13.70	84.62	38.69	***		***	
Equine	33.44	8.50	58.96	20.59	***		***	
Poultry and egg	20.88	9.04	***		***		***	
All other livestock**	17.14		9.09		30.60		10.69	
Total	**12.18**	**0.87**	**11.95**	**1.57**	**15.24**	**1.44**	**9.49**	**1.34**

* All other crop includes "Tobacco," "Cotton," "Nursery and floriculture," and "Other crop" farms.
** All other livestock includes "Dairy," "Aquaculture," and "Other livestock" farms.
*** Estimate is not reportable or is suppressed because of a non-reportable cell.

Table 2.75 National estimates of **injury rates for household youth** less than 20 years of age on racial minority farms by work status and type of farm, 2000

Type of Farm	Total Rate/1000	se	Working Rate/1000	se	Non-Working Rate/1000	se
All crop	**8.24**	**1.12**	**4.59**	**1.24**	**6.69**	**0.99**
Grain and oil seed	20.55	5.15	10.57	4.52	16.43	4.45
Vegetable and melon	4.05	1.80	0.00		4.05	
Fruit, nut, and berry	4.79	1.38	***		***	
All other crop*	7.32		2.83		6.30	
All livestock	**16.80**	**1.40**	**16.20**	**1.91**	**8.68**	**0.96**
Beef	14.03	1.44	14.45	2.08	6.86	0.91
Hog	16.72	7.18	***		***	
Sheep and goat	46.69	13.70	37.81	14.52	23.03	10.22
Equine	33.44	8.50	19.81	8.38	23.09	6.80
Poultry and egg	20.88	9.04	***		***	
All other livestock**	17.14		21.51		6.75	
Total	**12.18**	**0.87**	**11.78**	**1.27**	**7.34**	**0.65**

* All other crop includes "Tobacco," "Cotton," "Nursery and floriculture," and "Other crop" farms.
** All other livestock includes "Dairy," "Aquaculture," and "Other livestock" farms.
*** Estimate is not reportable or is suppressed because of a non-reportable cell.

Table 2.76 National estimates of **injury rates for household youth** less than 20 years of age on racial minority farms by sex and type of injury, 2000

Type of Injury	Total Rate/1000	se	Male Rate/1000	se	Female Rate/1000	se
Scrape, abrasion	0.93	0.21	1.27	0.34	0.62	0.25
Bruise, contusion	1.66	0.30	2.60	0.53	0.71	0.24
Sprain, strain	0.69	0.18	***		***	
Broken bone, fracture	2.74	0.36	4.00	0.61	1.53	0.41
Cut, laceration	3.32	0.43	4.70	0.67	2.00	0.57
Puncture, stab, jab	0.75	0.19	1.45	0.37	0.00	
Burn, blister, scald	0.25	0.10	0.49	0.19	0.00	
Multiple injuries	0.99	0.21	0.92	0.29	1.14	0.32
All other injuries*	0.75		***		***	
Total	12.18	0.87	16.72	1.37	7.92	1.00

* All other injuries includes "Dislocation," "Traumatic rupture," "Crushed," "Amputation," "Nerve injury," and "Other injury."
*** Estimate is not reportable or is suppressed because of a non-reportable cell.

Table 2.77   National estimates of **injury rates for household youth** less than 20 years of age on racial minority farms by age and type of injury, 2000

Type of Injury	Total Rate/1000	se	<10 years Rate/1000	se	10-15 years Rate/1000	se	16-19 years Rate/1000	se
Scrape, abrasion	0.93	0.21	***		1.38	0.38	***	
Bruise, contusion	1.66	0.30	1.19	0.44	2.20	0.52	1.70	0.60
Sprain, strain	0.69	0.18	***		***		1.03	0.41
Broken bone, fracture	2.74	0.36	3.40	0.73	3.00	0.60	1.95	0.60
Cut, laceration	3.32	0.43	4.83	1.03	3.08	0.60	1.90	0.52
Puncture, stab, jab	0.75	0.19	***		1.25	0.40	***	
Burn, blister, scald	0.25	0.10	***		***		***	
Multiple injuries	0.99	0.21	***		1.89	0.43	***	
All other injuries*	0.75		***		1.20		***	
Total	12.18	0.87	11.95	1.57	15.24	1.44	9.49	1.34

   * All other injuries includes "Dislocation," "Traumatic rupture," "Crushed," "Amputation," "Nerve injury," and "Other injury."

   *** Estimate is not reportable or is suppressed because of a non-reportable cell.

Table 2.78   National estimates of **injury rates for household youth** less than 20 years of age on racial minority farms by work status and type of injury, 2000

Type of Injury	Total Rate/1000	se	Working Rate/1000	se	Non-Working Rate/1000	se
Scrape, abrasion	0.93	0.21	***		***	
Bruise, contusion	1.66	0.30	1.73	0.50	0.94	0.22
Sprain, strain	0.69	0.18	***		***	
Broken bone, fracture	2.74	0.36	2.14	0.55	1.86	0.28
Cut, laceration	3.32	0.43	3.09	0.55	2.05	0.37
Puncture, stab, jab	0.75	0.19	1.16	0.37	0.27	0.11
Burn, blister, scald	0.25	0.10	***		***	
Multiple injuries	0.99	0.21	1.59	0.43	0.34	0.12
All other injuries*	0.75		0.71		0.45	
Total	12.18	0.87	11.78	1.27	7.34	0.65

   * All other injuries includes "Dislocation," "Traumatic rupture," "Crushed," "Amputation," "Nerve injury," and "Other injury."

   *** Estimate is not reportable or is suppressed because of a non-reportable cell.

Table 2.79   National estimates of **injury rates for household youth** less than 20 years of age on racial minority farms by sex and body part injured, 2000

Body Part Injured	Total Rate/1000	se	Male Rate/1000	se	Female Rate/1000	se
Head, skull	1.24	0.24	***		***	
Face	1.26	0.25	1.70	0.41	0.85	
Shoulder, chest, back	0.96	0.22	1.32	0.36	0.62	0.25
Arm	2.04	0.30	2.64	0.46	1.51	0.41
Hand, wrist, fingers	1.68	0.28	***		***	
Leg	1.90	0.31	2.36	0.49	1.53	0.41
Foot, ankle, toes	1.42	0.27	1.85	0.42	1.04	0.34
Multiple body parts	0.75	0.27	1.00	0.28	0.51	0.19
All other body parts*	0.84		0.75		1.00	
Total	12.18	0.87	16.72	1.37	7.92	1.00

* All other body parts includes "Neck," "Abdomen," "Pelvic region," "Internal injury," and "Other body parts."
*** Estimate is not reportable or is suppressed because of a non-reportable cell.

Table 2.80   National estimates of **injury rates for household youth** less than 20 years of age on racial minority farms by age and body part injured, 2000

Body Part Injured	Total Rate/1000	se	<10 years Rate/1000	se	10-15 years Rate/1000	se	16-19 years Rate/1000	se
Head, skull	1.24	0.24	***		2.13	0.53	***	
Face	1.26	0.25	2.49	0.65	***		***	
Shoulder, chest, back	0.96	0.22	***		***		2.22	0.67
Arm	2.04	0.30	***		2.78	0.58	***	
Hand, wrist, fingers	1.68	0.28	***		2.60	0.55	***	
Leg	1.90	0.31	0.81	0.32	2.68	0.57	2.41	0.64
Foot, ankle, toes	1.42	0.27	1.17	0.43	1.46	0.42	1.87	0.62
Multiple body parts	0.75	0.27	***		1.35	0.37	***	
All other body parts*	0.84		***		1.04		***	
Total	12.18	0.87	11.95	1.57	15.24	1.44	9.49	1.34

* All other body parts includes "Neck," "Abdomen," "Pelvic region," "Internal injury," and "Other body parts."
*** Estimate is not reportable or is suppressed because of a non-reportable cell.

Table 2.81 National estimates of **injury rates for household youth** less than 20 years of age on racial minority farms by work status and body part injured, 2000

Body Part Injured	Total		Working		Non-Working	
	Rate/1000	se	Rate/1000	se	Rate/1000	se
Head, skull	1.24	0.24	1.22	0.33	0.74	0.18
Face	1.26	0.25	***		***	
Shoulder, chest, back	0.96	0.22	1.03	0.38	0.54	0.15
Arm	2.04	0.30	1.60	0.41	1.39	0.23
Hand, wrist, fingers	1.68	0.28	1.33	0.37	1.14	0.24
Leg	1.90	0.31	2.15	0.51	1.02	0.23
Foot, ankle, toes	1.42	0.27	2.05	0.49	0.57	0.17
Multiple body parts	0.75	0.27	1.22	0.33	0.25	0.10
All other body parts*	0.84		***		***	
Total	12.18	0.87	11.78	1.27	7.34	0.65

* All other body parts includes "Neck," "Abdomen," "Pelvic region," "Internal injury," and "Other body parts."
*** Estimate is not reportable or is suppressed because of a non-reportable cell.

Table 2.82 National estimates of **injury rates for household youth** less than 20 years of age on racial minority farms by sex and source of injury, 2000

Source of Injury [†]	Total		Male		Female	
	Rate/1000	se	Rate/1000	se	Rate/1000	se
Containers (1)	**0.38**	**0.13**	***		***	
Parts/Materials (4)	**0.99**	**0.23**	***		***	
Fasteners (42)	0.31	0.13	***		***	
Vehicle Parts (48)	0.50	0.17	***		***	
Trailers (483)	*0.50*	*0.17*	***		***	
Persons/Animals/Plants/Minerals (5)	**1.41**	**0.26**	**1.80**	**0.40**	**1.05**	**0.33**
Animals (51)	1.24	0.25	1.47	0.38	1.05	0.33
Cattle (5152)	*0.40*	*0.14*	***		***	
Horses (5154)	*0.52*	*0.15*	***		***	
Structures and Surfaces (6)	**4.10**	**0.47**	**5.24**	**0.76**	**3.11**	**0.54**
Floors/Walkways/Ground (62)	3.22	0.41	4.06	0.68	2.51	0.48
Ground (623)	*2.77*	*0.38*	*3.33*	*0.62*	*2.33*	*0.45*
Other Structural Elements (63)	0.68	0.18	0.79	0.23	0.60	0.25
Fences (632)	*0.25*	*0.09*	***		***	
Tools/Instruments/Equipment (7)	**1.18**	**0.23**	***		***	
Nonpowered Hand Tools (71)	0.36	0.12	0.70	0.23	0.00	
Recreation Equipment (78)	0.56	0.16	***		***	
Gymnasium Equipment (782)	*0.23*	*0.08*	***		***	
Vehicles (8)	**1.71**	**0.29**	**2.54**	**0.44**	**0.90**	**0.39**
Off-Road Vehicles (84)	1.03	0.22	***		***	
All Terrain Vehicle (841)	*0.93*	*0.21*	***		***	
Other and Unknown Sources*	**2.41**		**3.16**		**1.73**	
Total	12.18	0.87	16.72	1.37	7.92	1.00

† Categories based on the Bureau of Labor Statistics Occupational Injury and Illness Coding Structure (OIICS). OIICS codes are provided in parentheses.
* Other and Unknown Sources includes "Chemicals," "Furniture and Fixtures," "Machinery," "Other Sources," and "Unknown Sources."
*** Estimate is not reportable or is suppressed because of a non-reportable cell.

Table 2.83 National estimates of **injury rates for household youth** less than 20 years of age on racial minority farms by age and source of injury, 2000

Source of Injury [†]	Total		<10 years		10-15 years		16-19 years	
	Rate/1000	se	Rate/1000	se	Rate/1000	se	Rate/1000	se
Containers (1)	**0.38**	**0.13**	***		***		***	
Parts/Materials (4)	**0.99**	**0.23**	***		**1.30**	**0.43**	***	
Fasteners (42)	0.31	0.13	***		***		***	
Vehicle Parts (48)	0.50	0.17	***		0.79	0.34	***	
Trailers (483)	*0.50*	*0.17*	***		*0.79*	*0.34*	***	
Persons/Animals/Plants/Minerals (5)	**1.41**	**0.26**	**1.34**	**0.50**	**1.41**	**0.38**	**1.69**	**0.54**
Animals (51)	1.24	0.25	1.34	0.50	0.94	0.31	1.69	0.54
Cattle (5152)	*0.40*	*0.14*	***		***		***	
Horses (5154)	*0.52*	*0.15*	***		***		*0.97*	*0.39*
Structures and Surfaces (6)	**4.10**	**0.47**	**4.58**	**0.89**	**5.64**	**0.85**	**1.95**	**0.62**
Floors/Walkways/Ground (62)	3.22	0.41	4.29	0.87	4.02	0.70	1.24	0.51
Ground (623)	*2.77*	*0.38*	*3.17*	*0.77*	*3.79*	*0.68*	*1.24*	*0.51*
Other Structural Elements (63)	0.68	0.18	***		1.38	0.39	***	
Fences (632)	*0.25*	*0.09*	*0.00*		*0.67*	*0.26*	*0.00*	
Tools/Instruments/Equipment (7)	**1.18**	**0.23**	**1.04**	**0.35**	**1.30**	**0.42**	**1.33**	**0.47**
Nonpowered Hand Tools (71)	0.36	0.12	***		***		***	
Recreation Equipment (78)	0.56	0.16	1.04	0.35	***		***	
Gymnasium Equipment (782)	*0.23*	*0.08*	*0.71*	*0.26*	*0.00*		*0.00*	
Vehicles (8)	**1.71**	**0.29**	***		**2.89**	**0.57**	***	
Off-Road Vehicles (84)	1.03	0.22	***		1.95	0.45	***	
All Terrain Vehicle (841)	*0.93*	*0.21*	***		*1.65*	*0.42*	***	
Other and Unknown Sources*	2.41		2.38		2.17		2.76	
Total	**12.18**	**0.87**	**11.95**	**1.57**	**15.24**	**1.44**	**9.49**	**1.34**

† Categories based on the Bureau of Labor Statistics Occupational Injury and Illness Coding Structure (OIICS). OIICS codes are provided in parentheses.

* Other and Unknown Sources includes "Chemicals," "Furniture and Fixtures," "Machinery," "Other Sources," and "Unknown Sources."

*** Estimate is not reportable or is suppressed because of a non-reportable cell.

Table 2.84 National estimates of **injury rates for household youth** less than 20 years of age on racial minority farms by work status and source of injury, 2000

Source of Injury [†]	Total		Working		Non-Working	
	Rate/1000	se	Rate/1000	se	Rate/1000	se
Containers (1)	**0.38**	**0.13**	***		***	
Parts/Materials (4)	**0.99**	**0.23**	***		***	
Fasteners (42)	0.31	0.13	***		***	
Vehicle Parts (48)	0.50	0.17	***		***	
Trailers (483)	*0.50*	*0.17*	***		***	
Persons/Animals/Plants/Minerals (5)	**1.41**	**0.26**	**1.63**	**0.43**	**0.74**	**0.19**
Animals (51)	1.24	0.25	1.42	0.42	0.65	0.18
Cattle (5152)	*0.40*	*0.14*	***		***	
Horses (5154)	*0.52*	*0.15*	***		***	
Structures and Surfaces (6)	**4.10**	**0.47**	**3.51**	**0.67**	**2.66**	**0.37**
Floors/Walkways/Ground (62)	3.22	0.41	2.27	0.49	2.29	0.34
Ground (623)	*2.77*	*0.38*	*2.27*	*0.49*	*1.84*	*0.31*
Other Structural Elements (63)	0.68	0.18	0.76	0.30	0.37	0.13
Fences (632)	*0.25*	*0.09*	***		***	
Tools/Instruments/Equipment (7)	**1.18**	**0.23**	**1.30**	**0.37**	**0.64**	**0.17**
Nonpowered Hand Tools (71)	0.36	0.12	***		***	
Recreation Equipment (78)	0.56	0.16	0.00		0.56	0.16
Gymnasium Equipment (782)	*0.23*	*0.08*	*0.00*		*0.23*	*0.08*
Vehicles (8)	**1.71**	**0.29**	**1.28**	**0.36**	**1.18**	**0.23**
Off-Road Vehicles (84)	1.03	0.22	0.81	0.27	0.70	0.17
All Terrain Vehicle (841)	*0.93*	*0.21*	*0.81*	*0.27*	*0.60*	*0.15*
Other and Unknown Sources*	2.41		1.51		1.79	
Total	**12.18**	**0.87**	**11.78**	**1.27**	**7.34**	**0.65**

† Categories based on the Bureau of Labor Statistics Occupational Injury and Illness Coding Structure (OIICS). OIICS codes are provided in parentheses.

* Other and Unknown Sources includes "Chemicals," "Furniture and Fixtures," "Machinery," "Other Sources," and "Unknown Sources."

*** Estimate is not reportable or is suppressed because of a non-reportable cell.

Table 2.85   National estimates of **injury rates for household youth** less than 20 years of age on racial minority farms by sex and type of injury event, 2000

Type of Injury Event [†]	Total		Male		Female	
	Rate/1000	se	Rate/1000	se	Rate/1000	se
Contact With Objects (0)	**3.77**	**0.43**	**5.60**	**0.71**	**1.96**	**0.48**
Contact With Object Unspecified (00)	0.39	0.14	***		***	
Struck Against Object (01)	1.36	0.25	1.71	0.38	1.07	0.35
Against Stationary Object (012)	*1.08*	*0.22*	*1.32*	*0.31*	*0.89*	*0.33*
Struck by Object (02)	1.76	0.28	***		***	
Struck by Falling Object (021)	*1.12*	*0.18*	***		***	
Struck by Slipping Handheld Object (0232)	*0.43*	*0.13*	*0.85*	*0.26*	*0.00*	
Caught in Objects (03)	0.26	0.10	***		***	
Caught in Objects n.e.c.* (039)	*0.26*	*0.10*	***		***	
Falls (1)	**3.80**	**0.44**	**4.96**	**0.73**	**2.75**	**0.51**
Fall to Lower Level (11)	2.13	0.32	2.94	0.54	1.38	0.35
Fall to Lower Level n.e.c.* (119)	*1.93*	*0.30*	*2.54*	*0.50*	*1.38*	*0.35*
Fall on Same Level (13)	1.42	0.26	1.71	0.40	1.19	0.35
Fall to Floor/Walkway/Ground (131)	*0.92*	*0.20*	*1.16*	*0.34*	*0.71*	*0.23*
Fall on Same Level n.e.c.* (139)	*0.29*	*0.12*	***		***	
Exposure to Substances/Environments (3)	**0.43**	**0.13**	***		***	
Exposure Caustic/Allergenic Substance (34)	0.35	0.12	***		***	
Transportation Events (4)	**1.72**	**0.29**	**2.78**	**0.48**	**0.65**	**0.35**
Non-highway Events (42)	1.53	0.27	2.39	0.44	0.65	0.35
Vehicle Struck Stationary Object (422)	*0.30*	*0.16*	*0.00*		*0.65*	*0.35*
Fall From Moving Vehicle (4231)	*0.36*	*0.12*	*0.70*	*0.24*	*0.00*	
Overturn (4233)	*0.43*	*0.13*	*0.83*	*0.25*	*0.00*	
Assaults and Violent Acts (6)	**0.78**	**0.20**	**0.74**	**0.27**	**0.88**	**0.31**
Assault by Animal (63)	0.78	0.20	0.74	0.27	0.88	0.31
Assault by Animal n.e.c.* (639)	*0.56*	*0.16*	***		***	
Other and Unknown Events**	**1.69**		**1.98**		**1.47**	
Total	**12.18**	**0.87**	**16.72**	**1.37**	**7.92**	**1.00**

† Categories based on the Bureau of Labor Statistics Occupational Injury and Illness Coding Structure (OIICS). OIICS codes are provided in parentheses.

* "n.e.c." is an abbreviation for "not elsewhere classified."

** Other and Unknown Events includes "Bodily Reaction/Exertion," "Fires and Explosions," "Other Events," and "Unknown Events."

*** Estimate is not reportable or is suppressed because of a non-reportable cell.

Table 2.86 National estimates of **injury rates** for **household youth** less than 20 years of age on racial minority farms by age and type of injury event, 2000

Type of Injury Event [†]	Total Rate/1000	se	<10 years Rate/1000	se	10-15 years Rate/1000	se	16-19 years Rate/1000	se
Contact With Objects (0)	**3.77**	**0.43**	**2.74**	**0.67**	**5.31**	**0.79**	**3.37**	**0.80**
Contact With Object Unspecified (00)	0.39	0.14	***		***		***	
Struck Against Object (01)	1.36	0.25	1.57	0.51	1.57	0.39	1.02	0.43
Against Stationary Object (012)	*1.08*	*0.22*	***		*1.34*	*0.37*	***	
Struck by Object (02)	1.76	0.28	0.89	0.37	2.75	0.58	1.67	0.52
Struck by Falling Object (021)	*0.73*	*0.18*	***		*1.07*	*0.39*	***	
Struck by Slipping Handheld Object (0232)	*0.43*	*0.13*	***		*0.96*	*0.33*	***	
Caught in Objects (03)	0.26	0.10	***		***		***	
Caught in Objects n.e.c. (039)*	*0.26*	*0.10*	***		***		***	
Falls (1)	**3.80**	**0.44**	**5.63**	**0.97**	**4.08**	**0.72**	**1.66**	**0.59**
Fall to Lower Level (11)	2.13	0.32	2.97	0.63	2.24	0.57	1.24	0.50
Fall to Lower Level n.e.c. (119)*	*1.93*	*0.30*	*2.36*	*0.54*	*2.24*	*0.57*	*1.24*	*0.50*
Fall on Same Level (13)	1.42	0.26	2.67	0.63	***		***	
Fall to Floor/Walkway/Ground (131)	*0.92*	*0.20*	*1.71*	*0.48*	***		***	
Fall on Same Level n.e.c. (139)*	*0.29*	*0.12*	***		***		***	
Exposure to Substances/Environments (3)	**0.43**	**0.13**	***		**0.69**	**0.26**	***	
Exposure Caustic/Allergenic Substance (34)	0.35	0.12	***		0.69	0.26	***	
Transportation Events (4)	**1.72**	**0.29**	***		**3.21**	**0.63**	***	
Non-highway Events (42)	1.53	0.27	***		2.99	0.61	***	
Vehicle Struck Stationary Object (422)	*0.30*	*0.16*	***		***		***	
Fall From Moving Vehicle (4231)	*0.36*	*0.12*	***		*0.72*	*0.28*	***	
Overturn (4233)	*0.43*	*0.13*	***		*0.95*	*0.32*	***	
Assaults and Violent Acts (6)	**0.78**	**0.20**	**1.00**	**0.44**	***		***	
Assault by Animal (63)	0.78	0.20	1.00	0.44	***		***	
Assault by Animal n.e.c. (639)*	*0.56*	*0.16*	***		***		***	
Other and Unknown Events**	1.69		1.24		1.43		2.47	
Total	**12.18**	**0.87**	**11.95**	**1.57**	**15.24**	**1.44**	**9.49**	**1.34**

† Categories based on the Bureau of Labor Statistics Occupational Injury and Illness Coding Structure (OIICS). OIICS codes are provided in parentheses.

* "n.e.c." is an abbreviation for "not elsewhere classified."

** Other and Unknown Events includes "Bodily Reaction/Exertion," "Fires and Explosions," "Other Events," and "Unknown Events."

*** Estimate is not reportable or is suppressed because of a non-reportable cell.

70

Table 2.87 National estimates of **injury rates for household youth** less than 20 years of age on racial minority farms by work status and type of injury event, 2000

Type of Injury Event [†]	Total		Working		Non-Working	
	Rate/1000	se	Rate/1000	se	Rate/1000	se
Contact With Objects (0)	**3.77**	**0.43**	**5.20**	**0.79**	**1.63**	**0.28**
Contact With Object Unspecified (00)	0.39	0.14	***		***	
Struck Against Object (01)	1.36	0.25	2.12	0.46	0.49	0.16
Against Stationary Object (012)	*1.08*	*0.22*	*1.63*	*0.38*	*0.41*	*0.15*
Struck by Object (02)	1.76	0.28	2.20	0.49	0.85	0.20
Struck by Falling Object (021)	*0.73*	*0.18*	*0.90*	*0.32*	*0.36*	*0.13*
Struck by Slipping Handheld Object (0232)	*0.43*	*0.13*	*****		*****	
Caught in Objects (03)	0.26	0.10	***		***	
Caught in Objects n.e.c. (039)*	*0.26*	*0.10*	*****		*****	
Falls (1)	**3.80**	**0.44**	**2.80**	**0.56**	**2.65**	**0.36**
Fall to Lower Level (11)	2.13	0.32	1.43	0.40	1.55	0.26
Fall to Lower Level n.e.c. (119)*	*1.93*	*0.30*	*1.43*	*0.40*	*1.34*	*0.24*
Fall on Same Level (13)	1.42	0.26	1.37	0.40	0.85	0.20
Fall to Floor/Walkway/Ground (131)	*0.92*	*0.20*	*0.92*	*0.32*	*0.54*	*0.15*
Fall on Same Level n.e.c. (139)*	*0.29*	*0.12*	*****		*****	
Exposure to Substances/Environments (3)	**0.43**	**0.13**	*******		*******	
Exposure Caustic/Allergenic Substance (34)	0.35	0.12				
Transportation Events (4)	**1.72**	**0.29**	**1.58**	**0.43**	**1.07**	**0.21**
Non-highway Events (42)	1.53	0.27	1.58	0.43	0.87	0.19
Vehicle Struck Stationary Object (422)	*0.30*	*0.16*	*****		*****	
Fall From Moving Vehicle (4231)	*0.36*	*0.12*	*0.00*		*0.36*	*0.12*
Overturn (4233)	*0.43*	*0.13*	*****		*****	
Assaults and Violent Acts (6)	**0.78**	**0.20**	*******		*******	
Assault by Animal (63)	0.78	0.20	***		***	
Assault by Animal n.e.c. (639)*	*0.56*	*0.16*	*****		*****	
Other and Unknown Events**	**1.69**		**1.09**		**1.24**	
Total	**12.18**	**0.87**	**11.78**	**1.27**	**7.34**	**0.65**

† Categories based on the Bureau of Labor Statistics Occupational Injury and Illness Coding Structure (OIICS). OIICS codes are provided in parentheses.

* "n.e.c." is an abbreviation for "not elsewhere classified."

** Other and Unknown Events includes "Bodily Reaction/Exertion," "Fires and Explosions," "Other Events," and "Unknown Events."

*** Estimate is not reportable or is suppressed because of a non-reportable cell.

71

Table 2.88 National estimates of **asthma among household youth** less than 20 years of age on racial minority farms by sex, 2000

Sex	Asthma Estimate	se	No Asthma Estimate	se	Unknown Estimate
Male	1,584	48	12,961	150	98
Female	920	35	12,085	145	37
Unknown	2		40		850
Total [†]	2,506	63	25,086	236	985

† Estimates may not add to the total because of rounding.

Table 2.89 National estimates of **asthma among household youth** less than 20 years of age on racial minority farms by age, 2000

Age	Asthma Estimate	se	No Asthma Estimate	se	Unknown Estimate
<10 years	708	33	8,602	130	29
10-15 years	1,081	38	9,465	126	32
10-11 years	356	21	2,855	60	8
12-13 years	368	21	3,127	63	18
14-15 years	357	21	3,482	66	5
16-19 years	706	30	6,896	100	46
16-17 years	430	23	3,770	70	22
18-19 years	276	19	3,126	63	24
Unknown	10		124		878
Total [†]	2,506	63	25,086	236	985

† Estimates may not add to the total because of rounding.

Table 2.90   National estimates of **asthma among household youth** less than 20 years of age on racial minority farms by sex and age, 2000

Age	Total † Estimate	se	Male Estimate	se	Female Estimate	se	Unknown Estimate
<10 years	**708**	**33**	**450**	**25**	**259**	**19**	**0**
10-15 years	**1,081**	**38**	**686**	**30**	**395**	**22**	**0**
10-11 years	356	21	247	17	109	11	0
12-13 years	368	21	237	17	131	13	0
14-15 years	357	21	203	16	154	14	0
16-19 years	**706**	**30**	**443**	**24**	**263**	**18**	**0**
16-17 years	430	23	249	18	181	15	0
18-19 years	276	19	194	16	82	10	0
Unknown	**10**		**4**		**3**		**2**
Total †	**2,506**	**63**	**1,584**	**48**	**920**	**35**	**2**

† Estimates may not add to the total because of rounding.

Table 2.91   National estimates of **asthma among household youth** less than 20 years of age on racial minority farms by sex and type of farm, 2000

Type of Farm	Total † Estimate	se	Male Estimate	se	Female Estimate	se	Unknown Estimate
All crop	**1,111**	**43**	**693**	**32**	**418**	**25**	**0**
Grain and oil seed	202	19	117	12	85	13	0
Tobacco	29	6	17	4	12	3	0
Cotton	56	11	38	8	18	5	0
Vegetable and melon	143	16	78	10	66	11	0
Fruit, nut, and berry	327	22	202	18	124	13	0
Nursery and floriculture	108	16	80	13	29	6	0
Other crop	246	20	161	16	85	11	0
All livestock	**1,324**	**45**	**834**	**34**	**488**	**25**	**2**
Beef	1,008	39	627	30	379	22	2
Dairy	31	7	22	6	9	5	0
Hog	68	11	42	8	26	6	0
Sheep and goat	51	8	31	6	21	5	0
Equine	98	13	63	11	35	7	0
Poultry and egg	30	6	18	5	12	4	0
Aquaculture	7	3	***		***		0
Other livestock	31	8	***		***		0
Unknown	**71**		**56**		**14**		**0**
Total †	**2,506**	**63**	**1,584**	**48**	**920**	**35**	**2**

† Estimates may not add to the total because of rounding.
*** Estimate is not reportable or is suppressed because of a non-reportable cell.

Table 2.92 National estimates of **asthma among household youth** less than 20 years of age on racial minority farms by age and type of farm, 2000

Type of Farm	Total[†] Estimate	se	<10 years Estimate	se	10-15 years Estimate	se	16-19 years Estimate	se	Unknown Estimate
All crop	**1,111**	**43**	**316**	**22**	**467**	**26**	**326**	**21**	**2**
Grain and oil seed	202	19	67	2	78	11	57	9	0
Tobacco	29	6	11	3	***		***		0
Cotton	56	11	11	4	30	7	15	4	0
Vegetable and melon	143	16	37	9	61	9	45	8	0
Fruit, nut, and berry	327	22	92	11	140	14	95	11	0
Nursery and floriculture	108	16	27	6	50	8	31	7	0
Other crop	246	20	71	10	***		***		2
All livestock	**1,324**	**45**	**377**	**24**	**571**	**27**	**368**	**22**	**8**
Beef	1,008	39	301	21	423	23	277	19	8
Dairy	31	7	***		17	5	***		0
Hog	68	11	18	6	38	8	12	3	0
Sheep and goat	51	8	20	5	14	4	18	5	0
Equine	98	13	25	8	44	7	29	7	0
Poultry and egg	30	6	***		18	5	***		0
Aquaculture	7	3	***		***		***		0
Other livestock	31	8	***		***		9	4	0
Unknown	**71**		**16**		**43**		**12**		**0**
Total[†]	**2,506**	**63**	**708**	**33**	**1,081**	**38**	**706**	**30**	**10**

† Estimates may not add to the total because of rounding.

*** Estimate is not reportable or is suppressed because of a non-reportable cell.

Table 2.93 National estimates of **asthmatic household youth** less than 20 years of age with 1 or more **asthma attacks while doing farm work** by sex on racial minority farms, 2000

Sex	Total[†] Estimate	se	Attack at Work Estimate	se	No Attack at Work Estimate	se	Unknown Estimate
Male	1,584	48	501	27	670	33	413
Female	920	35	309	22	374	22	236
Unknown	2		2		0		0
Total[†]	2,506	63	813	36	1,044	43	649

† Estimates may not add to the total because of rounding.

Table 2.94   National estimates of **asthmatic household youth** less than 20 years of age with 1 or more **asthma attacks while doing farm work** by age on racial minority farms, 2000

Age	Total [†] Estimate	se	Attack at Work Estimate	se	No Attack at Work Estimate	se	Unknown Estimate
<10 years	**708**	**33**	**203**	**19**	**238**	**19**	**268**
10-15 years	**1,081**	**38**	**338**	**21**	**431**	**25**	**313**
10-11 years	356	21	113	12	137	13	107
12-13 years	368	21	103	11	152	14	114
14-15 years	357	21	122	13	142	13	93
16-19 years	**706**	**30**	**270**	**19**	**371**	**23**	**65**
16-17 years	430	23	150	14	225	17	56
18-19 years	276	19	120	12	146	14	10
Unknown	**10**		**2**		**4**		**3**
Total [†]	**2,506**	**63**	**813**	**36**	**1,044**	**43**	**649**

† Estimates may not add to the total because of rounding.

Table 2.95   National estimates of **asthmatic household youth** less than 20 years of age with 1 or more **asthma attacks while doing farm work** by type of farm on racial minority farms, 2000

Type of Farm	Total [†] Estimate	se	Attack at Work Estimate	se	No Attack at Work Estimate	se	Unknown Estimate
All crop	**1,111**	**43**	**367**	**25**	**495**	**30**	**248**
Grain and oil seed	202	19	71	11	59	11	72
Tobacco	29	6	9	4	18	4	2
Cotton	56	11	25	8	28	7	4
Vegetable and melon	143	16	45	9	60	10	39
Fruit, nut, and berry	327	22	107	13	152	16	68
Nursery and floriculture	108	16	44	9	57	13	8
Other crop	246	20	67	11	123	15	56
All livestock	**1,324**	**45**	**422**	**25**	**526**	**30**	**375**
Beef	1,008	39	292	21	427	27	289
Dairy	31	7	9	4	8	4	15
Hog	68	11	29	8	16	4	22
Sheep and goat	51	8	32	6	8	4	11
Equine	98	13	43	8	38	10	17
Poultry and egg	30	6	8	3	12	4	10
Aquaculture	7	3	***		***		3
Other livestock	31	8	***		***		10
Unknown	**71**		**23**		**22**		**25**
Total [†]	**2,506**	**63**	**813**	**36**	**1,044**	**43**	**649**

† Estimates may not add to the total because of rounding.
*** Estimate is not reportable or is suppressed because of a non-reportable cell.

Table 2.96   National estimates of **asthmatic household youth** less than 20 years of age with 1 or more **asthma attacks requiring professional medical attention** by sex on racial minority farms, 2000

Sex	Total [†] Estimate	se	Medical Attention Estimate	se	No Medical Attention Estimate	se	Unknown Estimate
Male	1,584	48	354	21	1,230	43	0
Female	920	35	176	15	739	32	5
Unknown	2		0		2		0
Total [†]	2,506	63	530	26	1,971	56	5

† Estimates may not add to the total because of rounding.

Table 2.97   National estimates of **asthmatic household youth** less than 20 years of age with 1 or more **asthma attacks requiring professional medical attention** by age on racial minority farms, 2000

Age	Total [†] Estimate	se	Medical Attention Estimate	se	No Medical Attention Estimate	se	Unknown Estimate
<10 years	**708**	**33**	**210**	**16**	**498**	**28**	**0**
10-15 years	**1,081**	**38**	**220**	**16**	**859**	**31**	**2**
10-11 years	356	21	85	10	271	18	0
12-13 years	368	21	83	10	285	19	0
14-15 years	357	21	52	8	303	19	2
16-19 years	**706**	**30**	**97**	**11**	**607**	**28**	**3**
16-17 years	430	23	58	8	370	22	3
18-19 years	276	19	40	7	237	18	0
Unknown	**10**		**2**		**8**		**0**
Total [†]	**2,506**	**63**	**530**	**26**	**1,971**	**56**	**5**

† Estimates may not add to the total because of rounding.

Table 2.98   National estimates of **asthmatic household youth** less than 20 years of age with 1 or more **asthma attacks requiring professional medical attention** by type of farm on racial minority farms, 2000

Type of Farm	Total † Estimate	se	Medical Attention Estimate	se	No Medical Attention Estimate	se	Unknown Estimate
All crop	**1,111**	**43**	**192**	**16**	**919**	**40**	**0**
Grain and oil seed	202	19	37	7	165	17	0
Tobacco	29	6	7	2	22	5	0
Cotton	56	11	19	5	38	9	0
Vegetable and melon	143	16	26	7	117	14	0
Fruit, nut, and berry	327	22	52	8	275	21	0
Nursery and floriculture	108	16	10	4	98	15	0
Other crop	246	20	42	7	204	18	0
All livestock	**1,324**	**45**	**326**	**20**	**993**	**39**	**5**
Beef	1,008	39	258	18	746	33	5
Dairy	31	7	***		***		0
Hog	68	11	18	5	50	10	0
Sheep and goat	51	8	13	4	39	7	0
Equine	98	13	12	4	85	12	0
Poultry and egg	30	6	10	3	21	5	0
Aquaculture	7	3	***		***		0
Other livestock	31	8	10	4	21	7	0
Unknown	**71**		**11**		**60**		**0**
Total †	**2,506**	**63**	**530**	**26**	**1,971**	**56**	**5**

† Estimates may not add to the total because of rounding.
*** Estimate is not reportable or is suppressed because of a non-reportable cell.

Table 2.99   National estimates of **asthma prevalence rates for household youth** less than 20 years of age on racial minority farms by sex and age, 2000

Age	Total Rate/1000	se	Male Rate/1000	se	Female Rate/1000	se
<10 years	**75.85**	**3.69**	**93.75**	**5.40**	**56.97**	**4.41**
10-15 years	**102.18**	**3.81**	**122.08**	**5.67**	**79.65**	**4.59**
10-11 years	110.50	6.85	135.54	10.09	78.00	8.49
12-13 years	104.78	6.38	130.48	10.13	77.34	7.66
14-15 years	92.84	5.71	102.06	8.41	83.00	7.62
16-19 years	**92.35**	**4.17**	**106.84**	**6.15**	**75.18**	**5.37**
16-17 years	101.87	5.75	111.57	8.42	90.95	7.83
18-19 years	80.61	5.73	101.27	8.85	54.41	6.68
Total	**87.68**	**2.33**	**108.14**	**3.48**	**70.52**	**2.83**

Table 2.100 National estimates of **asthma prevalence rates for household youth** less than 20 years of age on racial minority farms by sex and type of farm, 2000

Type of Farm	Total Rate/1000	se	Male Rate/1000	se	Female Rate/1000	se
All crop	**90.58**	**3.78**	**107.27**	**5.36**	**73.32**	**4.60**
Grain and oil seed	97.87	9.78	107.54	12.31	87.78	13.64
Tobacco	63.98	13.56	76.65	20.44	51.20	15.33
Cotton	145.25	30.21	176.63	40.98	104.68	32.54
Vegetable and melon	65.90	7.68	68.35	9.45	67.43	11.28
Fruit, nut, and berry	93.11	6.91	107.77	10.01	76.99	8.43
Nursery and floriculture	84.98	13.08	118.82	20.65	48.81	11.08
Other crop	102.06	9.17	128.92	13.86	73.37	9.86
All livestock	**90.00**	**3.28**	**107.98**	**4.76**	**70.31**	**3.77**
Beef	87.30	3.62	102.60	5.15	70.20	4.20
Dairy	96.99	25.84	124.79	36.72	63.52	34.63
Hog	136.56	24.38	160.43	33.45	112.54	28.03
Sheep and goat	107.20	18.97	128.24	28.60	87.05	23.63
Equine	105.29	15.42	143.32	26.50	71.82	14.68
Poultry and egg	58.05	13.12	64.52	18.42	50.62	17.04
Aquaculture	76.43	32.21	***		***	
Other livestock	94.14	26.02	***		***	
Total	**87.68**	**2.33**	**108.14**	**3.48**	**70.52**	**2.83**

*** Estimate is not reportable or is suppressed because of a non-reportable cell.

Table 2.101 National estimates of **asthma prevalence rates for household youth** less than 20 years of age on racial minority farms by age and type of farm, 2000

Type of Farm	Total Rate/1000	se	<10 years Rate/1000	se	10-15 years Rate/1000	se	16-19 years Rate/1000	se
All crop	**90.58**	**3.78**	**74.39**	**5.48**	**101.88**	**5.93**	**98.43**	**6.58**
Grain and oil seed	97.87	9.78	98.48	6.04	103.80	16.02	92.25	14.53
Tobacco	63.98	13.56	66.87	20.29	***		***	
Cotton	145.25	30.21	77.61	29.08	205.44	50.93	162.10	50.70
Vegetable and melon	65.90	7.68	52.26	12.38	75.23	11.57	77.09	13.60
Fruit, nut, and berry	93.11	6.91	77.67	9.66	103.92	10.81	99.16	12.26
Nursery and floriculture	84.98	13.08	54.79	13.54	105.43	18.80	107.16	27.17
Other crop	102.06	9.17	81.24	12.41	***		***	
All livestock	**90.00**	**3.28**	**77.75**	**5.20**	**101.08**	**5.16**	**89.66**	**5.67**
Beef	87.30	3.62	79.16	5.76	94.01	5.52	87.57	6.30
Dairy	96.99	25.84	***		142.73	47.63	***	
Hog	136.56	24.38	94.04	34.36	204.26	45.80	101.81	31.35
Sheep and goat	107.20	18.97	170.94	48.47	72.11	24.46	103.96	29.97
Equine	105.29	15.42	79.90	26.65	135.46	24.95	100.07	25.93
Poultry and egg	58.05	13.12	***		93.65	28.26	***	
Aquaculture	76.43	32.21	***		***		***	
Other livestock	94.14	26.02	***		***		82.68	37.07
Total	**87.68**	**2.33**	**75.85**	**3.69**	**102.18**	**3.81**	**92.35**	**4.17**

*** Estimate is not reportable or is suppressed because of a non-reportable cell.

Table 2.102 National estimates of **asthma prevalence rates for household youth** less than 20 years of age with 1 or more **asthma attacks while doing farm work** by sex on racial minority farms, 2000

	Total	
Sex	Rate/1000	se
Male	68.66	3.80
Female	69.65	5.06
Total	69.18	3.20

Table 2.103 National estimates of **asthma prevalence rates for household youth** less than 20 years of age with 1 or more **asthma attacks while doing farm work** by age on racial minority farms, 2000

	Total	
Age	Rate/1000	se
<10 years	**124.99**	**12.32**
10-15 years	**60.14**	**3.83**
10-11 years	77.41	8.24
12-13 years	55.27	6.08
14-15 years	53.16	5.58
16-19 years	**60.53**	**4.31**
16-17 years	59.79	5.61
18-19 years	61.47	6.28
Total	**69.18**	**3.20**

Table 2.104 National estimates of **asthma prevalence rates for household youth** less than 20 years of age with 1 or more **asthma attacks while doing farm work** by type of farm on racial minority farms, 2000

	Total	
Type of Farm	Rate/1000	se
All crop	**88.72**	**6.47**
Grain and oil seed	87.89	14.91
Tobacco	48.48	19.72
Cotton	173.94	60.19
Vegetable and melon	63.03	13.03
Fruit, nut, and berry	106.98	14.01
Nursery and floriculture	149.69	33.02
Other crop	66.94	11.19
All livestock	**57.31**	**3.54**
Beef	51.04	3.78
Dairy	48.24	21.67
Hog	127.51	35.97
Sheep and goat	107.73	23.21
Equine	88.54	17.32
Poultry and egg	29.78	12.90
All other livestock*	49.33	
Total	**69.18**	**3.20**

* All other livestock includes "Aquaculture" and "Other livestock" farms.

Table 2.105 National estimates of **asthma prevalence rates for household youth** less than 20 years of age with 1 or more **asthma attacks requiring professional medical attention** by sex on racial minority farms, 2000

Sex	Total Rate/1000	se
Male	24.15	1.42
Female	13.50	1.14
Total	18.53	0.93

Table 2.106 National estimates of **asthma prevalence rates for household youth** less than 20 years of age with 1 or more **asthma attacks requiring professional medical attention** by age on racial minority farms, 2000

Age	Total Rate/1000	se
<10 years	**22.51**	**1.77**
10-15 years	**20.80**	**1.56**
10-11 years	26.41	3.18
12-13 years	23.65	2.83
14-15 years	13.50	2.02
16-19 years	**12.70**	**1.44**
16-17 years	13.64	1.96
18-19 years	11.53	2.00
Total	**18.53**	**0.93**

Table 2.107 National estimates of **asthma prevalence rates for household youth** less than 20 years of age with 1 or more **asthma attacks requiring professional medical attention** by type of farm on racial minority farms, 2000

Type of Farm	Total Rate/1000	se
All crop	**15.69**	**1.31**
Grain and oil seed	17.94	3.22
Tobacco	14.39	5.19
Cotton	48.67	14.57
Vegetable and melon	12.01	3.26
Fruit, nut, and berry	14.71	2.23
Nursery and floriculture	8.16	2.78
Other crop	17.45	3.05
All livestock	**22.17**	**1.42**
Beef	22.31	1.61
Hog	36.46	9.53
Sheep and goat	26.59	8.23
Equine	13.27	4.16
Poultry and egg	18.77	6.76
All other livestock*	21.06	
Total	**18.53**	**0.93**

* All other livestock includes "Dairy," "Aquaculture," and "Other livestock" farms.

Section III: National Demographic, Injury, and Asthma Estimates for Youth Less Than 20 Years of Age on Black Farm Operations

Table 3.1 National estimates of Black farms from the 1997 Census of Agriculture by business status, 2000

Status	Total [†]	
	Estimate	se
In business	15,301	49
Out of business	3,150	50
Total [†]	18,451	

† Estimates may not add to the total because of rounding.

Table 3.2 National estimates of **all youth** less than 20 years of age on Black farms by relationship to the farm and type of farm, 2000

Type of Farm	Total [†]		Household Youth		Hired Youth		Visiting Youth		Relatives		Non-Relatives	
	Estimate	se	Estimate	se	Estimate	se	Estimate	se	Estimate	se	Estimate	se
All crop	**49,346**	**1,833**	**2,451**	**71**	**918**	**68**	**45,977**	**1,812**	**25,922**	**608**	**20,055**	**1,570**
Grain and oil seed	16,293	1,111	917	46	105	19	15,272	1,098	8,707	375	6,565	945
Tobacco	6,488	372	373	28	287	34	5,828	355	3,793	227	2,036	215
Cotton	2,044	188	144	17	12	3	1,889	181	1,221	111	668	101
Vegetable and melon	10,617	1,125	378	29	386	51	9,863	1,114	4,798	275	5,055	1,037
Fruit, nut, and berry	2,609	314	139	20	***		***		1,351	161	***	
Nursery and floriculture	1,581	449	41	9	***		***		503	95	***	
Other crop	9,715	707	460	28	89	16	9,165	698	5,549	296	3,616	514
All livestock	**95,212**	**1,980**	**4,745**	**94**	**766**	**55**	**89,702**	**1,860**	**51,801**	**859**	**37,904**	**1,552**
Beef	79,387	1,623	3,988	86	608	49	74,791	1,596	44,822	804	29,968	1,163
Dairy	4,360	355	255	25	33	9	4,072	343	2,597	208	1,475	219
Hog	894	140	85	13	***		***		363	57	***	
Sheep and goat	5,429	738	203	22	55	12	5,172	726	1,998	194	3,174	622
Equine	1,759	218	113	18	***		***		915	111	692	134
Poultry and egg	434	109	13	4	0		421	6	180	48	241	62
All other livestock*	2,950		88		***		***		925		***	
Unknown	**3,014**		**492**		**15**		**2,508**		**595**		**913**	
Total [†]	**147,573**	**2,597**	**7,688**	**116**	**1,699**	**87**	**138,187**	**2,573**	**79,317**	**992**	**58,870**	**2,181**

† Estimates may not add to the total because of rounding.
* All other livestock includes "Aquaculture" and "Other livestock" farms.
*** Estimate is not reportable or is suppressed because of a non-reportable cell.

Table 3.3 National estimates of **all working youth** less than 20 years of age on Black farms by relationship to the farm and type of farm, 2000

Type of Farm	Total †		Working Household Youth		Non-Household Working Youth		Hired Youth		Working Relatives	
	Estimate	se	Estimate	se	Estimate	se	Estimate	se	Estimate	se
All crop	**3,300**	**132**	**889**	**39**	**2,411**	**118**	**918**	**68**	**1,493**	**89**
Grain and oil seed	822	62	324	25	498	52	105	19	393	46
Tobacco	791	64	153	15	638	58	287	34	351	42
Cotton	128	19	49	9	79	15	12	3	58	14
Vegetable and melon	915	79	152	16	763	74	386	51	378	47
All other crop*	644		212		433		129		304	
All livestock	**5,299**	**182**	**1,906**	**57**	**3,394**	**165**	**766**	**55**	**2,628**	**154**
Beef	4,354	152	1,566	50	2,788	138	608	49	2,179	128
Dairy	81	22	32	12	49	12	13	5	37	11
Hog	218	30	98	17	120	19	33	9	87	16
Sheep and goat	71	15	39	9	32	11	***		***	
Equine	280	39	99	15	181	32	55	12	126	29
Poultry and egg	124	24	49	9	75	21	***		***	
All other livestock**	171		22		150		***		***	
Unknown	**93**		**69**		**24**		**15**		**9**	
Total †	**8,693**	**221**	**2,864**	**68**	**5,829**	**202**	**1,699**	**87**	**4,130**	**177**

† Estimates may not add to the total because of rounding.
* All other crop includes "Fruit, nut, and berry," "Nursery and floriculture," and "Other crop" farms.
** All other livestock includes "Aquaculture" and "Other livestock" farms.
*** Estimate is not reportable or is suppressed because of a non-reportable cell.

Table 3.4 National estimates of **household youth** less than 20 years of age on Black farms by sex and age, 2000

Age	Total [†] Estimate	se	Male Estimate	se	Female Estimate	se	Unknown Estimate
<10 years	**2,353**	**59**	**1,206**	**38**	**1,147**	**38**	**0**
10-15 years	**2,882**	**63**	**1,515**	**42**	**1,365**	**40**	**2**
10-11 years	895	31	483	23	410	21	2
12-13 years	937	31	485	22	452	21	0
14-15 years	1,050	32	547	24	503	22	0
16-19 years	**2,118**	**49**	**1,151**	**35**	**967**	**32**	**0**
16-17 years	1,149	34	611	25	538	23	0
18-19 years	969	32	540	24	429	21	0
Unknown	**335**		**31**		**13**		**291**
Total [†]	**7,688**	**116**	**3,903**	**72**	**3,492**	**70**	**293**

† Estimates may not add to the total because of rounding.

Table 3.5 National estimates of **household youth** less than 20 years of age on Black farms by sex and type of farm, 2000

Type of Farm	Total [†] Estimate	se	Male Estimate	se	Female Estimate	se	Unknown Estimate
All crop	**2,451**	**71**	**1,259**	**44**	**1,183**	**44**	**9**
Grain and oil seed	917	46	489	29	428	28	0
Tobacco	373	28	182	16	191	18	0
Cotton	144	17	88	11	56	8	0
Vegetable and melon	378	29	185	17	191	17	2
Fruit, nut, and berry	139	20	75	12	64	12	0
Nursery and floriculture	41	9	19	5	18	6	5
Other crop	460	28	222	17	236	19	2
All livestock	**4,745**	**94**	**2,503**	**59**	**2,208**	**56**	**35**
Beef	3,988	86	2,086	53	1,868	51	35
Dairy	45	14	21	7	24	8	0
Hog	255	25	149	17	106	14	0
Sheep and goat	85	13	45	8	40	8	0
Equine	203	22	122	16	80	13	0
Poultry and egg	113	18	54	9	59	11	0
Aquaculture	13	4	***		***		0
Other livestock	43	9	***		***		0
Unknown	**492**		**141**		**102**		**249**
Total [†]	**7,688**	**116**	**3,903**	**72**	**3,492**	**70**	**293**

† Estimates may not add to the total because of rounding.
*** Estimate is not reportable or is suppressed because of a non-reportable cell.

Table 3.6 National estimates of **household youth** less than 20 years of age on Black farms by age and type of farm, 2000

Type of Farm	Total†		<10 years		10-15 years		16-19 years		Unknown
	Estimate	se	Estimate	se	Estimate	se	Estimate	se	Estimate
All crop	**2,451**	**71**	**802**	**36**	**931**	**37**	**707**	**30**	**12**
Grain and oil seed	917	46	284	22	339	23	294	20	0
Tobacco	373	28	136	15	152	15	85	9	0
Cotton	144	17	55	9	51	8	38	7	0
Vegetable and melon	378	29	94	11	165	16	117	12	2
Fruit, nut, and berry	139	20	41	9	67	11	31	7	0
Nursery and floriculture	41	9	17	6	***		***		5
Other crop	460	28	176	16	***		***		5
All livestock	**4,745**	**94**	**1,506**	**47**	**1,861**	**52**	**1,328**	**40**	**50**
Beef	3,988	86	1,254	43	1,556	46	1,128	36	50
Dairy	45	14	***		***		***		0
Hog	255	25	105	14	102	15	49	7	0
Sheep and goat	85	13	20	6	38	8	27	6	0
Equine	203	22	58	9	68	11	77	12	0
Poultry and egg	113	18	43	8	39	8	31	6	0
Aquaculture	13	4	***		***		***		0
Other livestock	43	9	***		***		***		0
Unknown	**492**		**44**		**90**		**84**		**274**
Total†	**7,688**	**116**	**2,353**	**59**	**2,882**	**63**	**2,118**	**49**	**335**

† Estimates may not add to the total because of rounding.
*** Estimate is not reportable or is suppressed because of a non-reportable cell.

86

Table 3.7   National estimates of **household youth** less than 20 years of age on Black farms by age, sex, and type of farm, 2000

	<10 years						
	Total [†]		Male		Female		Unknown
Type of Farm	Estimate	se	Estimate	se	Estimate	se	Estimate
All crop	**802**	**36**	**402**	**22**	**400**	**23**	**0**
Grain and oil seed	284	22	152	14	132	14	0
Tobacco	136	15	63	9	73	10	0
Cotton	55	9	36	6	20	5	0
Vegetable and melon	94	11	42	7	51	8	0
Fruit, nut, and berry	41	9	16	5	25	6	0
All other crop*	193		94		99		0
All livestock	**1,506**	**47**	**784**	**31**	**722**	**30**	**0**
Beef	1,254	43	653	29	601	27	0
Hog	105	14	58	10	47	8	0
Sheep and goat	20	6	***		***		0
Equine	58	9	25	5	33	7	0
Poultry and egg	43	8	20	4	23	6	0
All other livestock**	26		***		***		0
Unknown	**44**		**19**		**25**		**0**
Total [†]	**2,353**	**59**	**1,206**	**38**	**1,147**	**38**	**0**

	10-15 years						
	Total [†]		Male		Female		Unknown
Type of Farm	Estimate	se	Estimate	se	Estimate	se	Estimate
All crop	**931**	**37**	**502**	**26**	**429**	**23**	**0**
Grain and oil seed	339	23	193	17	147	14	0
Tobacco	152	15	86	11	66	9	0
Cotton	51	8	28	6	23	5	0
Vegetable and melon	165	16	81	10	83	10	0
Fruit, nut, and berry	67	11	45	8	23	6	0
All other crop*	158		69		89		0
All livestock	**1,861**	**52**	**971**	**34**	**888**	**33**	**2**
Beef	1,556	46	794	30	760	30	2
Hog	102	15	63	9	38	10	0
Sheep and goat	38	8	19	5	19	5	0
Equine	68	11	47	9	21	5	0
Poultry and egg	39	8	21	6	18	4	0
All other livestock**	59		27		32		0
Unknown	**90**		**43**		**48**		**0**
Total [†]	**2,882**	**63**	**1,515**	**42**	**1,365**	**40**	**2**

Continued

Table 3.7 National estimates of **household youth** less than 20 years of age on Black farms by age, sex, and type of farm, 2000 (Continued)

Type of Farm	Total † Estimate	se	Male Estimate	se	Female Estimate	se	Unknown Estimate
			16-19 years				
All crop	**707**	**30**	**353**	**20**	**353**	**20**	**0**
Grain and oil seed	294	20	144	13	150	14	0
Tobacco	85	9	33	5	52	7	0
Cotton	38	7	24	5	13	3	0
Vegetable and melon	117	12	61	8	57	8	0
Fruit, nut, and berry	31	7	15	5	16	5	0
All other crop*	142		76		66		0
All livestock	**1,328**	**40**	**736**	**28**	**592**	**26**	**0**
Beef	1,128	36	627	26	501	23	0
Hog	49	7	28	5	21	5	0
Sheep and goat	27	6	***		***		0
Equine	77	12	51	10	26	7	0
Poultry and egg	31	6	13	3	18	5	0
All other livestock**	16		***		***		0
Unknown	**83**		**61**		**22**		**0**
Total †	**2,118**	**49**	**1,151**	**35**	**967**	**32**	**0**

† Estimates may not add to the total because of rounding.
* All other crop includes "Nursery and floriculture" and "Other crop" farms.
** All other livestock includes "Dairy," "Aquaculture," and "Other livestock" farms.
*** Estimate is not reportable or is suppressed because of a non-reportable cell.

Table 3.8 National estimates of **household youth** less than 20 years of age on Black farms by work status and sex, 2000

Sex	Total † Estimate	se	Working Estimate	se	Non-Working Estimate	se	Unknown Estimate
Male	3,903	72	1,919	50	1,965	50	19
Female	3,492	70	941	37	2,540	58	12
Unknown	293		5		9		279
Total †	7,688	116	2,864	68	4,514	85	310

† Estimates may not add to the total because of rounding.

Table 3.9 National estimates of **household youth** less than 20 years of age on Black farms by work status and age, 2000

Age	Total[†] Estimate	se	Working Estimate	se	Non-Working Estimate	se	Unknown Estimate
<10 years	**2,353**	**59**	**296**	**20**	**2,053**	**55**	**3**
10-15 years	**2,882**	**63**	**1,388**	**44**	**1,487**	**45**	**7**
10-11 years	895	31	382	21	513	23	0
12-13 years	937	31	457	22	473	22	7
14-15 years	1,050	32	549	24	502	22	0
16-19 years	**2,118**	**49**	**1,162**	**38**	**949**	**32**	**7**
16-17 years	1,149	34	655	26	494	22	0
18-19 years	969	32	507	23	455	21	7
Unknown	**335**		**18**		**25**		**293**
Total[†]	**7,688**	**116**	**2,864**	**68**	**4,514**	**85**	**310**

† Estimates may not add to the total because of rounding.

Table 3.10 National estimates of **household youth** less than 20 years of age on Black farms by age, work status, and sex, 2000

Sex	Total[†] Estimate	se	Working Estimate	se	Non-Working Estimate	se	Unknown Estimate
<10 years							
Male	1,206	38	184	15	1,018	35	3
Female	1,147	38	112	11	1,035	36	0
Total[†]	2,353	59	296	20	2,053	55	3
10-15 years							
Male	1,515	42	909	33	604	27	2
Female	1,365	40	479	24	881	32	5
Unknown	2		0		2		0
Total[†]	2,882	63	1,388	44	1,487	45	7
16-19 years							
Male	1,151	35	814	30	332	19	5
Female	967	32	348	21	617	25	2
Total[†]	2,118	49	1,162	38	949	32	7

† Estimates may not add to the total because of rounding.

Table 3.11 National estimates of **household youth** less than 20 years of age on Black farms by whether they rode a horse and sex, 2000

Sex	Total [†] Estimate	se	Rode a Horse: Yes Estimate	se	Rode a Horse: No Estimate	se	Unknown Estimate
Male	3,903	72	907	35	2,966	63	30
Female	3,492	70	647	31	2,834	63	12
Unknown	293		2		11		279
Total [†]	7,688	116	1,556	52	5,811	101	320

† Estimates may not add to the total because of rounding.

Table 3.12 National estimates of **household youth** less than 20 years of age on Black farms by whether they rode a horse and age, 2000

Age	Total [†] Estimate	se	Rode a Horse: Yes Estimate	se	Rode a Horse: No Estimate	se	Unknown Estimate
<10 years	**2,353**	**59**	**379**	**23**	**1,971**	**54**	**3**
10-15 years	**2,882**	**63**	**699**	**31**	**2,172**	**54**	**11**
10-11 years	895	31	200	15	695	28	0
12-13 years	937	31	228	15	700	27	9
14-15 years	1,050	32	271	17	777	28	2
16-19 years	**2,118**	**49**	**472**	**24**	**1,630**	**43**	**16**
16-17 years	1,149	34	265	17	880	30	4
18-19 years	969	32	208	16	750	28	11
Unknown	**335**		**7**		**38**		**290**
Total [†]	**7,688**	**116**	**1,556**	**52**	**5,811**	**101**	**321**

† Estimates may not add to the total because of rounding.

Table 3.13 National estimates of **household youth** less than 20 years of age on Black farms by age, whether they rode a horse, and sex, 2000

	<10 years						
	Total [†]		Rode a Horse: Yes		Rode a Horse: No		Unknown
Sex	Estimate	se	Estimate	se	Estimate	se	Estimate
Male	1,206	38	211	16	991	34	3
Female	1,147	38	167	14	980	35	0
Total [†]	2,353	59	379	23	1,971	54	3
	10-15 years						
	Total [†]		Rode a Horse: Yes		Rode a Horse: No		Unknown
Sex	Estimate	se	Estimate	se	Estimate	se	Estimate
Male	1,515	42	394	22	1,117	36	4
Female	1,365	40	305	19	1,053	35	7
Unknown	2		0		2		0
Total [†]	2,882	63	699	31	2,172	54	11
	16-19 years						
	Total [†]		Rode a Horse: Yes		Rode a Horse: No		Unknown
Sex	Estimate	se	Estimate	se	Estimate	se	Estimate
Male	1,151	35	299	18	840	30	11
Female	967	32	173	15	790	29	5
Total [†]	2,118	49	472	24	1,630	43	16

† Estimates may not add to the total because of rounding.

Table 3.14 National estimates of **household youth** less than 20 years of age on Black farms by whether they drove an all-terrain vehicle (ATV) and sex, 2000

	Total [†]		Drove an ATV: Yes		Drove an ATV: No		Unknown
Sex	Estimate	se	Estimate	se	Estimate	se	Estimate
Male	3,903	72	999	36	2,536	58	368
Female	3,492	70	603	29	2,549	59	340
Unknown	293		0		2		291
Total [†]	7,688	116	1,602	51	5,087	93	999

† Estimates may not add to the total because of rounding.

Table 3.15 National estimates of **household youth** less than 20 years of age on Black farms by whether they drove an all-terrain vehicle (ATV) and age, 2000

Age	Total[†] Estimate	se	Drove an ATV: Yes Estimate	se	Drove an ATV: No Estimate	se	Unknown Estimate
<10 years	**2,353**	**59**	**177**	**15**	**1,537**	**44**	**639**
10-15 years	**2,882**	**63**	**760**	**31**	**2,115**	**55**	**7**
10-11 years	895	31	214	15	682	28	0
12-13 years	937	31	206	14	725	28	7
14-15 years	1,050	32	341	19	709	27	0
16-19 years	**2,118**	**49**	**665**	**29**	**1,435**	**40**	**18**
16-17 years	1,149	34	360	20	782	28	7
18-19 years	969	32	305	18	653	26	11
Unknown	**335**		**0**		**0**		**335**
Total[†]	**7,688**	**116**	**1,602**	**51**	**5,087**	**93**	**999**

† Estimates may not add to the total because of rounding.

Table 3.16 National estimates of **household youth** less than 20 years of age on Black farms by age, whether they drove an all-terrain vehicle (ATV), and sex, 2000

Sex	Total[†] Estimate	se	Drove an ATV: Yes Estimate	se	Drove an ATV: No Estimate	se	Unknown Estimate
			<10 years				
Male	1,206	38	104	11	779	30	324
Female	1,147	38	73	9	758	29	316
Total[†]	2,353	59	177	15	1,537	44	639
			10-15 years				
Male	1,515	42	448	23	1,065	36	2
Female	1,365	40	312	19	1,048	35	5
Unknown	2		0		2		0
Total[†]	2,882	63	760	31	2,115	55	7
			16-19 years				
Male	1,151	35	447	22	692	27	11
Female	967	32	218	16	743	28	7
Total[†]	2,118	49	665	29	1,435	40	18

† Estimates may not add to the total because of rounding.

Table 3.17 National estimates of **household youth** less than 20 years of age on Black farms by whether they drove a tractor and sex, 2000

Sex	Total [†]		Drove a Tractor: Yes		Drove a Tractor: No		Unknown
	Estimate	se	Estimate	se	Estimate	se	Estimate
Male	3,903	72	1,433	41	2,100	54	370
Female	3,492	70	480	26	2,670	59	342
Unknown	293		0		2		291
Total [†]	7,688	116	1,913	50	4,772	87	1,003

† Estimates may not add to the total because of rounding.

Table 3.18 National estimates of **household youth** less than 20 years of age on Black farms by whether they drove a tractor and age, 2000

Age	Total [†]		Drove a Tractor: Yes		Drove a Tractor: No		Unknown
	Estimate	se	Estimate	se	Estimate	se	Estimate
<10 years	**2,353**	**59**	**119**	**12**	**1,594**	**45**	**639**
10-15 years	**2,882**	**63**	**894**	**32**	**1,979**	**52**	**9**
10-11 years	895	31	194	14	701	28	0
12-13 years	937	31	271	16	660	26	7
14-15 years	1,050	32	429	21	619	25	2
16-19 years	**2,118**	**49**	**900**	**32**	**1,198**	**36**	**20**
16-17 years	1,149	34	470	22	674	26	4
18-19 years	969	32	429	22	525	23	15
Unknown	**335**		**0**		**0**		**335**
Total [†]	**7,688**	**116**	**1,913**	**50**	**4,772**	**87**	**1,003**

† Estimates may not add to the total because of rounding.

Table 3.19 National estimates of **household youth** less than 20 years of age on Black farms by age, whether they drove a tractor, and sex, 2000

	<10 years						
	Total [†]		Drove a Tractor: Yes		Drove a Tractor: No		Unknown
Sex	Estimate	se	Estimate	se	Estimate	se	Estimate
Male	1,206	38	79	9	804	31	324
Female	1,147	38	41	7	790	29	316
Total [†]	2,353	59	119	12	1,594	45	639

	10-15 years						
	Total [†]		Drove a Tractor: Yes		Drove a Tractor: No		Unknown
Sex	Estimate	se	Estimate	se	Estimate	se	Estimate
Male	1,515	42	654	26	857	33	4
Female	1,365	40	240	16	1,121	36	5
Unknown	2		0		2		0
Total [†]	2,882	63	894	32	1,979	52	9

	16-19 years						
	Total [†]		Drove a Tractor: Yes		Drove a Tractor: No		Unknown
Sex	Estimate	se	Estimate	se	Estimate	se	Estimate
Male	1,151	35	700	27	440	21	11
Female	967	32	200	16	759	28	9
Total [†]	2,118	49	900	32	1,198	36	20

[†] Estimates may not add to the total because of rounding.

Table 3.20 National estimates of **injuries to all youth** less than 20 years of age on Black farms by sex and relationship to the farm, 2000

	Total [†]		Male		Female	
Relationship to Farm	Estimate	se	Estimate	se	Estimate	se
Household youth	49	9	33	7	16	6
Hired youth	***		***		***	
Visiting youth	***		***		***	
Relatives	43	8	31	7	12	3
Non-relatives	***		***		***	
Total [†]	102	13	75	11	27	7

[†] Estimates may not add to the total because of rounding.
*** Estimate is not reportable or is suppressed because of a non-reportable cell.

Table 3.21 National estimates of **injuries to all youth** less than 20 years of age on Black farms by age and relationship to the farm, 2000

Relationship to Farm	Total [†] Estimate	se	<10 years Estimate	se	10-19 years Estimate	se
Household youth	49	9	17	6	32	
Hired youth	***		***		***	
Visiting youth	***		***		***	
Relatives	43	8	25	6	18	
Non-relatives	***		***		***	
Total [†]	102	13	42	9	60	

  † Estimates may not add to the total because of rounding.
  *** Estimate is not reportable or is suppressed because of a non-reportable cell.

Table 3.22 National estimates of **injuries to all youth** less than 20 years of age on Black farms by work status and relationship to the farm, 2000

Relationship to Farm	Total [†] Estimate	se	Working Estimate	se	Non-Working Estimate	se
Household youth	49	9	22	6	27	7
Hired youth	***		***		***	
Visiting youth	***		***		***	
Relatives	43	8	16	5	27	5
Non-relatives	***		***		***	
Total [†]	102	13	43	9	59	9

  † Estimates may not add to the total because of rounding.
  *** Estimate is not reportable or is suppressed because of a non-reportable cell.

Table 3.23 National estimates of **injuries to all youth** less than 20 years of age on Black farms by sex and race, 2000

Race	Total [†] Estimate	se	Male Estimate	se	Female Estimate	se
White	14	4	***		***	
Black	76	11	53	8	22	7
All other races*	13		***		***	
Total [†]	102	13	75	11	27	7

  † Estimates may not add to the total because of rounding.
  * All other races includes "Native American," "Asian," and "Other Races."
  *** Estimate is not reportable or is suppressed because of a non-reportable cell.

Table 3.24 National estimates of **injuries to all youth** less than 20 years of age on Black farms by age and race, 2000

Race	Total [†] Estimate	se	< 10 years Estimate	se	10-19 years Estimate	se
White	14	4	***		***	
Black	76	11	28	7	47	
All other races*	13		***		***	
Total [†]	102	13	42	9	60	

† Estimates may not add to the total because of rounding.
* All other races includes "Native American," "Asian," and "Other Races."
*** Estimate is not reportable or is suppressed because of a non-reportable cell.

Table 3.25 National estimates of **injuries to all youth** less than 20 years of age on Black farms by work status and race, 2000

Race	Total [†] Estimate	se	Working Estimate	se	Non-Working Estimate	se
Black	76	11	27	6	49	9
All other races*	27		16		10	
Total [†]	102	13	43	9	59	9

† Estimates may not add to the total because of rounding.
* All other races includes "White," "Native American," "Asian," and "Other races."

Table 3.26 National estimates of **injuries to all youth** less than 20 years of age on Black farms by sex and age, 2000

Age	Total [†] Estimate	se	Male Estimate	se	Female Estimate	se
< 10 years	**42**	**9**	**29**	**6**	**13**	**6**
10-15 years	**46**	**8**	**39**	**7**	**7**	**3**
10-11 years	14	4	***		***	
12-13 years	15	4	***		***	
14-15 years	17	5	***		***	
16-19 years	**15**	**4**	**8**	**3**	**7**	**3**
Total [†]	102	13	75	11	27	7

† Estimates may not add to the total because of rounding.
*** Estimate is not reportable or is suppressed because of a non-reportable cell.

Table 3.27 National estimates of **injuries to all youth** less than 20 years of age on Black farms by work status and age, 2000

Age	Total [†] Estimate	se	Working Estimate	se	Non-Working Estimate	se
< 10 years	**42**	**9**	***		***	
10-15 years	**46**	**8**	22	6	24	5
10-11 years	14	4	***		***	
12-13 years	15	4	***		***	
14-15 years	17	5	***		***	
16-19 years	**15**	**4**	***		***	
Total [†]	**102**	**13**	**43**	**9**	**59**	**9**

† Estimates may not add to the total because of rounding.
*** Estimate is not reportable or is suppressed because of a non-reportable cell.

Table 3.28 National estimates of **injuries to all youth** less than 20 years of age on Black farms by sex and type of farm, 2000

Type of Farm	Total [†] Estimate	se	Male Estimate	se	Female Estimate	se
All crop	**36**	**8**	21	5	16	6
Grain and oil seed	19	7	***		***	
All other crop*	17		***		***	
All livestock	**66**	**10**	55	9	12	4
Beef	49	9	***		***	
All other livestock**	17		***		***	
Total [†]	**102**	**13**	**75**	**11**	**27**	**7**

† Estimates may not add to the total because of rounding.
* All other crop includes "Tobacco," "Cotton," "Vegetable and melon," "Fruit, nut, and berry," "Nursery and floriculture," and "Other crop" farms.
** All other livestock includes "Dairy," "Hog," "Sheep and goat," "Equine," "Poultry and egg," "Aquaculture," and "Other livestock" farms.
*** Estimate is not reportable or is suppressed because of a non-reportable cell.

Table 3.29 National estimates of **injuries to all youth** less than 20 years of age on Black farms by age and type of farm, 2000

Type of Farm	Total [†] Estimate	se	<10 years Estimate	se	10-15 years Estimate	se	16-19 years Estimate	se
All crop	36	8	***		13	4	***	
All livestock	66	10	***		33	7	***	
Total [†]	102	13	42	9	46	8	15	4

† Estimates may not add to the total because of rounding.
*** Estimate is not reportable or is suppressed because of a non-reportable cell.

Table 3.30 National estimates of **injuries to all youth** less than 20 years of age on Black farms by work status and type of farm, 2000

Type of Farm	Total [†] Estimate	se	Working Estimate	se	Non-Working Estimate	se
All crop	36	8	11	4	25	7
All livestock	66	10	32	8	34	6
Total [†]	102	13	43	9	59	9

† Estimates may not add to the total because of rounding.

Table 3.31 National estimates of **injuries to all youth** less than 20 years of age on Black farms by sex and type of injury, 2000

Type of Injury	Total [†] Estimate	se	Male Estimate	se	Female Estimate	se
Bruise, contusion	8	3	8	3	0	
Sprain, strain	9	4	0		9	4
Broken bone, fracture	15	4	***		***	
Cut, laceration	34	8	25	6	9	5
Puncture, stab, jab	12	4	***		***	
All other injuries*	24		***		***	
Unknown	2		2		0	
Total [†]	102	13	75	11	27	7

† Estimates may not add to the total because of rounding.
* All other injuries includes "Scrape, abrasion," "Dislocation," "Traumatic rupture," "Crushed," "Amputation," "Nerve injury," "Burn, blister, scald," "Multiple injuries," and "Other injury."
*** Estimate is not reportable or is suppressed because of a non-reportable cell.

Table 3.32 National estimates of **injuries to all youth** less than 20 years of age on Black farms by age and type of injury, 2000

Type of Injury	Total [†] Estimate	se	< 10 years Estimate	se	10-15 years Estimate	se	16-19 years Estimate	se
Bruise, contusion	8	3	***		***		***	
Sprain, strain	9	4	***		***		***	
Broken bone, fracture	15	4	***		***		***	
Cut, laceration	34	8	27	8	***		***	
Puncture, stab, jab	12	4	***		***		***	
All other injuries*	24		***		***		***	
Unknown	2		0		2		0	
Total [†]	102	13	42	9	46	8	15	4

† Estimates may not add to the total because of rounding.
* All other injuries includes "Scrape, abrasion," "Dislocation," "Traumatic rupture," "Crushed," "Amputation," "Nerve injury," "Burn, blister, scald," "Multiple injuries," and "Other injury."
*** Estimate is not reportable or is suppressed because of a non-reportable cell.

Table 3.33 National estimates of **injuries to all youth** less than 20 years of age on Black farms by work status and type of injury, 2000

Type of Injury	Total [†] Estimate	se	Working Estimate	se	Non-Working Estimate	se
Bruise, contusion	8	3	***		***	
Sprain, strain	9	4	***		***	
Broken bone, fracture	15	4	***		***	
Cut, laceration	34	8	16	6	18	6
Puncture, stab, jab	12	4	***		***	
All other injuries*	24		12		12	
Unknown	2		0		2	
Total [†]	102	13	43	9	59	9

† Estimates may not add to the total because of rounding.
* All other injuries includes "Scrape, abrasion," "Dislocation," "Traumatic rupture," "Crushed," "Amputation," "Nerve injury," "Burn, blister, scald," "Multiple injuries," and "Other injury."
*** Estimate is not reportable or is suppressed because of a non-reportable cell.

Table 3.34 National estimates of **injuries to all youth** less than 20 years of age on Black farms by sex and body part injured, 2000

Body Part Injured	Total[†] Estimate	se	Male Estimate	se	Female Estimate	se
Head, skull	9	3	9	3	0	
Face	17	5	***		***	
Arm	19	4	***		***	
Hand, wrist, fingers	13	4	***		***	
Leg	19	6	10	5	9	4
Foot, ankle, toes	14	4	***		***	
All other body parts*	12		12		0	
Total[†]	102	13	75	11	27	7

† Estimates may not add to the total because of rounding.
* All other body parts includes "Neck," "Shoulder, chest, back," "Abdomen," "Pelvic region," "Internal injury," "Multiple body parts," and "Other body parts."
*** Estimate is not reportable or is suppressed because of a non-reportable cell.

Table 3.35 National estimates of **injuries to all youth** less than 20 years of age on Black farms by age and body part injured, 2000

Body Part Injured	Total[†] Estimate	se	< 10 years Estimate	se	10-15 years Estimate	se	16-19 years Estimate	se
Head, skull	9	3	***		***		0	
Face	17	5	***		***		0	
Arm	19	4	12	3	***		***	
Hand, wrist, fingers	13	4	***		***		***	
Leg	19	6	***		***		***	
Foot, ankle, toes	14	4	***		***		***	
All other body parts*	12		0		12		0	
Total[†]	102	13	42	9	46	8	15	4

† Estimates may not add to the total because of rounding.
* All other body parts includes "Neck," "Shoulder, chest, back," "Abdomen," "Pelvic region," "Internal injury," "Multiple body parts," and "Other body parts."
*** Estimate is not reportable or is suppressed because of a non-reportable cell.

Table 3.36 National estimates of **injuries to all youth** less than 20 years of age on Black farms by work status and body part injured, 2000

Body Part Injured	Total[†]		Working		Non-Working	
	Estimate	se	Estimate	se	Estimate	se
Head, skull	9	3	***		***	
Face	17	5	***		***	
Arm	19	4	***		***	
Hand, wrist, fingers	13	4	***		***	
Leg	19	6	12	5	7	4
Foot, ankle, toes	14	4	8	3	6	3
All other body parts*	12		***		***	
Total[†]	102	13	43	9	59	9

† Estimates may not add to the total because of rounding.
* All other body parts includes "Neck," "Shoulder, chest, back," "Abdomen," "Pelvic region," "Internal injury," "Multiple body parts," and "Other body parts."
*** Estimate is not reportable or is suppressed because of a non-reportable cell.

Table 3.37 National estimates of **injuries to all youth** less than 20 years of age on Black farms by sex and source of injury, 2000

Source of Injury[‡]	Total[†]		Male		Female	
	Estimate	se	Estimate	se	Estimate	se
Parts/Materials (4)	**12**	**4**	**12**	**4**	**0**	
Persons/Animals/Plants/Minerals (5)	**19**	**5**	***		***	
Structures and Surfaces (6)	**26**	**6**	***		***	
Floors/Walkways/Ground (62)	21	5	***		***	
Ground (623)	*16*	*4*	***		***	
Tools/Instruments/Equipment (7)	**11**	**3**	**11**	**3**	**0**	
Recreation Equipment (78)	7	2	7	2	0	
Other and Unknown Sources*	**35**		**17**		**18**	
Total[†]	**102**	**13**	**75**	**11**	**27**	**7**

† Estimates may not add to the total because of rounding.
‡ Categories based on the Bureau of Labor Statistics Occupational Injury and Illness Coding Structure (OIICS). OIICS codes are provided in parentheses.
* Other and Unknown Sources includes "Chemicals," "Containers," "Furniture and Fixtures," "Machinery," "Vehicles," "Other Sources," and "Unknown Sources."
*** Estimate is not reportable or is suppressed because of a non-reportable cell.

Table 3.38 National estimates of **injuries to all youth** less than 20 years of age on Black farms by age and source of injury, 2000

Source of Injury ‡	Total †		<10 years		10-15 years		16-19 years	
	Estimate	se	Estimate	se	Estimate	se	Estimate	se
Parts/Materials (4)	12	4	***		***		***	
Persons/Animals/Plants/Minerals (5)	19	5	***		10	4	***	
Animals (51)	14	4	***		8	3	***	
Structures and Surfaces (6)	26	6	9	3	17	5	0	
Floors/Walkways/Ground (62)	21	5	9	3	12	4	0	
Ground (623)	*16*	*4*	***		*12*	*4*	***	
Tools/Instruments/Equipment (7)	11	3	7	3	***		***	
Recreation Equipment (78)	7	2	***		***		0	
Other and Unknown Sources*	35		16		12		7	
Total †	102	13	42	9	46	8	15	4

† Estimates may not add to the total because of rounding.

‡ Categories based on the Bureau of Labor Statistics Occupational Injury and Illness Coding Structure (OIICS). OIICS codes are provided in parentheses.

* Other and Unknown Sources includes "Chemicals," "Containers," "Furniture and Fixtures," "Machinery," "Vehicles," "Other Sources," and "Unknown Sources."

*** Estimate is not reportable or suppressed because of a non-reportable cell.

Table 3.39 National estimates of **injuries to all youth** less than 20 years of age on Black farms by work status and source of injury, 2000

Source of Injury ‡	Total †		Working		Non-Working	
	Estimate	se	Estimate	se	Estimate	se
Parts/Materials (4)	12	4	12	4	0	
Persons/Animals/Plants/Minerals (5)	19	5	7	3	12	4
Animals (51)	14	4	***		***	
Structures and Surfaces (6)	26	6	12	4	14	4
Floors/Walkways/Ground (62)	21	5	10	3	11	3
Ground (623)	*16*	*4*	*10*	*3*	*7*	*3*
Tools/Instruments/Equipment (7)	11	3	***		***	
Recreation Equipment (78)	7	2	0		7	2
Other and Unknown Sources*	35		***		***	
Total †	102	13	43	9	59	9

† Estimates may not add to the total because of rounding.

‡ Categories based on the Bureau of Labor Statistics Occupational Injury and Illness Coding Structure (OIICS). OIICS codes are provided in parentheses.

* Other and Unknown Sources includes "Chemicals," "Containers," "Furniture and Fixtures," "Machinery," "Vehicles," "Other Sources," and "Unknown Sources."

*** Estimate is not reportable or is suppressed because of a non-reportable cell.

Table 3.40 National estimates of **injuries to all youth** less than 20 years of age on Black farms by sex and type of injury event, 2000

Type of Injury Event [‡]	Total [†] Estimate	se	Male Estimate	se	Female Estimate	se
Contact With Objects (0)	33	6	25	5	8	3
Contact With Object Unspecified (00)	7	3	7	3	0	
Struck Against Object (01)	11	4	***		***	
Against Stationary Object (012)	8	3	***		***	
Struck by Object (02)	11	4	***		***	
Falls (1)	31	6	***		***	
Fall to Lower Level (11)	18	4	***		***	
Fall to Lower Level n.e.c. (119)*	18	4	***		***	
Fall on Same Level (13)	10	4	***		***	
Exposure to Substances/Environments (3)	9	3	9	3	0	
Exposure Caustic/Allergenic Substance (34)	7	3	7	3	0	
Assaults and Violent Acts (6)	12	4	***		***	
Assault by Animal (63)	12	4	***		***	
Assault by Animal n.e.c. (639)*	7	3	***		***	
Other and Unknown Events**	18		9		9	
Total [†]	102	13	75	11	27	7

† Estimates may not add to the total because of rounding.

‡ Categories based on the Bureau of Labor Statistics Occupational Injury and Illness Coding Structure (OIICS). OIICS codes are provided in parentheses.

* "n.e.c." is an abbreviation for "not elsewhere classified."

** Other and Unknown Events includes "Bodily Reaction/Exertion," "Transportation Events," "Fires and Explosions," "Other Events," and "Unknown Events."

*** Estimate is not reportable or is suppressed because of a non-reportable cell.

Table 3.41 National estimates of **injuries to all youth** less than 20 years of age on Black farms by age and type of injury event, 2000

Type of Injury Event ‡	Total †		<10 years		10-15 years		16-19 years	
	Estimate	se	Estimate	se	Estimate	se	Estimate	se
Contact With Objects (0)	33	6	11	4	14	4	8	3
Contact With Object Unspecified (00)	7	3	0		***		***	
Struck Against Object (01)	11	4	***		7	3	***	
Against Stationary Object (012)	8	3	***	3	***		***	
Struck by Object (02)	11	4	8	3	***		***	
Falls (1)	31	6	17	4	14	4	0	
Fall to Lower Level (11)	18	4	11	3	7	3	0	
Fall to Lower Level n.e.c. (119)*	18	4	11	3	7	3	0	
Fall on Same Level (13)	10	4	***		***		***	
Exposure to Substances/Environments (3)	9	3	***		7	3	***	
Exposure Caustic/Allergenic Substance (34)	7	3	***		***		***	
Assaults and Violent Acts (6)	12	4	***		***		***	
Assault by Animal (63)	12	4	***		***		***	
Assault by Animal n.e.c. (639)*	7	3	***		***		***	
Other and Unknown Events	18		8		***		***	
Total †	102	13	42	9	46	8	15	4

† Estimates may not add to the total because of rounding.

‡ Categories based on the Bureau of Labor Statistics Occupational Injury and Illness Coding Structure (OIICS). OIICS codes are provided in parentheses.

* "n.e.c." is an abbreviation for "not elsewhere classified."

** Other and Unknown Events includes "Bodily Reaction/Exertion," "Transportation Events," "Other Events," and "Unknown Events."

*** Estimate is not reportable or is suppressed because of a non-reportable cell.

Table 3.42 National estimates of **injuries to all youth** less than 20 years of age on Black farms by work status and type of injury event, 2000

Type of Injury Event ‡	Total †		Working		Non-Working	
	Estimate	se	Estimate	se	Estimate	se
Contact With Objects (0)	33	6	16	5	17	4
Contact With Object Unspecified (00)	7	3	***		***	
Struck Against Object (01)	11	4	***		***	
Against Stationary Object (012)	8	3	***		***	
Struck by Object (02)	11	4	***		***	
Falls (1)	31	6	10	3	21	5
Fall to Lower Level (11)	18	4	***		***	
Fall to Lower Level n.e.c.* (119)	18	4	***		***	
Fall on Same Level (13)	10	4	***		***	
Exposure to Substances/Environments (3)	9	3	9	3	0	
Exposure Caustic/Allergenic Substance (34)	7	3	7	3	0	
Assaults and Violent Acts (6)	12	4	0		12	4
Assault by Animal (63)	12	4	0		12	4
Assault by Animal n.e.c.* (639)	7	3	***		***	
Other and Unknown Events**	18		9		9	
Total †	102	13	43	9	59	9

† Estimates may not add to the total because of rounding.

‡ Categories based on the Bureau of Labor Statistics Occupational Injury and Illness Coding Structure (OIICS). OIICS codes are provided in parentheses.

* "n.e.c." is an abbreviation for "not elsewhere classified."

** Other and Unknown Events includes "Bodily Reaction/Exertion," "Transportation Events," "Fires and Explosions," "Other Events," and "Unknown Events."

*** Estimate is not reportable or is suppressed because of a non-reportable cell.

Table 3.43 National estimates of **injuries to household youth** less than 20 years of age on Black farms by sex and age, 2000

Age	Total [†] Estimate	se	Male Estimate	se	Female Estimate	se
< 10 years	17	6	9	3	8	5
10-19 years	32		25		7	
Total [†]	49	9	33	7	16	6

† Estimates may not add to the total because of rounding.

Table 3.44 National estimates of **injuries to household youth** less than 20 years of age on Black farms by work status and age, 2000

Age	Total [†] Estimate	se	Working Estimate	se	Non-Working Estimate	se
< 10 years	17	6	0		17	6
10-19 years	32		22		10	
Total [†]	49	9	22	6	27	7

† Estimates may not add to the total because of rounding.

Table 3.45 National estimates of **injuries to household youth** less than 20 years of age on Black farms by sex and type of farm, 2000

Type of Farm	Total [†] Estimate	se	Male Estimate	se	Female Estimate	se
All crop	18	6	10	3	8	5
All livestock	31	7	24	6	7	4
Total [†]	49	9	33	7	16	6

† Estimates may not add to the total because of rounding.

Table 3.46 National estimates of **injuries to household youth** less than 20 years of age on Black farms by sex and type of injury, 2000

Type of Injury	Total [†] Estimate	se	Male Estimate	se	Female Estimate	se
Sprain, strain	7	3	0		7	3
Broken bone, fracture	7	3	7	3	0	
Cut, laceration	16	6	***		***	
All other injuries*	20		***		***	
Total [†]	49	9	33	7	16	6

† Estimates may not add to the total because of rounding.

* All other injuries includes "Scrape, abrasion," "Bruise, contusion," "Dislocation," "Puncture, stab, jab," "Traumatic rupture," "Crushed," "Amputation, " "Nerve injury," "Burn, blister, scald," "Multiple injuries," and "Other injury."

*** Estimate is not reportable or is suppressed because of a non-reportable cell.

Table 3.47 National estimates of **injuries to household youth** less than 20 years of age on Black farms by work status and type of injury, 2000

Type of Injury	Total [†] Estimate	se	Working Estimate	se	Non-Working Estimate	se
Sprain, strain	7	3	0		7	3
Broken bone, fracture	7	3	***		***	
Cut, laceration	16	6	***		***	
All other injuries*	20		***		***	
Total [†]	49	9	23	6	27	7

† Estimates may not add to the total because of rounding.

* All other injuries includes "Scrape, abrasion," "Bruise, contusion," "Dislocation," "Puncture, stab, jab," "Traumatic rupture," "Crushed," "Amputation, " "Nerve injury," "Burn, blister, scald," "Multiple injuries," and "Other injury."

*** Estimate is not reportable or is suppressed because of a non-reportable cell.

Table 3.48 National estimates of **injuries to household youth** less than 20 years of age on Black farms by sex and body part injured, 2000

Body Part Injured	Total [†] Estimate	se	Male Estimate	se	Female Estimate	se
Face	8	3	***		***	
Arm	9	3	9	3	0	
Leg	10	4	***		***	
Foot, ankle, toes	7	3	***		***	
All other body parts*	15		***		***	
Total [†]	49	9	33	7	16	6

† Estimates may not add to the total because of rounding.
* All other body parts includes "Head, skull," "Neck," "Shoulder, chest, back," "Abdomen," "Pelvic region," "Hand, wrist, fingers," "Internal injury," "Multiple body parts," and "Other body parts."
*** Estimate is not reportable or is suppressed because of a non-reportable cell.

Table 3.49 National estimates of **injuries to household youth** less than 20 years of age on Black farms by age and body part injured, 2000

Body Part Injured	Total [†] Estimate	se	< 10 years Estimate	se	10-19 years Estimate	se
Face	8	3	***		***	
Arm	9	3	***		***	
Leg	10	4	0		10	
Foot, ankle, toes	7	3	***		***	
All other body parts*	15		***		***	
Total [†]	49	9	17	6	32	

† Estimates may not add to the total because of rounding.
* All other body parts includes "Head, skull," "Neck," "Shoulder, chest, back," "Abdomen," "Pelvic region," "Hand, wrist, fingers," "Internal injury," "Multiple body parts," and "Other body parts."
*** Estimate is not reportable or is suppressed because of a non-reportable cell.

Table 3.50 National estimates of **injuries to household youth** less than 20 years of age on Black farms by work status and body part injured, 2000

Body Part Injured	Total [†]		Working		Non-Working	
	Estimate	se	Estimate	se	Estimate	se
Face	8	3	0		8	3
Arm	9	3	***		***	
Leg	10	4	***		***	
Foot, ankle, toes	7	3	***		***	
All other body parts*	15		***		***	
Total [†]	49	9	23	6	27	7

† Estimates may not add to the total because of rounding.

* All other body parts includes "Head, skull," "Neck," "Shoulder, chest, back," "Abdomen," "Pelvic region," "Hand, wrist, fingers," "Internal injury," "Multiple body parts," and "Other body parts."

*** Estimate is not reportable or is suppressed because of a non-reportable cell.

Table 3.51 National estimates of **injuries to household youth** less than 20 years of age on Black farms by sex and source of injury, 2000

Source of Injury [‡]	Total [†]		Male		Female	
	Estimate	se	Estimate	se	Estimate	se
Structures and Surfaces (6)	17	5	***		***	
Floors/Walkways/Ground (62)	12	4	***		***	
Ground (623)	9	3	***		***	
Tools/Instruments/Equipment (7)	7	3	7	3	0	
Other and Unknown Sources*	10		***		***	
Total [†]	49	9	33	7	16	6

† Estimates may not add to the total because of rounding.

‡ Categories based on the Bureau of Labor Statistics Occupational Injury and Illness Coding Structure (OIICS). OIICS codes are provided in parentheses.

* Other and Unknown Sources includes "Chemicals," "Containers," "Furniture and Fixtures," "Machinery," "Parts/Materials," "Persons/Animals/Plants/Minerals," "Vehicles," "Other Sources," and "Unknown Sources."

*** Estimate is not reportable or is suppressed because of a non-reportable cell.

Table 3.52 National estimates of **injuries to household youth** less than 20 years of age on Black farms by age and source of injury, 2000

Source of Injury ‡	Total †		<10 years		10-19 years	
	Estimate	se	Estimate	se	Estimate	se
Structures and Surfaces (6)	17	5	0		17	
Floors/Walkways/Ground (62)	12	4	0		12	
Ground (623)	9	3	***		***	
Tools/Instruments/Equipment (7)	7	3	***		***	
Other and Unknown Sources*	25		***		***	
Total †	49	9	17	6	27	

† Estimates may not add to the total because of rounding.
‡ Categories based on the Bureau of Labor Statistics Occupational Injury and Illness Coding Structure (OIICS). OIICS codes are provided in parentheses.
* Other and Unknown Sources includes "Chemicals," "Containers," "Furniture and Fixtures," "Machinery," "Parts/Materials," "Persons/Animals/Plants/Minerals," "Vehicles," "Other Sources," and "Unknown Sources."
*** Estimate is not reportable or is suppressed because of a non-reportable cell.

Table 3.53 National estimates of **injuries to household youth** less than 20 years of age on Black farms by work status and source of injury, 2000

Source of Injury ‡	Total †		Working		Non-Working	
	Estimate	se	Estimate	se	Estimate	se
Structures and Surfaces (6)	17	5	10	4	7	3
Floors/Walkways/Ground (62)	12	4	***		***	
Ground (623)	9	3	***		***	
Tools/Instruments/Equipment (7)	7	3	***		***	
Other and Unknown Sources*	25		***		***	
Total †	49	9	22	6	27	7

† Estimates may not add to the total because of rounding.
‡ Categories based on the Bureau of Labor Statistics Occupational Injury and Illness Coding Structure (OIICS). OIICS codes are provided in parentheses.
* Other and Unknown Sources includes "Chemicals," "Containers," "Furniture and Fixtures," "Machinery," "Parts/Materials," "Persons/Animals/Plants/Minerals," "Vehicles," "Other Sources," and "Unknown Sources."
*** Estimate is not reportable or is suppressed because of a non-reportable cell.

Table 3.54 National estimates of **injuries to household youth** less than 20 years of age on Black farms by age and type of injury event, 2000

Type of Injury Event ‡	Total †		<10 years		10-19 years	
	Estimate	se	Estimate	se	Estimate	se
Contact With Objects (0)	**15**	**4**	***		***	
Struck Against Object (01)	7	3	0		7	
Falls (1)	**22**	**5**	**10**	**4**	**12**	
Fall to Lower Level (11)	12	3	***		***	
Fall to Lower Level n.e.c. (119)	12	3	***		***	
Fall on Same Level (13)	8	3	***		***	
Other and Unknown Events**	**12**		***		***	
Total †	**49**	**9**	**17**	**6**	**32**	

† Estimates may not add to the total because of rounding.

‡ Categories based on the Bureau of Labor Statistics Occupational Injury and Illness Coding Structure (OIICS). OIICS codes are provided in parentheses.

* "n.e.c." is an abbreviation for "not elsewhere classified."

** Other and Unknown Events includes "Bodily Reaction/Exertion," "Exposure to Substances/Environments," "Transportation Events," "Fires and Explosions," "Assaults and Violent Acts," "Other Events," and "Unknown Events."

*** Estimate is not reportable or is suppressed because of a non-reportable cell.

Table 3.55 National estimates of **injuries to household youth** less than 20 years of age on Black farms by work status and type of injury event, 2000

Type of Injury Event ‡	Total †		Working		Non-Working	
	Estimate	se	Estimate	se	Estimate	se
Contact With Objects (0)	**15**	**4**	**7**	**3**	**8**	**3**
Struck Against Object (01)	7	3	***		***	
Falls (1)	**22**	**5**	**7**	**3**	**15**	**4**
Fall to Lower Level (11)	12	3	***		***	
Fall to Lower Level n.e.c. (119)	12	3	***		***	
Fall on Same Level (13)	8	3	***		***	
Other and Unknown Events**	**12**		**8**		**4**	
Total †	**49**	**9**	**22**	**6**	**27**	**7**

† Estimates may not add to the total because of rounding.

‡ Categories based on the Bureau of Labor Statistics Occupational Injury and Illness Coding Structure (OIICS). OIICS codes are provided in parentheses.

* "n.e.c." is an abbreviation for "not elsewhere classified."

** Other and Unknown Events includes "Bodily Reaction/Exertion," "Exposure to Substances/Environments," "Transportation Events," "Fires and Explosions," "Assaults and Violent Acts," "Other Events," and "Unknown Events."

*** Estimate is not reportable or is suppressed because of a non-reportable cell.

Table 3.56 National estimates of **injury rates for all youth** less than 20 years of age on Black farms by work status and relationship to the farm, 2000

	Total		Working		Non-Working	
Relationship to Farm	Rate/1000	se	Rate/1000	se	Rate/1000	se
Household youth	**6.36**	**1.21**	**7.68**	**2.10**	**3.51**	**0.91**
Hired youth	***		***		***	
Visiting youth	***		***		***	
Relatives	0.54	0.10	3.87	1.22	0.34	0.06
Non-relatives	***		***		***	
Total	**0.69**	**0.09**	**4.98**	**1.00**	**0.40**	**0.06**

*** Estimate is not reportable or is suppressed because of a non-reportable cell.

Table 3.57 National estimates of **injury rates for all youth** less than 20 years of age on Black farms by work status and type of farm, 2000

	Total		Working		Non-Working	
Type of Farm	Rate/1000	se	Rate/1000	se	Rate/1000	se
All crop	**0.73**	**0.16**	**3.33**	**1.22**	**0.51**	**0.14**
Grain and oil seed	1.19	0.42	***		***	
All other crop*	0.51		***		***	
All livestock	**0.70**	**0.11**	**6.10**	**1.45**	**0.35**	**0.07**
Beef	0.62	0.11	***		***	
All other livestock**	1.07		***		***	
Total	**0.69**	**0.09**	**4.98**	**1.00**	**0.40**	**0.06**

* All other crop includes "Tobacco," "Cotton," "Vegetable and melon," "Fruit, nut, and berry," "Nursery and floriculture," and "Other crop" farms.

** All other livestock includes "Dairy," "Hog," "Sheep and goat," "Equine," "Poultry and egg," "Aquaculture," and "Other livestock" farms.

*** Estimate is not reportable or is suppressed because of a non-reportable cell.

Table 3.58 National estimates of **injury rates for all youth** less than 20 years of age on Black farms by work status and type of injury, 2000

Type of Injury	Total Rate/1000	se	Working Rate/1000	se	Non-Working Rate/1000	se
Bruise, contusion	0.05	0.02	***		***	
Sprain, strain	0.06	0.02	***		***	
Broken bone, fracture	0.10	0.03	***		***	
Cut, laceration	0.23	0.06	1.83	0.63	0.12	0.04
Puncture, stab, jab	0.08	0.03	***		***	
All other injuries*	0.16		1.36		0.08	
Total	0.69	0.09	4.98	1.00	0.40	0.06

* All other injuries includes "Scrape, abrasion," "Dislocation," "Traumatic rupture," "Crushed," "Amputation," "Nerve injury," "Burn, blister, scald," "Multiple injuries," and "Other injury."

*** Estimate is not reportable or is suppressed because of a non-reportable cell.

Table 3.59 National estimates of **injury rates for all youth** less than 20 years of age on Black farms by work status and body part injured, 2000

Body Part Injured	Total Rate/1000	se	Working Rate/1000	se	Non-Working Rate/1000	se
Head, skull	0.06	0.02	***		***	
Face	0.11	0.03	***		***	
Arm	0.13	0.03	***		***	
Hand, wrist, fingers	0.09	0.03	***		***	
Leg	0.13	0.04	1.37	0.62	0.05	0.02
Foot, ankle, toes	0.09	0.03	0.90	0.37	0.04	0.02
All other body parts*	0.08		***		***	
Total	0.69	0.09	4.98	1.00	0.40	0.06

* All other body parts includes "Neck," "Shoulder, chest, back," "Abdomen," "Pelvic region," "Internal injury," "Multiple body parts," and "Other body parts."

*** Estimate is not reportable or is suppressed because of a non-reportable cell.

Table 3.60 National estimates of **injury rates for all youth** less than 20 years of age on Black farms by work status and source of injury, 2000

Source of Injury [†]	Total Rate/1000	se	Working Rate/1000	se	Non-Working Rate/1000	se
Parts/Materials (4)	**0.08**	**0.03**	**1.37**	**0.51**	**0.00**	
Persons/Animals/Plants/Minerals (5)	**0.13**	**0.03**	**0.81**	**0.30**	**0.08**	**0.03**
Animals (51)	0.10	0.03	***		***	
Structures and Surfaces (6)	**0.18**	**0.04**	**1.38**	**0.50**	**0.09**	**0.03**
Floors/Walkways/Ground (62)	0.14	0.03	1.09	0.36	0.08	0.02
Ground (623)	*0.11*	*0.03*	*1.09*	*0.36*	*0.05*	*0.02*
Tools/Instruments/Equipment (7)	**0.08**	**0.02**	***		***	
Recreation Equipment (78)	0.04	0.02	0.00		0.04	0.02
Other and Unknown Sources*	**0.23**		***		***	
Total	**0.69**	**0.09**	**4.98**	**1.00**	**0.40**	**0.06**

† Categories based on the Bureau of Labor Statistics Occupational Injury and Illness Coding Structure (OIICS). OIICS codes are provided in parentheses.

* Other and Unknown Sources includes "Chemicals," "Containers," "Furniture and Fixtures," "Machinery," "Vehicles," "Other Sources," and "Unknown Sources."

*** Estimate is not reportable or is suppressed because of a non-reportable cell.

Table 3.61 National estimates of **injury rates for all youth** less than 20 years of age on Black farms by work status and type of injury event, 2000

Type of Injury Event [†]	Total Rate/1000	se	Working Rate/1000	se	Non-Working Rate/1000	se
Contact With Objects (0)	**0.22**	**0.04**	**1.83**	**0.53**	**0.11**	**0.03**
Contact With Object Unspecified (00)	0.05	0.02	***		***	
Struck Against Object (01)	0.07	0.03	***		***	
Against Stationary Object (012)	*0.06*	*0.02*	***		***	
Struck by Object (02)	0.07	0.03	***		***	
Falls (1)	**0.21**	**0.04**	**1.09**	**0.36**	**0.15**	**0.03**
Fall to Lower Level (11)	0.12	0.03	***		***	
Fall to Lower Level n.e.c.* (119)	*0.12*	*0.03*	***		***	
Fall on Same Level (13)	0.07	0.02	***		***	
Exposure to Substances/Environments (3)	**0.06**	**0.02**	**1.07**	**0.35**	**0.00**	
Exposure Caustic/Allergenic Substance (34)	**0.05**	**0.02**	0.81	0.30	0.00	
Assaults and Violent Acts (6)	**0.08**	**0.03**	**0.00**		**0.08**	**0.03**
Assault by Animal (63)	0.08	0.03	0.00		0.08	0.03
Assault by Animal n.e.c.* (639)	*0.05*	*0.02*	***		***	
Other and Unknown Events**	**0.12**		**1.00**		**0.06**	
Total	**0.69**	**0.09**	**4.98**	**1.00**	**0.40**	**0.06**

† Categories based on the Bureau of Labor Statistics Occupational Injury and Illness Coding Structure (OIICS). OIICS codes are provided in parentheses.

* "n.e.c." is an abbreviation for "not elsewhere classified."

** Other and Unknown Events includes "Bodily Reaction/Exertion," "Transportation Events," "Fires and Explosions," "Other Events," and "Unknown Events."

*** Estimate is not reportable or is suppressed because of a non-reportable cell.

Table 3.62 National estimates of **injury rates for household youth** less than 20 years of age on Black farms by sex and age, 2000

Age	Total Rate/1000	se	Male Rate/1000	se	Female Rate/1000	se
<10 years	7.31	2.56	7.30	2.33	7.33	4.37
10-19 years	6.34		9.19		3.04	
Total	6.36	1.21	8.53	1.75	4.44	1.75

Table 3.63 National estimates of **injury rates for household youth** less than 20 years of age on Black farms by work status and age, 2000

Age	Total Rate/1000	se	Working Rate/1000	se	Non-Working Rate/1000	se
<10 years	7.31	2.56	0.00		7.31	2.56
10-19 years	6.34		8.71		1.90	
Total	6.36	1.21	7.75	2.03	3.47	0.93

Table 3.64 National estimates of **injury rates for household youth** less than 20 years of age on Black farms by sex and type of farm, 2000

Type of Farm	Total Rate/1000	se	Male Rate/1000	se	Female Rate/1000	se
All crop	7.38	2.58	7.70	2.71	7.10	4.24
All livestock	6.49	1.46	9.47	2.37	3.22	1.59
Total	6.36	1.21	8.53	1.75	4.44	1.75

Table 3.65 National estimates of **injury rates for household youth** less than 20 years of age on Black farms by sex and type of injury, 2000

Type of Injury	Total Rate/1000	se	Male Rate/1000	se	Female Rate/1000	se
Sprain, strain	0.86	0.43	0.00		1.89	0.95
Broken bone, fracture	0.86	0.43	1.69	0.85	0.00	
Cut, laceration	2.04	0.76	***		***	
All other injuries*	2.60		***		***	
Total	6.36	1.21	8.53	1.75	4.44	1.75

* All other injuries includes "Scrape, abrasion," "Bruise, contusion," "Dislocation," "Puncture, stab, jab," "Traumatic rupture," "Crushed," "Amputation," "Nerve injury," "Burn, blister, scald," "Multiple injuries," and "Other injury."

*** Estimate is not reportable or is suppressed because of a non-reportable cell.

Table 3.66 National estimates of **injury rates for household youth** less than 20 years of age on Black farms by work status and type of injury, 2000

Type of Injury	Total Rate/1000	se	Working Rate/1000	se	Non-Working Rate/1000	se
Sprain, strain	0.86	0.43	0.00		0.86	0.43
Broken bone, fracture	0.86	0.43	***		***	
Cut, laceration	2.04	0.76	***		***	
All other injuries*	2.60		***		***	
Total	6.36	1.21	7.89	2.10	3.47	0.93

* All other injuries includes "Scrape, abrasion," "Bruise, contusion," "Dislocation," "Puncture, stab, jab," "Traumatic rupture," "Crushed," "Amputation," "Nerve injury," "Burn, blister, scald," "Multiple injuries," and "Other injury."

*** Estimate is not reportable or is suppressed because of a non-reportable cell.

Table 3.67 National estimates of **injury rates for household youth** less than 20 years of age on Black farms by sex and body part injured, 2000

Body Part Injured	Total Rate/1000	se	Male Rate/1000	se	Female Rate/1000	se
Face	1.03	0.42	***		***	
Arm	1.20	0.39	2.36	0.77	0.00	
Leg	1.34	0.56	***		***	
Foot, ankle, toes	0.87	0.33	***		***	
All other body parts*	1.93		***		***	
Total	6.36	1.21	8.53	1.75	4.44	1.75

* All other body parts includes "Head, skull," "Neck," "Shoulder, chest, back," "Abdomen," "Pelvic region," "Hand, wrist, fingers," "Internal injury," "Multiple body parts," and "Other body parts."

*** Estimate is not reportable or is suppressed because of a non-reportable cell.

Table 3.68 National estimates of **injury rates for household youth** less than 20 years of age on Black farms by age and body part injured, 2000

Body Part Injured	Total Rate/1000	se	<10 years Rate/1000	se	10-19 years Rate/1000	se
Face	1.03	0.42	***		***	
Arm	1.20	0.39	***		***	
Leg	1.34	0.56	0.00		2.06	
Foot, ankle, toes	0.87	0.33	***		***	
All other body parts*	1.93		***		***	
Total	6.36	1.21	7.31	2.56	6.34	

* All other body parts includes "Head, skull," "Neck," "Shoulder, chest, back," "Abdomen," "Pelvic region," "Hand, wrist, fingers," "Internal injury," "Multiple body parts," and "Other body parts."

*** Estimate is not reportable or is suppressed because of a non-reportable cell.

Table 3.69 National estimates of **injury rates for household youth** less than 20 years of age on Black farms by work status and body part injured, 2000

Body Part Injured	Total Rate/1000	se	Working Rate/1000	se	Non-Working Rate/1000	se
Face	1.03	0.42	0.00		1.03	0.42
Arm	1.20	0.39	***		***	
Leg	1.34	0.56	***		***	
Foot, ankle, toes	0.87	0.33	***		***	
All other body parts*	1.93		***		***	
Total	6.36	1.21	7.89	2.10	3.47	0.93

* All other body parts includes "Head, skull," "Neck," "Shoulder, chest, back," "Abdomen," "Pelvic region," "Hand, wrist, fingers," "Internal injury," "Multiple body parts," and "Other body parts."

*** Estimate is not reportable or is suppressed because of a non-reportable cell.

Table 3.70 National estimates of **injury rates for household youth** less than 20 years of age on Black farms by sex and source of injury, 2000

Source of Injury †	Total		Male		Female	
	Rate/1000	se	Rate/1000	se	Rate/1000	se
Structures and Surfaces (6)	**2.19**	**0.64**	***		***	
Floors/Walkways/Ground (62)	1.52	0.46	***		***	
Ground (623)	*1.22*	*0.40*	***		***	
Tools/Instruments/Equipment (7)	**0.88**	**0.33**	**1.74**	**0.64**	**0.00**	
Other and Unknown Sources*	**3.29**		***		***	
Total	**6.36**	**1.21**	**8.53**	**1.75**	**4.44**	**1.75**

† Categories based on the Bureau of Labor Statistics Occupational Injury and Illness Coding Structure (OIICS). OIICS codes are provided in parentheses.

* Other and Unknown Sources includes "Chemicals," "Containers," "Furniture and Fixtures," "Machinery," "Parts/Materials," "Persons/Animals/Plants/Minerals," "Vehicles," "Other Sources," and "Unknown Sources."

*** Estimate is not reportable or suppressed because of a non-reportable cell.

Table 3.71 National estimates of **injury rates for household youth** less than 20 years of age on Black farms by age and source of injury, 2000

Source of Injury †	Total		<10 years		10-19 years	
	Rate/1000	se	Rate/1000	se	Rate/1000	se
Structures and Surfaces (6)	**2.19**	**0.64**	**0.00**		**3.36**	
Floors/Walkways/Ground (62)	1.52	0.46	0.00		2.34	
Ground (623)	*1.22*	*0.40*	***		***	
Tools/Instruments/Equipment (7)	**0.88**	**0.33**	***		***	
Other and Unknown Sources*	**3.29**		***		***	
Total	**6.36**	**1.21**	**7.31**	**2.56**	**5.40**	

† Categories based on the Bureau of Labor Statistics Occupational Injury and Illness Coding Structure (OIICS). OIICS codes are provided in parentheses.

* Other and Unknown Sources includes "Chemicals," "Containers," "Furniture and Fixtures," "Machinery," "Parts/Materials," "Persons/Animals/Plants/Minerals," "Vehicles," "Other Sources," and "Unknown Sources."

*** Estimate is not reportable or suppressed because of a non-reportable cell.

Table 3.72 National estimates of **injury rates for household youth** less than 20 years of age on Black farms by work status and source of injury, 2000

Source of Injury [†]	Total Rate/1000	se	Working Rate/1000	se	Non-Working Rate/1000	se
Structures and Surfaces (6)	2.19	0.64	3.35	1.40	0.92	0.35
Floors/Walkways/Ground (62)	1.52	0.46	***		***	
Ground (623)	*1.22*	*0.40*	***		***	
Tools/Instruments/Equipment (7)	0.88	0.33	***		***	
Other and Unknown Sources*	3.29		***		***	
Total	6.36	1.21	7.75	2.10	3.47	0.93

† Categories based on the Bureau of Labor Statistics Occupational Injury and Illness Coding Structure (OIICS). OIICS codes are provided in parentheses.

* Other and Unknown Sources includes "Chemicals," "Containers," "Furniture and Fixtures," "Machinery," "Parts/Materials," "Persons/Animals/Plants/Minerals," "Vehicles," "Other Sources," and "Unknown Sources."

*** Estimate is not reportable or suppressed because of a non-reportable cell.

Table 3.73 National estimates of **injury rates for household youth** less than 20 years of age on Black farms by age and type of injury event, 2000

Type of Injury Event [†]	Total Estimate	se	<10 years Estimate	se	10-19 years Estimate	se
Contact With Objects (0)	1.95	0.56	***		***	
Struck Against Object (01)	0.96	0.38	0.00		1.48	
Falls (1)	2.81	0.64	4.21	1.49	2.34	
Fall to Lower Level (11)	1.50	0.44	***		***	
Fall to Lower Level n.e.c. (119)*	*1.50*	*0.44*	***		***	
Fall on Same Level (13)	1.00	0.42	***		***	
Other and Unknown Events**	1.60		***		***	
Total	6.36	1.21	7.31	2.56	6.34	

† Categories based on the Bureau of Labor Statistics Occupational Injury and Illness Coding Structure (OIICS). OIICS codes are provided in parentheses.

* "n.e.c." is an abbreviation for "not elsewhere classified."

** Other and Unknown Events includes "Bodily Reaction/Exertion," "Exposure to Substances/Environments," "Transportation Events," "Fires and Explosions," "Assaults and Violent Acts," "Other Events," and "Unknown Events."

*** Estimate is not reportable or is suppressed because of a non-reportable cell.

Table 3.74 National estimates of **injury rates for household youth** less than 20 years of age on Black farms by work status and type of injury event, 2000

Type of Injury Event [†]	Total Rate/1000	se	Working Rate/1000	se	Non-Working Rate/1000	se
Contact With Objects (0)	**1.95**	**0.56**	2.51	0.98	1.01	0.42
Struck Against Object (01)	0.96	0.38	***		***	
Falls (1)	**2.81**	**0.64**	2.48	0.94	1.89	0.53
Fall to Lower Level (11)	1.50	0.44	***		***	
Fall to Lower Level n.e.c.* (119)	*1.50*	*0.44*	***		***	
Fall on Same Level (13)	1.00	0.42	***		***	
Other and Unknown Events**	**1.60**		2.76		0.57	
Total	**6.36**	**1.21**	**7.75**	**2.10**	**3.47**	**0.93**

† Categories based on the Bureau of Labor Statistics Occupational Injury and Illness Coding Structure (OIICS). OIICS codes are provided in parentheses.

* "n.e.c." is an abbreviation for "not elsewhere classified."

** Other and Unknown Events includes "Bodily Reaction/Exertion," "Exposure to Substances/Environments," "Transportation Events," "Fires and Explosions," "Assaults and Violent Acts," "Other Events," and "Unknown Events."

*** Estimate is not reportable or is suppressed because of a non-reportable cell.

Table 3.75 National estimates of **asthma among household youth** less than 20 years of age on Black farms by sex, 2000

Sex	Asthma Estimate	se	No Asthma Estimate	se	Unknown Estimate
Male	473	24	3390	67	39
Female	270	17	3209	67	13
Unknown	2		16		275
Total [†]	745	30	6615	107	328

† Estimates may not add to the total because of rounding.

Table 3.76 National estimates of **asthma among household youth** less than 20 years of age on Black farms by age, 2000

Age	Asthma Estimate	se	No Asthma Estimate	se	Unknown Estimate
<10 years	**235**	**17**	**2108**	**55**	**10**
10-15 years	**314**	**19**	**2559**	**58**	**9**
10-11 years	118	11	777	29	0
12-13 years	102	10	827	29	9
14-15 years	95	10	956	32	0
16-19 years	**189**	**15**	**1906**	**47**	**23**
16-17 years	119	11	1021	32	9
18-19 years	71	9	885	30	14
Unknown	**7**		**43**		**286**
Total [†]	**745**	**30**	**6615**	**107**	**327**

† Estimates may not add to the total because of rounding.

Table 3.77 National estimates of **asthma among household youth** less than 20 years of age on Black farms by sex and age, 2000

Age	Total † Estimate	se	Male Estimate	se	Female Estimate	se	Unknown Estimate
<10 years	**235**	**17**	**157**	**13**	**78**	**9**	**0**
10-15 years	**314**	**19**	**189**	**15**	**125**	**11**	**0**
10-11 years	118	11	75	9	43	7	0
12-13 years	102	10	65	9	36	6	0
14-15 years	95	10	49	7	45	7	0
16-19 years	**189**	**15**	**123**	**12**	**66**	**8**	**0**
16-17 years	119	11	71	9	48	7	0
18-19 years	71	9	52	8	19	4	0
Unknown	**7**		**4**		**0**		**2**
Total †	**745**	**30**	**473**	**24**	**270**	**17**	**2**

† Estimates may not add to the total because of rounding.

Table 3.78 National estimates of **asthma among household youth** less than 20 years of age on Black farms by sex and type of farm, 2000

Type of Farm	Total † Estimate	se	Male Estimate	se	Female Estimate	se	Unknown Estimate
All crop	**261**	**19**	**163**	**14**	**97**	**10**	**0**
Grain and oil seed	77	11	49	8	28	5	0
Tobacco	29	6	17	4	12	3	0
Cotton	31	8	24	6	7	3	0
Vegetable and melon	38	7	24	5	14	4	0
Fruit, nut, and berry	21	5	14	4	7	3	0
All other crop*	65		35		30		0
All livestock	**465**	**24**	**297**	**19**	**166**	**13**	**2**
Beef	371	21	222	15	147	12	2
Hog	34	7	***		***		0
Sheep and goat	14	4	***		***		0
Equine	24	7	***		***		0
Poultry and egg	11	3	***		***		0
All other livestock**	12		12		0		0
Unknown	**20**		**13**		**7**		**0**
Total †	**745**	**30**	**473**	**24**	**270**	**17**	**2**

† Estimates may not add to the total because of rounding.
* All other crop includes "Nursery and floriculture" and "Other crop" farms.
** All other livestock includes "Dairy," "Aquaculture," and "Other livestock" farms.
*** Estimate is not reportable or is suppressed because of a non-reportable cell.

Table 3.79 National estimates of **asthma among household youth** less than 20 years of age on Black farms by age and type of farm, 2000

Type of Farm	Total [†] Estimate	se	<10 years Estimate	se	10-15 years Estimate	se	16-19 years Estimate	se
All crop	**261**	**19**	**83**	**9**	**123**	**13**	**52**	**7**
Grain and oil seed	77	11	28	5	35	9	14	4
Tobacco	29	6	***		14	4	***	
Cotton	31	8	11	4	11	3	9	3
Vegetable and melon	38	7	***		20	5	9	3
Fruit, nut, and berry	21	5	***		16	5	***	
All other crop*	65		21		28		14	
All livestock	**465**	**24**	**148**	**14**	**181**	**13**	**132**	**13**
Beef	371	21	116	11	143	12	108	11
Hog	34	7	15	6	14	4	***	
Sheep and goat	14	4	7	3	***		***	
Equine	24	7	***		***		11	5
Poultry and egg	11	3	***		***		***	
All other livestock**	12		***		12		***	
Unknown	**20**		**4**		**11**		**5**	
Total [†]	**745**	**30**	**235**	**17**	**314**	**19**	**189**	**15**

† Estimates may not add to the total because of rounding.
* All other crop includes "Nursery and floriculture" and "Other crop" farms.
** All other livestock includes "Dairy," "Aquaculture," and "Other livestock" farms.
*** Estimate is not reportable or is suppressed because of a non-reportable cell.

Table 3.80 National estimates of **asthmatic household youth** less than 20 years of age with 1 or more **asthma attacks while doing farm work** by sex on Black farms, 2000

Sex	Total [†] Estimate	se	Attack at Work Estimate	se	No Attack at Work Estimate	se	Unknown Estimate
Male	473	24	156	13	182	15	135
Female	270	17	70	9	131	12	69
Unknown	2		2		0		0
Total [†]	745	30	228	17	313	313	204

† Estimates may not add to the total because of rounding.

Table 3.81 National estimates of **asthmatic household youth** less than 20 years of age with 1 or more **asthma attacks while doing farm work** by age on Black farms, 2000

Age	Total [†] Estimate	se	Attack at Work Estimate	se	No Attack at Work Estimate	se	Unknown Estimate
<10 years	**235**	**17**	**58**	**8**	**78**	**9**	**99**
10-15 years	**314**	**19**	**106**	**11**	**119**	**12**	**90**
10-11 years	118	11	46	7	45	7	27
12-13 years	102	10	23	5	45	4	34
14-15 years	95	10	37	6	30	5	29
16-19 years	**189**	**15**	**62**	**9**	**112**	**11**	**15**
16-17 years	119	11	32	6	76	9	11
18-19 years	71	9	30	6	36	7	4
Unknown	**7**		**2**		**4**		**0**
Total [†]	**745**	**30**	**228**	**17**	**313**	**20**	**204**

† Estimates may not add to the total because of rounding.

Table 3.82 National estimates of **asthmatic household youth** less than 20 years of age with 1 or more **asthma attacks while doing farm work** by type of farm on Black farms, 2000

Type of Farm	Total [†] Estimate	se	Attack at Work Estimate	se	No Attack at Work Estimate	se	Unknown Estimate
All crop	**261**	**19**	**83**	**11**	**119**	**14**	**58**
Grain and oil seed	77	11	23	5	24	8	30
Tobacco	29	6	9	4	18	4	2
Cotton	31	8	13	6	14	4	4
Vegetable and melon	38	7	11	3	20	5	7
Fruit, nut, and berry	21	5	***		***		8
All other crop*	65		***		***		7
All livestock	**465**	**24**	**138**	**13**	**185**	**15**	**142**
Beef	371	21	102	11	163	13	107
Hog	34	7	9	3	9	3	16
Sheep and goat	14	4	9	3	0		5
Equine	24	7	9	4	9	5	6
Poultry and egg	11	3	***		***		***
All other livestock**	12		***		***		***
Unknown	**20**		**7**		**9**		**3**
Total [†]	**745**	**30**	**228**	**17**	**313**	**20**	**204**

† Estimates may not add to the total because of rounding.
* All other crop includes "Nursery and floriculture" and "Other crop" farms.
** All other livestock includes "Dairy," "Aquaculture," and "Other livestock" farms.
*** Estimate is not reportable or is suppressed because of a non-reportable cell.

Table 3.83 National estimates of **asthmatic household youth** less than 20 years of age with 1 or more **asthma attacks requiring professional medical attention** by sex on Black farms, 2000

Sex	Total [†] Estimate	se	Medical Attention Estimate	se	No Medical Attention Estimate	se	Unknown Estimate
Male	473	24	159	13	315	20	0
Female	270	17	66	9	201	14	2
Unknown	2		0		2		0
Total [†]	745	30	225	16	518	25	2

† Estimates may not add to the total because of rounding.

Table 3.84 National estimates of **asthmatic household youth** less than 20 years of age with 1 or more **asthma attacks requiring professional medical attention** by age on Black farms, 2000

Age	Total [†] Estimate	se	Medical Attention Estimate	se	No Medical Attention Estimate	se	Unknown Estimate
<10 years	**235**	**17**	**86**	**9**	**149**	**13**	**0**
10-15 years	**314**	**19**	**89**	**10**	**223**	**16**	**2**
10-11 years	118	11	42	7	76	9	0
12-13 years	102	10	26	5	76	9	0
14-15 years	95	10	21	5	71	8	2
16-19 years	**189**	**15**	**49**	**7**	**141**	**13**	**0**
16-17 years	119	11	25	5	93	10	0
18-19 years	71	9	23	5	48	8	0
Unknown	**7**		**2**		**2**		**0**
Total [†]	**745**	**30**	**225**	**16**	**518**	**25**	**2**

† Estimates may not add to the total because of rounding.

Table 3.85 National estimates of **asthmatic household youth** less than 20 years of age with 1 or more **asthma attacks requiring professional medical attention** by type of farm on Black farms, 2000

Type of Farm	Total† Estimate	se	Medical Attention Estimate	se	No Medical Attention Estimate	se	Unknown Estimate
All crop	**261**	**19**	**72**	**9**	**188**	**16**	**0**
Grain and oil seed	77	11	19	5	58	10	0
Tobacco	29	6	***		***		0
Cotton	31	8	13	5	18	5	0
Vegetable and melon	38	7	***		***		0
Fruit, nut, and berry	21	5	8	3	13	4	0
All other crop*	65		21		44		0
All livestock	**465**	**24**	**151**	**13**	**312**	**19**	**2**
Beef	371	21	109	11	260	17	2
Hog	34	7	18	5	16	6	0
Sheep and goat	14	4	7	3	6	2	0
Equine	24	7	***		***		0
Poultry and egg	11	3	***		***		0
All other livestock**	12		12		0		0
Unknown	**20**		**2**		**17**		**0**
Total†	**745**	**30**	**225**	**16**	**518**	**25**	**2**

† Estimates may not add to the total because of rounding.
* All other crop includes "Nursery and floriculture" and "Other crop" farms.
** All other livestock includes "Dairy," "Aquaculture," and "Other livestock" farms.
*** Estimate is not reportable or is suppressed because of a non-reportable cell.

Table 3.86 National estimates of **asthma prevalence rates for household youth** less than 20 years of age on Black farms by sex and age, 2000

Age	Total Rate/1000	se	Male Rate/1000	se	Female Rate/1000	se
<10 years	**99.85**	**7.44**	**130.04**	**11.77**	**68.11**	**8.00**
10-15 years	**109.05**	**6.97**	**124.98**	**10.37**	**91.52**	**8.42**
10-11 years	132.19	13.44	155.17	19.65	105.83	16.73
12-13 years	108.31	11.66	134.53	18.73	80.14	13.60
14-15 years	90.08	9.64	89.90	13.57	90.26	13.72
16-19 years	**89.40**	**7.38**	**106.82**	**10.84**	**68.64**	**8.98**
16-17 years	103.25	10.06	115.81	14.85	88.98	13.38
18-19 years	72.95	9.99	96.67	15.95	43.11	10.24
Total	**96.94**	**4.19**	**121.29**	**6.45**	**77.18**	**5.08**

Table 3.87 National estimates of **asthma prevalence rates for household youth** less than 20 years of age on Black farms by sex and type of farm, 2000

Type of Farm	Total Rate/1000	se	Male Rate/1000	se	Female Rate/1000	se
All crop	**106.27**	**8.23**	**129.74**	**11.99**	**82.10**	**9.30**
Grain and oil seed	83.76	12.31	100.22	17.60	64.97	13.08
Tobacco	77.54	16.60	95.50	25.63	60.37	18.22
Cotton	215.73	57.77	273.86	72.26	123.88	63.77
Vegetable and melon	100.50	19.55	132.18	31.58	71.17	19.91
Fruit, nut, and berry	150.68	42.93	179.76	63.63	116.35	50.29
All other crop*	129.26		145.05		117.76	
All livestock	**98.07**	**5.34**	**118.80**	**7.98**	**75.06**	**6.24**
Beef	93.00	5.52	106.33	7.82	78.66	6.98
Hog	131.76	31.32	***		***	
Sheep and goat	161.56	49.98	***		***	
Equine	116.49	36.79	***		***	
Poultry and egg	98.85	32.32	***		***	
All other livestock**	120.91		262.93		0.00	
Total	**96.94**	**4.19**	**121.29**	**6.45**	**77.18**	**5.08**

* All other crop includes "Nursery and floriculture" and "Other crop" farms.
** All other livestock includes "Dairy," "Aquaculture," and "Other livestock" farms.
*** Estimate is not reportable or is suppressed because of a non-reportable cell.

Table 3.88 National estimates of **asthma prevalence rates for household youth** less than 20 years of age on Black farms by age and type of farm, 2000

Type of Farm	Total Rate/1000	se	<10 years Rate/1000	se	10-15 years Rate/1000	se	16-19 years Rate/1000	se
All crop	**106.27**	**8.23**	**103.08**	**12.46**	**132.23**	**14.92**	**74.16**	**10.51**
Grain and oil seed	83.76	12.31	97.67	20.14	104.42	26.08	46.57	12.64
Tobacco	77.54	16.60	***		88.87	28.33	***	
Cotton	215.73	57.77	203.97	79.60	214.99	69.32	234.04	85.66
Vegetable and melon	100.50	19.55	***		119.61	32.05	79.22	26.81
Fruit, nut, and berry	150.68	42.93	***		233.28	76.97	***	
All other crop*	129.26		108.98		176.66		97.18	
All livestock	**98.07**	**5.34**	**98.14**	**9.48**	**97.14**	**7.68**	**99.64**	**10.23**
Beef	93.00	5.52	92.41	9.64	91.83	7.93	95.66	10.56
Hog	131.76	31.32	142.58	58.52	137.93	42.50	***	
Sheep and goat	161.56	49.98	339.90	158.73	***		***	
Equine	116.49	36.79	***		***		146.21	74.18
Poultry and egg	98.85	32.32	***		***		***	
All other livestock**	120.91		***		208.55		***	
Total	**96.94**	**4.19**	**99.85**	**7.44**	**109.05**	**6.97**	**89.40**	**7.38**

* All other crop includes "Nursery and floriculture" and "Other crop" farms.
** All other livestock includes "Dairy," "Aquaculture," and "Other livestock" farms.
*** Estimate is not reportable or is suppressed because of a non-reportable cell.

Table 3.89 National estimates of **asthma prevalence rates for household youth** less than 20 years of age with 1 or more **asthma attacks while doing farm work** by sex on Black farms, 2000

Sex	Total Rate/1000	se
Male	81.24	7.25
Female	74.53	10.20
Total	79.71	6.23

Table 3.90 National estimates of **asthma prevalence rates for household youth** less than 20 years of age with 1 or more **asthma attacks while doing farm work** by age on Black farms, 2000

Age	Total Rate/1000	se
<10 years	**195.07**	**29.43**
10-15 years	**76.30**	**8.08**
10-11 years	121.14	19.22
12-13 years	50.56	10.77
14-15 years	66.52	11.12
16-19 years	**53.61**	**7.93**
16-17 years	49.02	8.92
18-19 years	59.52	11.36
Total	**79.71**	**6.23**

Table 3.91 National estimates of **asthma prevalence rates for household youth** less than 20 years of age with 1 or more **asthma attacks while doing farm work** by type of farm on Black farms, 2000

Type of Farm	Total Rate/1000	se
All crop	**93.45**	**12.61**
Grain and oil seed	72.31	16.44
Tobacco	59.55	24.31
Cotton	266.80	129.13
Vegetable and melon	73.07	22.38
All other crop*	124.65	
All livestock	**72.42**	**7.16**
Beef	64.82	7.38
Hog	88.50	36.97
Sheep and goat	232.14	92.59
Equine	94.85	40.94
All other livestock**	90.20	
Total	**79.71**	**6.23**

* All other crop includes "Fruit, nut, and berry," "Nursery and floriculture," and "Other crop" farms.
** All other livestock includes "Dairy," "Poultry and egg," "Aquaculture," and "Other livestock" farms.

Table 3.92 National estimates of **asthma prevalence rates for household youth** less than 20 years of age with 1 or more **asthma attacks requiring professional medical attention** by sex on Black farms, 2000

	Total	
Sex	Rate/1000	se
Male	40.71	3.39
Female	18.99	2.46
Total	29.31	2.12

Table 3.93 National estimates of **asthma prevalence rates for household youth** less than 20 years of age with 1 or more **asthma attacks requiring professional medical attention** by age on Black farms, 2000

	Total	
Age	Rate/1000	se
<10 years	**36.43**	**4.10**
10-15 years	**30.84**	**3.47**
10-11 years	46.93	7.55
12-13 years	27.43	5.52
14-15 years	20.09	4.42
16-19 years	**22.90**	**3.49**
16-17 years	22.11	4.40
18-19 years	23.73	5.11
Total	**29.31**	**2.12**

Table 3.94 National estimates of **asthma prevalence rates for household youth** less than 20 years of age with 1 or more **asthma attacks requiring professional medical attention** by type of farm on Black farms, 2000

	Total	
Type of Farm	Rate/1000	se
All crop	**29.45**	**3.89**
Grain and oil seed	21.05	5.13
Cotton	93.25	33.75
Fruit, nut, and berry	56.96	23.87
All other crop*	25.24	
All livestock	**31.78**	**2.77**
Beef	27.36	2.75
Hog	70.98	18.93
Sheep and goat	86.08	35.48
All other livestock**	39.11	
Total	**29.31**	**2.12**

* All other crop includes "Tobacco," "Vegetable and melon," "Nursery and floriculture," and "Other crop" farms.
** All other livestock includes "Dairy," "Equine," "Poultry and egg," "Aquaculture," and "Other livestock" farms.

Section IV: National Demographic, Injury, and Asthma Estimates for Youth Less Than 20 Years of Age on Native American Farm Operations

Table 4.1 National estimates of Native American farms from the 1997 Census of Agriculture by business status, 2000

Status	Total† Estimate	se
In business	9,556	34
Out of business	1,082	33
Total†	10,638	

† Estimates may not add to the total because of rounding.

Table 4.2 National estimates of **all youth** less than 20 years of age on Native American farms by relationship to the farm and type of farm, 2000

Type of Farm	Total† Estimate	se	Household Youth Estimate	se	Hired Youth Estimate	se	Visiting Youth Estimate	se	Relatives Estimate	se	Non-Relatives Estimate	se
All crop	**29,858**	**1,547**	**1,583**	**68**	**657**	**89**	**27,618**	**1,518**	**11,084**	**463**	**16,534**	**1,354**
Grain and oil seed	10,382	1,152	576	43	116	21	9,691	1,135	3,104	250	6,587	1,068
Tobacco	1,444	227	63	12	70	16	1,311	220	822	149	489	100
Vegetable and melon	1,840	368	122	24	***		***		751	132	***	
Fruit, nut, and berry	2,634	292	142	17	119	30	2,372	280	1,194	128	1,178	202
Nursery and floriculture	1,402	399	38	8	***		***		312	105	***	
All other crop*	12,157		641		142		11,373		4,900		6,473	
All livestock	**94,314**	**2,297**	**5,454**	**109**	**1,390**	**82**	**87,470**	**2,263**	**39,887**	**748**	**47,583**	**1,958**
Beef	69,643	1,763	4,370	100	1,078	73	64,196	1,724	31,623	678	32,573	1,402
Dairy	2,160	571	122	21	***		***		711	119	***	
Hog	1,210	216	80	13	***		***		611	120	***	
Sheep and goat	4,007	736	143	22	48	13	3,816	725	1,053	144	2,763	648
Equine	11,437	1,094	488	35	161	29	10,789	1,082	4,013	279	6,776	982
Poultry and egg	1,790	238	119	18	35	10	1,636	224	783	105	853	148
All other livestock**	4,067		133		27		3,097		1,094		2,814	
Unknown	**3,776**		**345**		**10**		**3,421**		**1,300**		**2,122**	
Total†	127,947	2,765	7,381	123	2,057	121	118,509	2,740	52,271	827	66,239	2,463

† Estimates may not add to the total because of rounding.
* All other crop includes "Cotton" and "Other crop" farms.
** All other livestock includes "Aquaculture" and "Other livestock" farms.
*** Estimate is not reportable or is suppressed because of a non-reportable cell.

Table 4.3 National estimates of **all working youth** less than 20 years of age on Native American farms by relationship to the farm and type of farm, 2000

Type of Farm	Total †		Working Household Youth		Non-Household Working Youth		Hired Youth		Working Relatives	
	Estimate	se	Estimate	se	Estimate	se	Estimate	se	Estimate	se
All crop	**2,372**	**147**	**840**	**47**	**1,532**	**130**	**657**	**89**	**875**	**85**
Grain and oil seed	691	66	294	28	397	50	116	21	282	42
Tobacco	190	32	33	9	157	30	70	16	87	25
Vegetable and melon	258	70	***		***		74	21	***	
Fruit, nut, and berry	272	41	81	12	191	36	119	30	72	14
Nursery and floriculture	173	75	***		***		137	74	***	
All other crop*	789		353		436		142		410	
All livestock	**9,887**	**270**	**3,309**	**82**	**6,577**	**246**	**1,390**	**82**	**5,187**	**229**
Beef	7,812	241	2,652	75	5,160	217	1,078	73	4,083	201
Dairy	223	47	63	14	160	40	34	14	126	37
Hog	124	27	58	11	***		***		***	
Sheep and goat	270	46	104	17	166	38	48	13	117	35
Equine	1,026	109	281	24	745	101	161	29	585	94
Poultry and egg	200	30	83	14	117	23	35	10	82	20
All other livestock**	232		69		163		27		126	
Unknown	**101**		**74**		**28**		**10**		**18**	
Total †	**12,359**	**298**	**4,222**	**92**	**8,137**	**274**	**2,057**	**121**	**6,080**	**241**

† Estimates may not add to the total because of rounding.

* All other crop includes "Cotton" and "Other crop" farms.

** All other livestock includes "Aquaculture" and "Other livestock" farms.

*** Estimate is not reportable or is suppressed because of a non-reportable cell.

Table 4.4 National estimates of **household youth** less than 20 years of age on Native American farms by sex and age, 2000

Age	Total[†] Estimate	se	Male Estimate	se	Female Estimate	se	Unknown Estimate
<10 years	**2,355**	**65**	**1,181**	**41**	**1,173**	**43**	**0**
10-15 years	**2,800**	**67**	**1,431**	**44**	**1,369**	**44**	**0**
10-11 years	813	32	431	22	382	21	0
12-13 years	898	32	423	22	474	24	0
14-15 years	1,090	36	577	26	513	26	0
16-19 years	**2,069**	**53**	**1,099**	**38**	**970**	**35**	**0**
16-17 years	1,084	36	548	26	536	25	0
18-19 years	985	34	550	26	435	23	0
Unknown	**158**		**8**		**15**		**135**
Total[†]	**7,381**	**123**	**3,718**	**77**	**3,528**	**76**	**135**

† Estimates may not add to the total because of rounding.

Table 4.5 National estimates of **household youth** less than 20 years of age on Native American farms by sex and type of farm, 2000

Type of Farm	Total[†] Estimate	se	Male Estimate	se	Female Estimate	se	Unknown Estimate
All crop	**1,583**	**68**	**847**	**41**	**736**	**41**	**0**
Grain and oil seed	576	43	300	25	276	26	0
Tobacco	63	12	31	8	31	7	0
Vegetable and melon	122	24	59	12	63	15	0
Fruit, nut, and berry	142	17	86	12	57	9	0
Nursery and floriculture	38	8	23	6	15	4	0
All other crop*	641		347		294		0
All livestock	**5,454**	**109**	**2,759**	**68**	**2,683**	**67**	**11**
Beef	4,370	100	2,264	62	2,101	59	4
Dairy	122	21	54	11	69	14	0
Hog	80	13	28	5	48	10	4
Sheep and goat	143	22	72	12	71	13	0
Equine	488	35	207	20	279	23	2
Poultry and egg	119	18	63	11	55	12	0
Aquaculture	40	11	***		***		0
Other livestock	92	14	***		***		0
Unknown	**345**		**113**		**108**		**124**
Total[†]	**7,381**	**123**	**3,718**	**77**	**3,528**	**76**	**135**

† Estimates may not add to the total because of rounding.
* All other crop includes "Cotton" and "Other crop" farms.
*** Estimate is not reportable or is suppressed because of a non-reportable cell.

Table 4.6 National estimates of **household youth** less than 20 years of age on Native American farms by age and type of farm, 2000

Type of Farm	Total † Estimate	se	<10 years Estimate	se	10-15 years Estimate	se	16-19 years Estimate	se	Unknown Estimate
All crop	**1,583**	**68**	**472**	**32**	**592**	**34**	**514**	**29**	**4**
Grain and oil seed	576	43	181	20	216	20	179	18	0
Tobacco	63	12	35	6	28	6	19	6	0
Vegetable and melon	122	24	24	8	51	13	47	10	0
Fruit, nut, and berry	142	17	31	8	58	9	54	8	0
Nursery and floriculture	38	8	***		***		24	6	0
All other crop*	641		***		***		192		4
All livestock	**5,454**	**109**	**1,824**	**58**	**2,107**	**59**	**1,495**	**46**	**27**
Beef	4,370	100	1,480	52	1,722	53	1,150	40	18
Dairy	122	21	43	11	49	12	31	9	0
Hog	80	13	***		***		30	7	7
Sheep and goat	143	22	36	10	56	10	51	10	0
Equine	488	35	162	18	177	18	147	15	2
Poultry and egg	119	18	29	7	47	10	43	8	0
Aquaculture	40	11	***		***		11	3	0
Other livestock	92	14	37	9	21	6	35	7	0
Unknown	**345**		**59**		**101**		**59**		**126**
Total †	**7,381**	**123**	**2,355**	**65**	**2,800**	**67**	**2,069**	**53**	**158**

† Estimates may not add to the total because of rounding.
* All other crop includes "Cotton" and "Other crop" farms.
*** Estimate is not reportable or is suppressed because of a non-reportable cell.

Table 4.7 National estimates of **household youth** less than 20 years of age on Native American farms by age, sex, and type of farm, 2000

	<10 years					
	Total †		Male		Female	
Type of Farm	Estimate	se	Estimate	se	Estimate	se
All crop	**472**	**32**	**250**	**20**	**222**	**21**
Grain and oil seed	181	20	92	12	89	14
Fruit, nut, and berry	31	8	***		***	
All other crop*	260		***		***	
All livestock	**1,824**	**58**	**903**	**36**	**921**	**37**
Beef	1,480	52	739	33	741	32
Diary	43	11	***		***	
Sheep and goat	36	10	***		***	
Equine	162	18	70	10	92	13
Poultry and egg	29	7	20	5	9	3
All other livestock**	75		37		37	
Unknown	**59**		**28**		**31**	
Total †	**2,355**	**65**	**1,181**	**41**	**1,173**	**43**

Continued

Table 4.7 National estimates of **household youth** less than 20 years of age on Native American farms by age, sex, and type of farm, 2000 (Continued)

	10-15 years					
	Total [†]		Male		Female	
Type of Farm	Estimate	se	Estimate	se	Estimate	se
All crop	**592**	**34**	**316**	**21**	**276**	**21**
Grain and oil seed	216	20	119	14	97	13
Fruit, nut, and berry	58	9	36	7	21	5
All other crop*	318		161		158	
All livestock	**2,107**	**59**	**1,060**	**38**	**1,047**	**39**
Beef	1,722	53	891	34	832	34
Dairy	49	12	24	7	24	7
Sheep and goat	56	10	33	7	24	6
Equine	177	18	71	12	106	13
Poultry and egg	47	10	21	6	26	7
All other livestock**	56		21		35	
Unknown	**101**		**56**		**45**	
Total [†]	**2,800**	**67**	**1,431**	**44**	**1,369**	**44**

	16-19 years					
	Total [†]		Male		Female	
Type of Farm	Estimate	se	Estimate	se	Estimate	se
All crop	**514**	**29**	**278**	**21**	**236**	**18**
Grain and oil seed	179	18	90	11	90	12
Fruit, nut, and berry	54	8	***		***	
All other crop*	282		***		***	
All livestock	**1,495**	**46**	**791**	**32**	**704**	**30**
Beef	1,150	40	632	29	517	25
Dairy	31	9	***		***	
Sheep and goat	51	10	***		***	
Equine	147	15	67	10	80	11
Poultry and egg	43	8	22	6	20	5
All other livestock**	75		39		36	
Unknown	59		29		30	
Total [†]	**2,069**	**53**	**1,099**	**38**	**970**	**35**

† Estimates may not add to the total because of rounding.
* All other crop includes "Tobacco," "Cotton," "Vegetable and melon," "Nursery and floriculture," and "Other crop" farms.
** All other livestock includes "Hog," "Aquaculture," and "Other livestock" farms.
*** Estimate is not reportable or is suppressed because of a non-reportable cell.

Table 4.8 National estimates of **household youth** less than 20 years of age on Native American farms by work status and sex, 2000

Sex	Total † Estimate	se	Working Estimate	se	Non-Working Estimate	se	Unknown Estimate
Male	3,718	77	2,443	62	1,273	43	2
Female	3,528	76	1,775	55	1,750	52	2
Unknown	135		4		0		131
Total †	7,381	123	4,222	92	3,023	74	135

† Estimates may not add to the total because of rounding.

Table 4.9 National estimates of **household youth** less than 20 years of age on Native American farms by work status and age, 2000

Age	Total † Estimate	se	Working Estimate	se	Non-Working Estimate	se	Unknown Estimate
<10 years	**2,355**	**65**	**697**	**34**	**1,658**	**54**	**0**
10-15 years	**2,800**	**67**	**2,000**	**55**	**797**	**36**	**2**
10-11 years	813	32	527	25	286	18	0
12-13 years	898	32	654	27	244	18	0
14-15 years	1,090	36	819	31	268	19	2
16-19 years	**2,069**	**53**	**1,508**	**46**	**558**	**26**	**2**
16-17 years	1,084	36	797	31	287	18	0
18-19 years	985	34	711	30	272	18	2
Unknown	**158**		**18**		**10**		**131**
Total †	7,381	123	4,222	92	3,023	74	135

† Estimates may not add to the total because of rounding.

Table 4.10 National estimates of **household youth** less than 20 years of age on Native American farms by age, work status, and sex, 2000

| | <10 years | | | | | | |
| | Total [†] | | Working | | Non-Working | | Unknown |
Sex	Estimate	se	Estimate	se	Estimate	se	Estimate
Male	1,181	41	372	22	809	33	0
Female	1,173	43	325	22	849	36	0
Total [†]	2,355	65	697	34	1,658	54	0

| | 10-15 years | | | | | | |
| | Total [†] | | Working | | Non-Working | | Unknown |
Sex	Estimate	se	Estimate	se	Estimate	se	Estimate
Male	1,431	44	1,150	39	279	20	2
Female	1,369	44	850	35	518	28	0
Total [†]	2,800	67	2,000	55	797	36	2

| | 16-19 years | | | | | | |
| | Total [†] | | Working | | Non-Working | | Unknown |
Sex	Estimate	se	Estimate	se	Estimate	se	Estimate
Male	1,099	38	917	35	182	14	0
Female	970	35	591	27	377	22	2
Total [†]	2,069	53	1,508	46	558	26	2

† Estimates may not add to the total because of rounding.

Table 4.11 National estimates of **household youth** less than 20 years of age on Native American farms by whether they rode a horse and sex, 2000

| | Total [†] | | Rode a Horse: Yes | | Rode a Horse: No | | Unknown |
Sex	Estimate	se	Estimate	se	Estimate	se	Estimate
Male	3,718	77	1,781	56	1,932	55	4
Female	3,528	76	1,705	54	1,818	55	5
Unknown	135		0		4		131
Total [†]	7,381	123	3,486	86	3,755	88	140

† Estimates may not add to the total because of rounding.

Table 4.12 National estimates of **household youth** less than 20 years of age on Native American farms by whether they rode a horse and age, 2000

Age	Total [†] Estimate	se	Rode a Horse: Yes Estimate	se	Rode a Horse: No Estimate	se	Unknown Estimate
<10 years	**2,355**	**65**	**971**	**41**	**1,383**	**50**	**0**
10-15 years	**2,800**	**67**	**1,493**	**49**	**1,305**	**47**	**2**
10-11 years	813	32	442	23	371	21	0
12-13 years	898	32	510	25	387	21	0
14-15 years	1,090	36	540	26	547	27	2
16-19 years	**2,069**	**53**	**1,015**	**38**	**1,049**	**37**	**5**
16-17 years	1,084	36	546	26	538	25	0
18-19 years	985	34	469	24	512	25	5
Unknown	**158**		**8**		**17**		**133**
Total [†]	**7,381**	**123**	**3,486**	**86**	**3,755**	**88**	**140**

† Estimates may not add to the total because of rounding.

Table 4.13 National estimates of **household youth** less than 20 years of age on Native American farms by age, whether they rode a horse, and sex, 2000

	<10 years						
Sex	Total [†] Estimate	se	Rode a Horse: Yes Estimate	se	Rode a Horse: No Estimate	se	Unknown Estimate
Male	1,181	41	487	27	694	31	0
Female	1,173	43	484	27	689	33	0
Total [†]	2,355	65	971	41	1,383	50	0

	10-15 years						
Sex	Total [†] Estimate	se	Rode a Horse: Yes Estimate	se	Rode a Horse: No Estimate	se	Unknown Estimate
Male	1,431	44	723	32	706	31	2
Female	1,369	44	770	34	599	29	0
Total [†]	2,800	67	1,493	49	1,305	47	2

	16-19 years						
Sex	Total [†] Estimate	se	Rode a Horse: Yes Estimate	se	Rode a Horse: No Estimate	se	Unknown Estimate
Male	1,099	38	571	28	525	26	2
Female	970	35	443	24	524	26	2
Total [†]	2,069	53	1,015	38	1,049	37	5

† Estimates may not add to the total because of rounding.

Table 4.14 National estimates of **household youth** less than 20 years of age on Native American farms by whether they drove an all-terrain vehicle (ATV) and sex, 2000

Sex	Total[†] Estimate	se	Drove an ATV: Yes Estimate	se	Drove an ATV: No Estimate	se	Unknown Estimate
Male	3,718	77	1,499	49	1,887	56	332
Female	3,528	76	1,097	41	2,049	59	382
Unknown	135		0		0		135
Total[†]	7,381	123	2,597	71	3,936	91	848

† Estimates may not add to the total because of rounding.

Table 4.15 National estimates of **household youth** less than 20 years of age on Native American farms by whether they drove an all-terrain vehicle (ATV) and age, 2000

Age	Total[†] Estimate	se	Drove an ATV: Yes Estimate	se	Drove an ATV: No Estimate	se	Unknown Estimate
<10 years	2,355	65	324	22	1,349	47	681
10-15 years	2,800	67	1,306	46	1,491	46	2
10-11 years	813	32	330	20	482	24	0
12-13 years	898	32	392	21	506	25	0
14-15 years	1,090	36	584	27	504	26	2
16-19 years	2,069	53	966	36	1,095	41	7
16-17 years	1,084	36	492	24	589	28	2
18-19 years	985	34	474	24	506	26	5
Unknown	158		0		0		158
Total[†]	7,381	123	2,597	71	3,936	91	848

† Estimates may not add to the total because of rounding.

Table 4.16 National estimates of **household youth** less than 20 years of age on Native American farms by age, whether they drove an all-terrain vehicle (ATV), and sex, 2000

| | <10 years | | | | | | |
Sex	Total † Estimate	se	Drove an ATV: Yes Estimate	se	Drove an ATV: No Estimate	se	Unknown Estimate
Male	1,181	41	181	16	683	30	317
Female	1,173	43	143	13	667	31	364
Total †	2,355	65	324	22	1,349	47	681

| | 10-15 years | | | | | | |
Sex	Total † Estimate	se	Drove an ATV: Yes Estimate	se	Drove an ATV: No Estimate	se	Unknown Estimate
Male	1,431	44	757	32	672	31	2
Female	1,369	44	549	28	820	34	0
Total †	2,800	67	1,306	46	1,491	46	2

| | 16-19 years | | | | | | |
Sex	Total † Estimate	se	Drove an ATV: Yes Estimate	se	Drove an ATV: No Estimate	se	Unknown Estimate
Male	1,099	38	561	27	533	28	2
Female	970	35	405	22	562	28	2
Total †	2,069	53	966	36	1,095	41	5

† Estimates may not add to the total because of rounding.

Table 4.17 National estimates of **household youth** less than 20 years of age on Native American farms by whether they drove a tractor and sex, 2000

Sex	Total † Estimate	se	Drove a Tractor: Yes Estimate	se	Drove a Tractor: No Estimate	se	Unknown Estimate
Male	3,718	77	1,605	50	1,782	53	332
Female	3,528	76	739	34	2,407	61	382
Unknown	135		0		0		135
Total †	7,381	123	2,344	63	4,189	89	848

† Estimates may not add to the total because of rounding.

Table 4.18 National estimates of **household youth** less than 20 years of age on Native American farms by whether they drove a tractor and age, 2000

Age	Total [†] Estimate	se	Drove a Tractor: Yes Estimate	se	Drove a Tractor: No Estimate	se	Unknown Estimate
<10 years	**2,355**	**65**	**93**	**10**	**1,581**	**51**	**681**
10-15 years	**2,800**	**67**	**1,037**	**38**	**1,760**	**53**	**2**
10-11 years	813	32	173	14	639	28	0
12-13 years	898	32	329	20	569	26	0
14-15 years	1,090	36	536	25	552	27	2
16-19 years	**2,069**	**53**	**1,214**	**42**	**848**	**33**	**7**
16-17 years	1,084	36	605	28	477	24	2
18-19 years	985	34	609	27	372	21	5
Unknown	**158**		**0**		**0**		**158**
Total [†]	**7,381**	**123**	**2,344**	**63**	**4,189**	**89**	**848**

† Estimates may not add to the total because of rounding.

Table 4.19 National estimates of **household youth** less than 20 years of age on Native American farms by age, whether they drove a tractor, and sex, 2000

	<10 years						
Sex	Total [†] Estimate	se	Drove a Tractor: Yes Estimate	se	Drove a Tractor: No Estimate	se	Unknown Estimate
Male	1,181	41	53	8	811	33	317
Female	1,173	43	40	7	769	34	364
Total [†]	2,355	65	93	10	1,581	51	681

	10-15 years						
Sex	Total [†] Estimate	se	Drove a Tractor: Yes Estimate	se	Drove a Tractor: No Estimate	se	Unknown Estimate
Male	1,431	44	718	31	711	31	2
Female	1,369	44	319	21	1,049	38	0
Total [†]	2,800	67	1,037	38	1,760	53	2

	16-19 years						
Sex	Total [†] Estimate	se	Drove a Tractor: Yes Estimate	se	Drove a Tractor: No Estimate	se	Unknown Estimate
Male	1,099	38	834	33	260	18	5
Female	970	35	380	22	588	27	2
Total [†]	2,069	53	1,214	42	848	33	7

† Estimates may not add to the total because of rounding.

Table 4.20 National estimates of **injuries to all youth** less than 20 years of age on Native American farms by sex and relationship to the farm, 2000

Relationship to Farm	Total † Estimate	se	Male Estimate	se	Female Estimate	se	Unknown Estimate
Household youth	177	16	112	11	65	9	0
Hired youth	9	4	9	4	0		0
Visiting youth	78	11	49	8	29	6	0
Relatives	52	8	35	6	17	5	0
Non-relatives	26	7	13	4	12	4	0
Unknown	2		0		0		2
Total †	266	20	170	15	94	11	2

† Estimates may not add to the total because of rounding.

Table 4.21 National estimates of **injuries to all youth** less than 20 years of age on Native American farms by age and relationship to farm, 2000

Relationship to Farm	Total † Estimate	se	<10 years Estimate	se	10-15 years Estimate	se	16-19 years Estimate	se	Unknown Estimate
Household youth	177	16	52	9	87	11	38	7	0
Hired youth	9	4	***		***		***		0
Visiting youth	78	11	***		***		***		0
Relatives	52	8	12	3	30	6	11	4	0
Non-relatives	26	7	***		***		***		0
Unknown	2		0		0		0		2
Total †	266	20	72	10	129	13	63	9	2

† Estimates may not add to the total because of rounding.
*** Estimate is not reportable or is suppressed because of a non-reportable cell.

Table 4.22 National estimates of **injuries to all youth** less than 20 years of age on Native American farms by work status and relationship to the farm, 2000

Relationship to Farm	Total † Estimate	se	Working Estimate	se	Non-Working Estimate	se	Unknown Estimate
Household youth	177	16	75	11	102	12	0
Hired youth	9	4	9	4	0		0
Visiting youth	78	11	14	5	64	10	0
Relatives	52	8	14	5	38	7	0
Non-relatives	26	7	0		26	7	0
Unknown	2		0		0		2
Total †	266	20	98	12	166	15	2

† Estimates may not add to the total because of rounding.

Table 4.23 National estimates of **injuries to all youth** less than 20 years of age on Native American farms by sex and race, 2000

Race	Total [†] Estimate	se	Male Estimate	se	Female Estimate	se	Unknown Estimate
Native American	201	17	127	13	74	10	0
All other races*	62		43		20		0
Unknown	2		0		0		2
Total [†]	266	20	170	15	94	11	2

† Estimates may not add to the total because of rounding.
* All other races includes "White," "Black," "Asian," and "Other races."

Table 4.24 National estimates of **injuries to all youth** less than 20 years of age on Native American farms by age and race, 2000

Race	Total [†] Estimate	se	<10 years Estimate	se	10-15 years Estimate	se	16-19 years Estimate	se	Unknown Estimate
Native American	201	17	56	9	104	12	41	7	0
All other races*	62		15		25		22		0
Unknown	2		0		0		0		2
Total [†]	266	20	72	10	129	13	63	9	2

† Estimates may not add to the total because of rounding.
* All other races includes "White," "Black," "Asian," and "Other races."

Table 4.25 National estimates of **injuries to all youth** less than 20 years of age on Native American farms by work status and race, 2000

Race	Total [†] Estimate	se	Working Estimate	se	Non-Working Estimate	se	Unknown Estimate
Native American	201	17	81	11	121	13	0
All other races*	62		17		45		0
Unknown	2		0		0		2
Total [†]	266	20	98	12	166	15	2

† Estimates may not add to the total because of rounding.
* All other races includes "White," "Black," "Asian," and "Other races."

Table 4.26 National estimates of **injuries to all youth** less than 20 years of age on Native American farms by sex and age, 2000

Age	Total [†] Estimate	se	Male Estimate	se	Female Estimate	se	Unknown Estimate
< 10 years	72	10	36	7	35	7	0
10-15 years	129	13	85	10	44	8	0
10-11 years	32	7	19	5	13	4	0
12-13 years	32	6	22	5	10	4	0
14-15 years	64	9	44	7	21	5	0
16-19 years	63	9	49	8	15	4	0
16-17 years	38	7	***		***		0
18-19 years	26	6	***		***		0
Unknown	2		0		0		2
Total [†]	266	20	170	15	94	11	2

† Estimates may not add to the total because of rounding.
*** Estimate is not reportable or is suppressed because of a non-reportable cell.

Table 4.27 National estimates of **injuries to all youth** less than 20 years of age on Native American farms by work status and age, 2000

Age	Total [†] Estimate	se	Working Estimate	se	Non-Working Estimate	se	Unknown Estimate
< 10 years	72	10	15	5	56	9	0
10-15 years	129	13	43	7	86	11	0
10-11 years	32	7	***		***		0
12-13 years	32	6	***		***		0
14-15 years	64	9	27	6	38	6	0
16-19 years	63	9	40	7	24	6	0
16-17 years	38	7	27	6	11	4	0
18-19 years	26	6	13	4	13	4	0
Unknown	2		0		0		2
Total [†]	266	20	98	12	166	15	2

† Estimates may not add to the total because of rounding.
*** Estimate is not reportable or is suppressed because of a non-reportable cell.

Table 4.28 National estimates of **injuries to all youth** less than 20 years of age on Native American farms by sex and type of farm, 2000

Type of Farm	Total [†] Estimate	se	Male Estimate	se	Female Estimate	se	Unknown Estimate
All crop	**48**	**9**	**34**	**7**	**15**	**6**	**0**
Grain and oil seed	21	7	15	5	6	5	0
All other crop*	27		19		8		0
All livestock	**212**	**18**	**131**	**13**	**79**	**10**	**2**
Beef	157	15	101	12	54	8	2
Equine	28	6	13	5	15	4	0
All other livestock**	33		17		11		0
Unknown	**6**		**6**		**0**		**0**
Total [†]	**266**	**20**	**170**	**15**	**94**	**11**	**2**

† Estimates may not add to the total because of rounding.
* All other crop includes "Tobacco," "Cotton," "Vegetable and melon," "Fruit, nut, and berry," "Nursery and floriculture," and "Other crop" farms.
** All other livestock includes "Dairy," "Hog," "Sheep and goat," "Poultry and egg," "Aquaculture," and "Other livestock" farms.

Table 4.29 National estimates of **injuries to all youth** less than 20 years of age on Native American farms by age and type of farm, 2000

Type of Farm	Total [†] Estimate	se	<10 years Estimate	se	10-15 years Estimate	se	16-19 years Estimate	se	Unknown Estimate
All crop	**48**	**9**	**12**	**6**	**24**	**5**	**13**	**5**	**0**
Grain and oil seed	21	7	***		***		***		0
All other crop*	27		***		***		***		0
All livestock	**212**	**18**	**60**	**9**	**102**	**11**	**49**	**8**	**2**
Beef	157	15	36	7	82	10	37	7	2
Equine	28	6	12	4	8	3	9	4	0
All other livestock**	33		12		13		8		0
Unknown	**6**		**0**		**3**		**2**		**0**
Total [†]	**266**	**20**	**72**	**10**	**129**	**13**	**63**	**9**	**2**

† Estimates may not add to the total because of rounding.
* All other crop includes "Tobacco," "Cotton," "Vegetable and melon," "Fruit, nut, and berry," "Nursery and floriculture," and "Other crop" farms.
** All other livestock includes "Dairy," "Hog," "Sheep and goat," "Poultry and egg," "Aquaculture," and "Other livestock" farms.
*** Estimate is not reportable or is suppressed because of a non-reportable cell.

Table 4.30 National estimates of **injuries to all youth** less than 20 years of age on Native American farms by work status and type of farm, 2000

Type of Farm	Total[†] Estimate	se	Working Estimate	se	Non-working Estimate	se	Unknown Estimate
All crop	**48**	**9**	**14**	**5**	**34**	**8**	**0**
Grain and oil seed	21	7	***		***		0
All other crop*	27		***		***		0
All livestock	**212**	**18**	**84**	**11**	**126**	**13**	**2**
Beef	157	15	63	10	92	11	2
Equine	28	6	11	4	17	5	0
All other livestock**	33		10		22		0
Unknown	**6**		**0**		**6**		**0**
Total[†]	**266**	**20**	**98**	**12**	**166**	**15**	**2**

† Estimates may not add to the total because of rounding.
* All other crop includes "Tobacco," "Cotton," "Vegetable and melon," "Fruit, nut, and berry," "Nursery and floriculture," and "Other crop" farms.
** All other livestock includes "Dairy," "Hog," "Sheep and goat," "Poultry and egg," "Aquaculture," and "Other livestock" farms.
*** Estimate is not reportable or is suppressed because of a non-reportable cell.

Table 4.31 National estimates of **injuries to all youth** less than 20 years of age on Native American farms by sex and type of injury, 2000

Type of Injury	Total[†] Estimate	se	Male Estimate	se	Female Estimate	se	Unknown Estimate
Scrape, abrasion	15	4	7	3	8	3	0
Bruise, contusion	33	6	16	4	17	4	0
Sprain, strain	16	5	***		***		0
Broken bone, fracture	84	11	70	10	14	4	0
Cut, laceration	55	8	39	7	16	5	0
Puncture, stab, jab	17	4	***		***		0
Multiple injuries	12	3	***		***		0
All other injuries*	30		18		12		0
Unknown	5		0		3		2
Total[†]	266	20	170	15	94	11	2

† Estimates may not add to the total because of rounding.
* All other injuries includes "Dislocation," "Traumatic rupture," "Crushed," "Amputation," "Nerve injury," "Burn, blister, scald," and "Other injury."
*** Estimate is not reportable or is suppressed because of a non-reportable cell.

Table 4.32 National estimates of **injuries to all youth** less than 20 years of age on Native American farms by age and type of injury, 2000

Type of Injury	Total † Estimate	se	< 10 years Estimate	se	10-15 years Estimate	se	16-19 years Estimate	se	Unknown Estimate
Scrape, abrasion	15	4	***		9	3	***		0
Bruise, contusion	33	6	***		19	4	***		0
Sprain, strain	16	5	***		***		11	4	0
Broken bone, fracture	84	11	24	6	39	7	21	6	0
Cut, laceration	55	8	18	5	25	5	13	4	0
Puncture, stab, jab	17	4	***		9	3	***		0
Multiple injuries	12	3	***		9	3	***		0
All other injuries*	30		13		***		***		0
Unknown	5		0		3		0		2
Total †	266	20	72	10	129	13	63	9	2

† Estimates may not add to the total because of rounding.
* All other injuries includes "Dislocation," "Traumatic rupture," "Crushed," "Amputation," "Nerve injury," "Burn, blister, scald," and "Other injury."
*** Estimate is not reportable or is suppressed because of a non-reportable cell.

Table 4.33 National estimates of **injuries to all youth** less than 20 years of age on Native American farms by work status and type of injury, 2000

Type of Injury	Total † Estimate	se	Working Estimate	se	Non-Working Estimate	se	Unknown Estimate
Scrape, abrasion	15	4	***		***		0
Bruise, contusion	33	6	9	4	24	5	0
Sprain, strain	16	5	9	4	7	3	0
Broken bone, fracture	84	11	32	7	52	8	0
Cut, laceration	55	8	26	5	29	6	0
Puncture, stab, jab	17	4	***		***		0
Multiple injuries	12	3	***		***		0
All other injuries*	30		7		23		0
Unknown	5		3		0		2
Total †	266	20	98	12	166	15	2

† Estimates may not add to the total because of rounding.
* All other injuries includes "Dislocation," "Traumatic rupture," "Crushed," "Amputation," "Nerve injury," "Burn, blister, scald," and "Other injury."
*** Estimate is not reportable or is suppressed because of a non-reportable cell.

Table 4.34 National estimates of **injuries to all youth** less than 20 years of age on Native American farms by sex and body part injured, 2000

Body Part Injured	Total [†] Estimate	se	Male Estimate	se	Female Estimate	se	Unknown Estimate
Head, skull	26	6	***		***		0
Face	13	4	***		***		0
Shoulder, chest, back	21	5	13	4	8	3	0
Arm	58	9	41	7	17	5	0
Hand, wrist, fingers	44	7	***		***		0
Leg	41	7	19	5	22	5	0
Foot, ankle, toes	24	5	14	4	10	3	0
Multiple body parts	17	4	8	3	9	3	0
All other body parts*	20		8		13		0
Unknown	2		0		0		2
Total [†]	266	20	170	15	94	11	2

† Estimates may not add to the total because of rounding.
* All other body parts includes "Neck," "Abdomen," "Pelvic region," "Internal injury," and "Other body parts."
*** Estimate is not reportable or is suppressed because of a non-reportable cell.

Table 4.35 National estimates of **injuries to all youth** less than 20 years of age on Native American farms by age and body part injured, 2000

Body Part Injured	Total [†] Estimate	se	< 10 years Estimate	se	10-15 years Estimate	se	16-19 years Estimate	se	Unknown Estimate
Head, skull	26	6	9	3	12	4	***		0
Face	13	4	***		***		***		0
Shoulder, chest, back	21	5	8	3	***		***		0
Arm	58	9	20	6	30	6	8	3	0
Hand, wrist, fingers	44	7	8	3	24	5	12	4	0
Leg	41	7	7	3	24	6	10	3	0
Foot, ankle, toes	24	5	***		14	4	***		0
Multiple body parts	17	4	***		9	3	***		0
All other body parts*	20		***		10		***		0
Unknown	2		0		0		0		2
Total [†]	266	20	72	10	129	13	63	9	2

† Estimates may not add to the total because of rounding.
* All other body parts includes "Neck," "Abdomen," "Pelvic region," "Internal injury," and "Other body parts."
*** Estimate is not reportable or is suppressed because of a non-reportable cell.

Table 4.36 National estimates of **injuries to all youth** less than 20 years of age on Native American farms by work status and body part injured, 2000

Body Part Injured	Total [†] Estimate	se	Working Estimate	se	Non-Working Estimate	se	Unknown Estimate
Head, skull	26	6	9	3	17	4	0
Face	13	4	***		***		0
Shoulder, chest, back	21	5	***		***		0
Arm	58	9	20	5	37	7	0
Hand, wrist, fingers	44	7	24	6	20	5	0
Leg	41	7	17	5	25	6	0
Foot, ankle, toes	24	5	8	3	17	4	0
Multiple body parts	17	4	7	3	10	3	0
All other body parts*	20		***		***		0
Unknown	2		0		0		2
Total [†]	266	20	98	12	166	15	2

† Estimates may not add to the total because of rounding.

* All other body parts includes "Neck," "Abdomen," "Pelvic region," "Internal injury," and "Other body parts."

*** Estimate is not reportable or is suppressed because of a non-reportable cell.

Table 4.37 National estimates of **injuries to all youth** less than 20 years of age on Native American farms by sex and source of injury, 2000

Source of Injury ‡	Total † Estimate	se	Male Estimate	se	Female Estimate	se	Unknown Estimate
Parts/Materials (4)	15	4	***		***		0
Vehicle Parts (48)	7	3	***		***		0
Trailers (483)	7	3	***		***		*0*
Persons/Animals/Plants/Minerals (5)	44	8	21	5	23	5	0
Animals (51)	39	8	***		***		0
Cattle (5152)	*11*	*4*	***		***		*0*
Horses (5154)	*17*	*4*	***		***		*0*
Structures and Surfaces (6)	96	11	64	9	33	6	0
Floors/Walkways/Ground (62)	72	9	***		***		0
Ground (623)	*65*	*9*	*40*	*7*	*25*	*5*	*0*
Other Structural Elements (63)	22	5	***		***		0
Tools/Instruments/Equipment (7)	26	6	16	4	10	4	0
Recreation Equipment (78)	16	5	***		***		0
Water Sports Equipment (786)	*8*	*3*	***		***		*0*
Vehicles (8)	40	7	***		***		0
Highway Vehicles (82)	9	4	***		***		0
Off-Road Vehicles (84)	22	5	***		***		0
All Terrain Vehicle (841)	*22*	*5*	***		***		*0*
Industrial Vehicles (85)	7	3	***		***		0
Tractors (853)	*7*	*3*	***		***		*0*
Other and Unknown Sources*	45		21		22		2
Total †	266	20	170	15	94	11	2

† Estimates may not add to the total because of rounding.

‡ Categories based on the Bureau of Labor Statistics Occupational Injury and Illness Coding Structure (OIICS). OIICS codes are provided in parentheses.

* Other and Unknown Sources includes "Chemicals," "Containers," "Furniture and Fixtures," "Machinery," "Other Sources," and "Unknown Sources."

*** Estimate is not reportable or is suppressed because of a non-reportable cell.

Table 4.38 National estimates of **injuries to all youth** less than 20 years of age on Native American farms by age and source of injury, 2000

Source of Injury [‡]	Total [†]	se	<10 years	se	10-15 years	se	16-19 years	se	Unknown Estimate
	Estimate	se	Estimate	se	Estimate	se	Estimate	se	Estimate
Parts/Materials (4)	**15**	**4**	***		***		***		**0**
Vehicle Parts (48)	7	3	***		***		***		0
Trailers (483)	7	3	***		***		***		0
Persons/Animals/Plants/Minerals (5)	**44**	**8**	19	6	15	4	10	4	**0**
Animals (51)	39	8	19	6	13	4	7	3	0
Cattle (5152)	11	4	***		***		***		0
Horses (5154)	17	4	8	3	***		***		0
Structures and Surfaces (6)	**96**	**11**	21	5	50	8	26	6	**0**
Floors/Walkways/Ground (62)	72	9	19	5	35	7	17	5	0
Ground (623)	65	9	17	4	33	7	15	5	0
Other Structural Elements (63)	22	5	***		14	4	***		0
Tools/Instruments/Equipment (7)	**26**	**6**	***		13	4	***		**0**
Recreation Equipment (78)	16	5	***		9	4	***		0
Water Sports Equipment (786)	8	3	***		***		***		0
Vehicles (8)	**40**	**7**	***		28	6	***		**0**
Highway Vehicles (82)	9	4	***		***		***		0
Off-Road Vehicles (84)	22	5	***		15	4	***		0
All Terrain Vehicle (841)	22	5	***		15	4	***		0
Industrial Vehicles (85)	7	3	***		***		***		0
Tractors (853)	7	3	***		***		***		0
Other and Unknown Sources*	**45**		12		19		12		**2**
Total [†]	**266**	**20**	**72**	**10**	**129**	**13**	**63**	**9**	**2**

† Estimates may not add to the total because of rounding.

‡ Categories based on the Bureau of Labor Statistics Occupational Injury and Illness Coding Structure (OIICS). OIICS codes are provided in parentheses.

* Other and Unknown Sources includes "Chemicals," "Containers," "Furniture and Fixtures," "Machinery," "Other Sources," and "Unknown Sources."

*** Estimate is not reportable or is suppressed because of a non-reportable cell.

Table 4.39 National estimates of **injuries to all youth** less than 20 years of age on Native American farms by work status and source of injury, 2000

Source of Injury ‡	Total †		Working		Non-Working		Unknown
	Estimate	se	Estimate	se	Estimate	se	Estimate
Parts/Materials (4)	**15**	**4**	***		***		**0**
Vehicle Parts (48)	7	3	***		***		0
Trailers (483)	*7*	*3*	***		***		*0*
Persons/Animals/Plants/Minerals (5)	**44**	**8**	**15**	**5**	**30**	**7**	**0**
Animals (51)	39	8	***		***		0
Cattle (5152)	*11*	*4*	***		***		*0*
Horses (5154)	*17*	*4*	***		***		*0*
Structures and Surfaces (6)	**96**	**11**	**38**	**7**	**59**	**8**	**0**
Floors/Walkways/Ground (62)	72	9	23	6	49	7	0
Ground (623)	*65*	*9*	***		***		*0*
Other Structural Elements (63)	22	5	12	4	10	3	0
Tools/Instruments/Equipment (7)	**26**	**6**	***		***		**0**
Recreation Equipment (78)	16	5	***		***		0
Water Sports Equipment (786)	*8*	*3*	***		***		*0*
Vehicles (8)	**40**	**7**	**17**	**4**	**23**	**5**	**0**
Highway Vehicles (82)	9	4	***		***		0
Off-Road Vehicles (84)	22	5	***		***		0
All Terrain Vehicle (841)	*22*	*5*	***		***		*0*
Industrial Vehicles (85)	7	3	***		***		0
Tractors (853)	*7*	*3*	***		***		*0*
Other and Unknown Sources*	**45**		**14**		**29**		**2**
Total †	**266**	**20**	**98**	**12**	**166**	**15**	**2**

† Estimates may not add to the total because of rounding.

‡ Categories based on the Bureau of Labor Statistics Occupational Injury and Illness Coding Structure (OIICS). OIICS codes are provided in parentheses.

* Other and Unknown Sources includes "Chemicals," "Containers," "Furniture and Fixtures," "Machinery," "Other Sources," and "Unknown Sources."

*** Estimate is not reportable or is suppressed because of a non-reportable cell.

Table 4.40 National estimates of **injuries to all youth** less than 20 years of age on Native American farms by sex and type of injury event, 2000

Type of Injury Event ‡	Total †		Male		Female		Unknown
	Estimate	se	Estimate	se	Estimate	se	Estimate
Contact With Objects (0)	78	10	59	9	19	5	0
Struck Against Object (01)	30	6	***		***		0
Against Stationary Object (012)	25	6	***		***		0
Struck by Object (02)	33	6	***		***		0
Struck by Falling Object (021)	8	3	***		***		0
Struck by Slipping Handheld Object (0232)	7	3	***		***		0
Caught in Objects (03)	12	4	***		***		0
Caught in Objects n.e.c. (039)*	10	3	***		***		0
Falls (1)	72	9	44	8	27	5	0
Fall to Lower Level (11)	48	8	30	7	18	5	0
Fall to Lower Level n.e.c. (119)*	42	8	***		***		0
Fall on Same Level (13)	17	4	10	3	7	3	0
Fall to Floor/Walkway/Ground (131)	14	4	***		***		0
Exposure to Substances/Environments (3)	13	5	***		***		0
Exposure Caustic/Allergenic Substance (34)	8	5	***		***		0
Transportation Events (4)	38	7	***		***		0
Non-highway Events (42)	33	6	***		***		0
Fall From Moving Vehicle (4231)	7	3	***		***		0
Overturn (4233)	13	4	***		***		0
Loss of Control (4234)	7	3	***		***		0
Assaults and Violent Acts (6)	23	5	***		***		0
Assault by Animal (63)	23	5	***		***		0
Assault by Animal n.e.c. (639)*	20	5	***		***		0
Other and Unknown Events**	43		22		19		2
Total †	266	20	170	15	94	11	2

† Estimates may not add to the total because of rounding.

‡ Categories based on the Bureau of Labor Statistics Occupational Injury and Illness Coding Structure (OIICS). OIICS codes are provided in parentheses.

* "n.e.c." is an abbreviation for "not elsewhere classified."

** Other and Unknown Events includes "Bodily Reaction/Exertion," "Fires and Explosions," "Other Events," and "Unknown Events."

*** Estimate is not reportable or is suppressed because of a non-reportable cell.

Table 4.41 National estimates of **injuries to all youth** less than 20 years of age on Native American farms by age and type of injury event, 2000

Type of Injury Event ‡	Total †		<10 years		10-15 years		16-19 years		Unknown	
	Estimate	se	Estimate	se	Estimate	se	Estimate	se	Estimate	se
Contact With Objects (0)	78	10	13	4	44	7	21	6	0	
Struck Against Object (01)	30	6	11	4	12	3	8	3	0	
Against Stationary Object (012)	25	6	9	3	9	3	8	3	0	
Struck by Object (02)	33	6	***		20	5	***		0	
Struck by Falling Object (021)	8	3	***		***		***		0	
Struck by Slipping Handheld Object (0232)	7	3	***		***		***		0	
Caught in Objects (03)	12	4	***		9	3	***		0	
*Caught in Objects n.e.c. * (039)*	10	3	***		7	3	***		0	
Falls (1)	72	9	24	5	31	6	17	5	0	
Fall to Lower Level (11)	48	8	14	4	22	6	13	4	0	
*Fall to Lower Level n.e.c. * (119)*	42	8	11	3	18	5	13	4	0	
Fall on Same Level (13)	17	4	10	3	***		***		0	
Fall to Floor/Walkway/Ground (131)	14	4	10	3	***		***		0	
Exposure to Substances/Environments (3)	13	5	8	5	***		***		0	
Exposure Caustic/Allergenic Substance (34)	8	5	***		***		***		0	
Transportation Events (4)	38	7	7	3	23	5	8	4	0	
Non-highway Events (42)	33	6	***		21	5	***		0	
Fall From Moving Vehicle (4231)	7	3	***		***		***		0	
Overturn (4233)	13	4	***		10	4	***		0	
Loss of Control (4234)	7	3	***		***		***		0	
Assaults and Violent Acts (6)	23	5	10	3	10	4	***		0	
Assault by Animal (63)	23	5	***		10	4	***		0	
*Assault by Animal n.e.c. * (639)*	20	5	***		8	3	***		0	
Other and Unknown Events	43		10		19		12		2	
Total †	266	20	72	10	129	13	63	9	2	

† Estimates may not add to the total because of rounding.

‡ Categories based on the Bureau of Labor Statistics Occupational Injury and Illness Coding Structure (OIICS). OIICS codes are provided in parentheses.

* "n.e.c." is an abbreviation for "not elsewhere classified."

** Other and Unknown Events includes "Bodily Reaction/Exertion," "Fires and Explosions," "Other Events," and "Unknown Events."

*** Estimate is not reportable or is suppressed because of a non-reportable cell.

154

Table 4.42 National estimates of **injuries to all youth** less than 20 years of age on Native American farms by work status and type of injury event, 2000

Type of Injury Event ‡	Total †		Working		Non-Working		Unknown
	Estimate	se	Estimate	se	Estimate	se	Estimate
Contact With Objects (0)	**78**	**10**	**39**	**7**	**39**	**7**	**0**
Struck Against Object (01)	30	6	20	5	10	3	0
Against Stationary Object (012)	25	6	***		***		0
Struck by Object (02)	33	6	12	4	21	5	0
Struck by Falling Object (021)	8	3	***		***		0
Struck by Slipping Handheld Object (0232)	7	3	***		***		0
Caught in Objects (03)	12	4	***		***		0
Caught in Objects n.e.c. (039)*	10	3	***		***		0
Falls (1)	**72**	**9**	**26**	**6**	**46**	**7**	**0**
Fall to Lower Level (11)	48	8	***		***		0
Fall to Lower Level n.e.c. (119)*	42	8	***		***		0
Fall on Same Level (13)	17	4	***		***		0
Fall to Floor/Walkway/Ground (131)	14	4	***		***		0
Exposure to Substances/Environments (3)	**13**	**5**	***		***		**0**
Exposure Caustic/Allergenic Substance (34)	8	5	***		***		0
Transportation Events (4)	**38**	**7**	**13**	**4**	**26**	**6**	**0**
Non-highway Events (42)	33	6	13	4	20	5	0
Fall From Moving Vehicle (4231)	7	3	***		***		0
Overturn (4233)	13	4	***		***		0
Loss Of Control (4234)	7	3	***		***		0
Assaults and Violent Acts (6)	**23**	**5**	***		***		**0**
Assault by Animal (63)	23	5	***		***		0
Assault by Animal n.e.c. (639)*	20	5	***		***		0
Other and Unknown Events**	**43**		**15**		**26**		**2**
Total †	**266**	**20**	**98**	**12**	**166**	**15**	**2**

† Estimates may not add to the total because of rounding.

‡ Categories based on the Bureau of Labor Statistics Occupational Injury and Illness Coding Structure (OIICS). OIICS codes are provided in parentheses.

* "n.e.c." is an abbreviation for "not elsewhere classified."

** Other and Unknown Events includes "Bodily Reaction/Exertion," "Fires and Explosions," "Other Events," and "Unknown Events."

*** Estimate is not reportable or is suppressed because of a non-reportable cell.

155

Table 4.43 National estimates of **injuries to household youth** less than 20 years of age on Native American farms by sex and age, 2000

Age	Total [†] Estimate	se	Male Estimate	se	Female Estimate	se
< 10 years	**52**	**9**	**29**	**6**	**23**	**6**
10-15 years	**87**	**11**	**58**	**9**	**30**	**6**
10-11 years	30	6	19	5	11	4
12-13 years	23	6	15	5	8	3
14-15 years	35	7	24	6	11	4
16-19 years	**38**	**7**	**26**	**6**	**12**	**4**
16-17 years	26	6	***		***	
18-19 years	12	4	***		***	
Total [†]	**177**	**16**	**112**	**13**	**65**	**9**

† Estimates may not add to the total because of rounding.
*** Estimate is not reportable or is suppressed because of a non-reportable cell.

Table 4.44 National estimates of **injuries to household youth** less than 20 years of age on Native American farms by work status and age, 2000

Age	Total [†] Estimate	se	Working Estimate	se	Non-Working Estimate	se
< 10 years	**52**	**9**	**15**	**5**	**37**	**7**
10-15 years	**87**	**11**	**33**	**6**	**55**	**9**
10-11 years	30	6	***		***	
12-13 years	23	6	***		***	
14-15 years	35	7	21	5	14	4
16-19 years	**38**	**7**	**27**	**6**	**11**	**4**
16-17 years	26	6	***		***	
18-19 years	12	4	***		***	
Total [†]	**177**	**16**	**75**	**11**	**102**	**12**

† Estimates may not add to the total because of rounding.
*** Estimate is not reportable or is suppressed because of a non-reportable cell.

Table 4.45 National estimates of **injuries to household youth** less than 20 years of age on Native American farms by sex and type of farm, 2000

Type of Farm	Total [†] Estimate	se	Male Estimate	se	Female Estimate	se
All crop	30	7	18	5	12	5
Grain and oil seed	12	5	***		***	
All other crop*	18		***		***	
All livestock	147	15	94	12	53	8
Beef	115	13	78	11	37	6
Equine	17	5	***		***	
All other livestock**	15		***		***	
Total [†]	177	16	112	13	65	9

† Estimates may not add to the total because of rounding.
* All other crop includes "Tobacco," "Cotton," "Vegetable and melon," "Fruit, nut, and berry," "Nursery and floriculture," and "Other crop" farms.
** All other livestock includes "Dairy," "Hog," "Sheep and goat," "Poultry and egg," "Aquaculture," and "Other livestock" farms.
*** Estimate is not reportable or is suppressed because of a non-reportable cell.

Table 4.46 National estimates of **injuries to household youth** less than 20 years of age on Native American farms by age and type of farm, 2000

Type of Farm	Total [†] Estimate	se	<10 years Estimate	se	10-15 years Estimate	se	16-19 years Estimate	se
All crop	30	7	***		20	5	***	
Grain and oil seed	12	5	***		***		***	
All other crop*	18		***		***		***	
All livestock	147	15	***		67	10	***	
Beef	115	13	29	6	54	8	33	7
Equine	17	5	10	4	***		***	
All other livestock**	15		***		***		***	
Total [†]	177	16	52	9	87	11	38	7

† Estimates may not add to the total because of rounding.
* All other crop includes "Tobacco," "Cotton," "Vegetable and melon," "Fruit, nut, and berry," "Nursery and floriculture," and "Other crop" farms.
** All other livestock includes "Dairy," "Hog," "Sheep and goat," "Poultry and egg," "Aquaculture," and "Other livestock" farms.
*** Estimate is not reportable or is suppressed because of a non-reportable cell.

Table 4.47 National estimates of **injuries to household youth** less than 20 years of age on Native American farms by sex and type of injury, 2000

Type of Injury	Total † Estimate	se	Male Estimate	se	Female Estimate	se
Scrape, abrasion	12	4	***		***	
Bruise, contusion	21	5	12	4	9	3
Sprain, strain	10	4	***		***	
Broken bone, fracture	58	9	47	8	12	4
Cut, laceration	44	7	28	5	16	5
Multiple injuries	12	3	***		***	
All other injuries*	12		***		***	
Unknown	3		0		3	
Total †	177	16	112	13	65	9

† Estimates may not add to the total because of rounding.
* All other injuries includes "Dislocation," "Puncture, stab, jab," "Traumatic rupture," "Crushed," "Amputation," "Nerve injury," "Burn, blister, scald," and "Other injury."
*** Estimate is not reportable or is suppressed because of a non-reportable cell.

Table 4.48 National estimates of **injuries to household youth** less than 20 years of age on Native American farms by age and type of injury, 2000

Type of Injury	Total † Estimate	se	< 10 years Estimate	se	10-15 years Estimate	se	16-19 years Estimate	se
Scrape, abrasion	12	4	***		7	3	***	
Bruise, contusion	21	5	***		12	4	***	
Sprain, strain	10	4	***		***		***	
Broken bone, fracture	58	9	22	6	27	6	10	4
Cut, laceration	44	7	15	4	19	5	10	3
Multiple injuries	12	3	***		9	3	***	
All other injuries*	12		***		***		***	
Unknown	3		0		3		0	
Total †	177	16	52	9	87	11	38	7

† Estimates may not add to the total because of rounding.
* All other injuries includes "Dislocation," "Puncture, stab, jab," "Traumatic rupture," "Crushed," "Amputation," "Nerve injury," "Burn, blister, scald," and "Other injury."
*** Estimate is not reportable or is suppressed because of a non-reportable cell.

Table 4.49 National estimates of **injuries to household youth** less than 20 years of age on Native American farms by work status and type of injury, 2000

Type of Injury	Total[†] Estimate	se	Working Estimate	se	Non-Working Estimate	se
Scrape, abrasion	12	4	***		***	
Bruise, contusion	21	5	9	4	12	4
Sprain, strain	10	4	***		***	
Broken bone, fracture	58	9	20	6	38	7
Cut, laceration	44	7	23	5	21	5
Multiple injuries	12	3	***		***	
All other injuries*	12		***		***	
Unknown	3		3		0	
Total[†]	177	16	75	11	102	12

† Estimates may not add to the total because of rounding.
* All other injuries includes "Dislocation," "Puncture, stab, jab," "Traumatic rupture," "Crushed," "Amputation," "Nerve injury," "Burn, blister, scald," and "Other injury."
*** Estimate is not reportable or is suppressed because of a non-reportable cell.

Table 4.50 National estimates of **injuries to household youth** less than 20 years of age on Native American farms by sex and body part injured, 2000

Body Part Injured	Total[†] Estimate	se	Male Estimate	se	Female Estimate	se
Head, skull	19	5	***		***	
Face	10	3	***		***	
Shoulder, chest, back	15	4	***		***	
Arm	41	7	27	6	14	5
Hand, wrist, fingers	31	6	***		***	
Leg	27	6	17	5	10	3
Foot, ankle, toes	10	3	***		***	
Multiple body parts	11	3	***		***	
All other body parts*	13		***		***	
Total[†]	177	16	112	13	65	9

† Estimates may not add to the total because of rounding.
* All other body parts includes "Neck," "Abdomen," "Pelvic region," "Internal injury," and "Other body parts."
*** Estimate is not reportable or is suppressed because of a non-reportable cell.

Table 4.51 National estimates of **injuries to household youth** less than 20 years of age on Native American farms by age and body part injured, 2000

Body Part Injured	Total [†] Estimate	se	< 10 years Estimate	se	10-15 years Estimate	se	16-19 years Estimate	se
Head, skull	19	5	***		12	4	***	
Face	10	3	8	3	***		***	
Shoulder, chest, back	15	4	***		***		8	3
Arm	41	7	***		24	6	***	
Hand, wrist, fingers	31	6	***		19	5	***	
Leg	27	6	***		15	4	***	
Foot, ankle, toes	10	3	***		***		***	
Multiple body parts	11	3	***		7	3	***	
All other body parts*	13		***		***		***	
Total [†]	177	16	52	9	87	11	38	7

† Estimates may not add to the total because of rounding.
* All other body parts includes "Neck," "Abdomen," "Pelvic region," "Internal injury," and "Other body parts."
*** Estimate is not reportable or is suppressed because of a non-reportable cell.

Table 4.52 National estimates of **injuries to household youth** less than 20 years of age on Native American farms by work status and body part injured, 2000

Body Part Injured	Total [†] Estimate	se	Working Estimate	se	Non-Working Estimate	se
Head, skull	19	5	9	3	10	3
Face	10	3	***		***	
Shoulder, chest, back	15	4	***		***	
Arm	41	7	14	4	27	6
Hand, wrist, fingers	31	6	13	4	18	5
Leg	27	6	17	5	10	4
Foot, ankle, toes	10	3	***		***	
Multiple body parts	11	3	***		***	
All other body parts*	13		***		***	
Total [†]	177	16	75	11	102	12

† Estimates may not add to the total because of rounding.
* All other body parts includes "Neck," "Abdomen," "Pelvic region," "Internal injury," and "Other body parts."
*** Estimate is not reportable or is suppressed because of a non-reportable cell.

Table 4.53 National estimates of **injuries to household youth** less than 20 years of age on Native American farms by sex and source of injury, 2000

Source of Injury [‡]	Total [†] Estimate	se	Male Estimate	se	Female Estimate	se
Parts/Materials (4)	10	3	***		***	
Persons/Animals/Plants/Minerals (5)	23	5	13	4	11	4
Animals (51)	23	5	13	4	11	4
Cattle (5152)	11	4	***		***	
Horses (5154)	12	4	***		***	
Structures and Surfaces (6)	70	10	40	7	30	6
Floors/Walkways/Ground (62)	53	8	***		***	
Ground (623)	48	8	***		***	
Other Structural Elements (63)	14	5	***		***	
Tools/Instruments/Equipment (7)	16	4	***		***	
Recreation Equipment (78)	9	4	***		***	
Vehicles (8)	30	6	***		***	
Highway Vehicles (82)	9	4	***		***	
Off-Road Vehicles (84)	16	4	***		***	
All Terrain Vehicle (841)	16	4	***		***	
Other and Unknown Sources*	28		16		12	
Total [†]	177	16	112	13	65	9

† Estimates may not add to the total because of rounding.

‡ Categories based on the Bureau of Labor Statistics Occupational Injury and Illness Coding Structure (OIICS). OIICS codes are provided in parentheses.

* Other and Unknown Sources includes "Chemicals," "Containers," "Furniture and Fixtures," "Machinery," "Other Sources," and "Unknown Sources."

*** Estimate is not reportable or is suppressed because of a non-reportable cell.

Table 4.54 National estimates of **injuries to household youth** less than 20 years of age on Native American farms by age and source of injury, 2000

Source of Injury ‡	Total † Estimate	se	<10 years Estimate	se	10-15 years Estimate	se	16-19 years Estimate	se
Parts/Materials (4)	**10**	**3**	***		***		***	
Persons/Animals/Plants/Minerals (5)	**23**	**5**	**9**	**3**	**8**	**3**	**7**	**3**
Animals (51)	23	5	9	3	8	3	7	3
Cattle (5152)	*11*	*4*	***		***		***	
Horses (5154)	*12*	*4*	***		***		***	
Structures and Surfaces (6)	**70**	**10**	**29**	**6**	**40**	**7**	**12**	**4**
Floors/Walkways/Ground (62)	53	8	***		28	6	***	
Ground (623)	*48*	*8*	***		25	6	***	
Other Structural Elements (63)	14	5	***		12	4	***	
Tools/Instruments/Equipment (7)	**16**	**4**	***		**11**	**4**	***	
Recreation Equipment (78)	9	4	***		***		***	
Vehicles (8)	**30**	**6**	***		**20**	**5**	***	
Highway Vehicles (82)	9	4	***		***		***	
Off-Road Vehicles (84)	16	4	***		9	3	***	
All Terrain Vehicle (841)	*16*	*4*	***		9	3	***	
Other and Unknown Sources*	**28**		**12**		**7**		**9**	
Total †	**177**	**16**	**52**	**9**	**87**	**10**	**38**	**7**

† Estimates may not add to the total because of rounding.

‡ Categories based on the Bureau of Labor Statistics Occupational Injury and Illness Coding Structure (OIICS). OIICS codes are provided in parentheses.

* Other and Unknown Sources includes "Chemicals," "Containers," "Furniture and Fixtures," "Machinery," "Other Sources," and "Unknown Sources."

*** Estimate is not reportable or is suppressed because of a non-reportable cell.

Table 4.55 National estimates of **injuries to household youth** less than 20 years of age on Native American farms by work status and source of injury, 2000

Source of Injury ‡	Total †		Working		Non-Working	
	Estimate	se	Estimate	se	Estimate	se
Parts/Materials (4)	10	3	***		***	
Persons/Animals/Plants/Minerals (5)	23	5	11	4	12	4
Animals (51)	23	5	11	4	12	4
Cattle (5152)	11	4	***		***	
Horses (5154)	12	4	***		***	
Structures and Surfaces (6)	70	10	29	6	42	7
Floors/Walkways/Ground (62)	53	8	17	5	37	6
Ground (623)	48	8	17	5	32	6
Other Structural Elements (63)	14	5	***		***	
Tools/Instruments/Equipment (7)	16	4	***		***	
Recreation Equipment (78)	9	4	0		9	4
Vehicles (8)	30	6	13	4	17	4
Highway Vehicles (82)	9	4	***		***	
Off-Road Vehicles (84)	16	4	7	3	9	3
All Terrain Vehicle (841)	16	4	7	3	9	3
Other and Unknown Sources*	28		11		17	
Total †	177	16	75	11	102	12

† Estimates may not add to the total because of rounding.

‡ Categories based on the Bureau of Labor Statistics Occupational Injury and Illness Coding Structure (OIICS). OIICS codes are provided in parentheses.

* Other and Unknown Sources includes "Chemicals," "Containers," "Furniture and Fixtures," "Machinery," "Other Sources," and "Unknown Sources."

*** Estimate is not reportable or is suppressed because of a non-reportable cell.

Table 4.56 National estimates of **injuries to household youth** less than 20 years of age on Native American farms by sex and type of injury event, 2000

Type of Injury Event ‡	Total †		Male		Female	
	Estimate	se	Estimate	se	Estimate	se
Contact With Objects (0)	55	9	39	7	16	5
Struck Against Object (01)	25	5	17	4	8	3
Against Stationary Object (012)	22	5	***		***	
Struck by Object (02)	20	5	***		***	
Struck by Slipping Handheld Object (0232)	7	3	7	3	0	
Caught in Objects (03)	7	3	***		***	
Caught in Objects n.e.c. (039)*	7	3	***		***	
Falls (1)	54	8	29	6	25	5
Fall to Lower Level (11)	37	7	***		***	
Fall to Lower Level n.e.c. (119)*	35	7	*19*	*5*	*16*	*4*
Fall on Same Level (13)	12	4	***		***	
Fall to Floor/Walkway/Ground (131)	12	4	***		***	
Transportation Events (4)	27	6	***		***	
Non-highway Events (42)	22	5	***		***	
Overturn (4233)	7	3	***		***	
Assaults and Violent Acts (6)	13	4	***		***	
Assault by Animal (63)	13	4	***		***	
Assault by Animal n.e.c. (639)*	13	4	***		***	
Other and Unknown Events**	28		16		12	
Total †	177	16	112	13	65	9

† Estimates may not add to the total because of rounding.

‡ Categories based on the Bureau of Labor Statistics Occupational Injury and Illness Coding Structure (OIICS). OIICS codes are provided in parentheses.

* "n.e.c." is an abbreviation for "not elsewhere classified."

** Other and Unknown Events includes "Bodily Reaction/Exertion," "Exposure to Substances/Environments," "Fires and Explosions," "Other Events," and "Unknown Events."

*** Estimate is not reportable or is suppressed because of a non-reportable cell.

Table 4.57 National estimates of **injuries to household youth** less than 20 years of age on Native American farms by age and type of injury event, 2000

Type of Injury Event ‡	Total †		<10 years		10-15 years		16-19 years	
	Estimate	se	Estimate	se	Estimate	se	Estimate	se
Contact With Objects (0)	**55**	**9**	**11**	**4**	**32**	**6**	**12**	**4**
Struck Against Object (01)	25	5	11	4	***		***	
Against Stationary Object (012)	22	5	***		9	3	***	
Struck by Object (02)	20	5	***		16	4	***	
Struck by Slipping Handheld Object (0232)	7	3	***		***		***	
Caught in Objects (03)	7	3	***		***		***	
Caught in Objects n.e.c. * (039)	7	3	***		***		***	
Falls (1)	**54**	**8**	**21**	**5**	**23**	**6**	**10**	**4**
Fall to Lower Level (11)	37	7	12	3	16	5	10	4
Fall to Lower Level n.e.c. * (119)	35	7	9	3	16	5	10	4
Fall on Same Level (13)	12	4	10	3	***		***	
Fall to Floor/Walkway/Ground (131)	12	4	10	3	***		***	
Transportation Events (4)	**27**	**6**	***		**17**	**4**	***	
Non-highway Events (42)	22	5	***		15	4	***	
Overturn (4233)	7	3	***		***		***	
Assaults and Violent Acts (6)	**13**	**4**	***		***		***	
Assault by Animal (63)	13	4	***		***		***	
Assault by Animal n.e.c. * (639)	13	4	***		***		***	
Other and Unknown Events**	**28**		**10**		**10**		**9**	
Total †	**177**	**16**	**52**	**9**	**87**	**10**	**38**	**7**

† Estimates may not add to the total because of rounding.

‡ Categories based on the Bureau of Labor Statistics Occupational Injury and Illness Coding Structure (OIICS). OIICS codes are provided in parentheses.

* "n.e.c." is an abbreviation for "not elsewhere classified."

** Other and Unknown Events includes "Bodily Reaction/Exertion," "Exposure to Substances/Environments," "Fires and Explosions," "Other Events," and "Unknown Events."

*** Estimate is not reportable or is suppressed because of a non-reportable cell.

Table 4.58 National estimates of **injuries to household youth** less than 20 years of age on Native American farms by work status and type of injury event, 2000

Type of Injury Event [‡]	Total [†]		Working		Non-Working	
	Estimate	se	Estimate	se	Estimate	se
Contact With Objects (0)	55	9	31	6	24	6
Struck Against Object (01)	25	5	17	4	8	3
Against Stationary Object (012)	22	5	***		***	
Struck by Object (02)	20	5	9	3	11	4
Struck by Slipping Handheld Object (0232)	7	3	***		***	
Caught in Objects (03)	7	3	***		***	
Caught in Objects n.e.c. (039)*	7	3	***		***	
Falls (1)	54	8	20	5	34	6
Fall to Lower Level (11)	37	7	***		***	
Fall to Lower Level n.e.c. (119)*	35	7	*14*	*4*	*20*	*5*
Fall on Same Level (13)	12	4	***		***	
Fall to Floor/Walkway/Ground (131)	12	4	***		***	
Transportation Events (4)	27	6	10	3	17	4
Non-highway Events (42)	22	5	10	3	12	3
Overturn (4233)	7	3	***		***	
Assaults and Violent Acts (6)	13	4	***		***	
Assault by Animal (63)	13	4	***		***	
Assault by Animal n.e.c. (639)*	13	4	***		***	
Other and Unknown Events**	28		11		17	
Total [†]	177	16	75	11	102	12

† Estimates may not add to the total because of rounding.

‡ Categories based on the Bureau of Labor Statistics Occupational Injury and Illness Coding Structure (OIICS). OIICS codes are provided in parentheses.

* "n.e.c." is an abbreviation for "not elsewhere classified."

** Other and Unknown Events includes "Bodily Reaction/Exertion," "Exposure to Substances/Environments," "Fires and Explosions," "Other Events," and "Unknown Events."

*** Estimate is not reportable or is suppressed because of a non-reportable cell.

Table 4.59 National estimates of **injury rates for all youth** less than 20 years of age on Native American farms by work status and relationship to the farm, 2000

Relationship to Farm	Total Rate/1000	se	Working Rate/1000	se	Non-Working Rate/1000	se
Household youth	**23.98**	**2.24**	**17.74**	**2.59**	**13.82**	**1.64**
Hired youth	**4.23**	**1.77**	**4.38**	**1.96**	**0.00**	
Visiting youth	**0.66**	**0.09**	**2.30**	**0.83**	**0.54**	**0.09**
Relatives	1.00	0.16	2.30	0.83	0.73	0.13
Non-relatives	0.39	0.10	0.00		0.39	0.11
Total	**2.08**	**0.16**	**7.91**	**1.01**	**1.30**	**0.12**

Table 4.60 National estimates of **injury rates for all youth** less than 20 years of age on Native American farms by work status and type of farm, 2000

Type of Farm	Total Rate/1000	se	Working Rate/1000	se	Non-Working Rate/1000	se
All crop	**1.61**	**0.33**	**5.94**	**1.93**	**1.14**	**0.28**
Grain and oil seed	2.06	0.67	***		***	
All other crop*	1.37		***		***	
All livestock	**2.25**	**0.19**	**8.47**	**1.18**	**1.34**	**0.14**
Beef	2.25	0.22	8.06	1.33	1.32	0.15
Equine	2.46	0.60	10.53	3.87	1.51	0.43
All other livestock**	2.46		9.44		1.62	
Total	**2.08**	**0.16**	**7.91**	**1.01**	**1.30**	**0.12**

* All other crop includes "Tobacco," "Cotton," "Vegetable and melon," "Fruit, nut, and berry," "Nursery and floriculture," and "Other crop" farms.

** All other livestock includes "Dairy," "Hog," "Sheep and goat," "Poultry and egg," "Aquaculture," and "Other livestock" farms.

*** Estimate is not reportable or is suppressed because of a non-reportable cell.

Table 4.61 National estimates of **injury rates for all youth** less than 20 years of age on Native American farms by work status and type of injury, 2000

Type of Injury	Total Rate/1000	se	Working Rate/1000	se	Non-Working Rate/1000	se
Scrape, abrasion	0.11	0.03	***		***	
Bruise, contusion	0.25	0.05	0.72	0.32	0.19	0.04
Sprain, strain	0.12	0.04	0.70	0.29	0.06	0.02
Broken bone, fracture	0.66	0.09	2.61	0.59	0.41	0.06
Cut, laceration	0.43	0.06	2.11	0.44	0.22	0.05
Puncture, stab, jab	0.13	0.03	***		***	
Multiple injuries	0.09	0.03	***		***	
All other injuries*	0.23		0.56		0.18	
Total	2.08	0.16	7.91	1.01	1.30	0.12

* All other injuries includes "Dislocation," "Traumatic rupture," "Crushed," "Amputation," "Nerve injury," "Burn, blister, scald," and "Other injury."

*** Estimate is not reportable or is suppressed because of a non-reportable cell.

Table 4.62 National estimates of **injury rates for all youth** less than 20 years of age on Native American farms by work status and body part injured, 2000

Body Part Injured	Total Rate/1000	se	Working Rate/1000	se	Non-Working Rate/1000	se
Head, skull	0.20	0.04	0.75	0.25	0.13	0.03
Face	0.10	0.03	***		***	
Shoulder, chest, back	0.16	0.04	***		***	
Arm	0.45	0.07	1.65	0.44	0.29	0.06
Hand, wrist, fingers	0.34	0.06	1.94	0.45	0.16	0.04
Leg	0.32	0.06	1.34	0.37	0.19	0.04
Foot, ankle, toes	0.19	0.04	0.62	0.26	0.13	0.03
Multiple body parts	0.13	0.03	0.57	0.21	0.08	0.03
All other body parts*	0.16		***		***	
Total	2.08	0.16	7.91	1.01	1.30	0.12

* All other body parts includes "Neck," "Abdomen," "Pelvic region," "Internal injury," and "Other body parts."

*** Estimate is not reportable or is suppressed because of a non-reportable cell.

Table 4.63 National estimates of **injury rates for all youth** less than 20 years of age on Native American farms by work status and source of injury, 2000

Source of Injury [†]	Total		Working		Non-Working	
	Rate/1000	se	Rate/1000	se	Rate/1000	se
Parts/Materials (4)	0.12	0.03	***		***	
Vehicle Parts (48)	0.05	0.02	***		***	
Trailers (483)	*0.05*	*0.02*	***		***	
Persons/Animals/Plants/Minerals (5)	0.35	0.06	1.17	0.38	0.23	0.05
Animals (51)	0.30	0.06	***		***	
Cattle (5152)	*0.09*	*0.03*	***		***	
Horses (5154)	*0.13*	*0.03*	***		***	
Structures and Surfaces (6)	0.75	0.09	3.07	0.60	0.46	0.06
Floors/Walkways/Ground (62)	0.56	0.07	1.84	0.45	0.38	0.06
Ground (623)	*0.50*	*0.07*	***		***	
Other Structural Elements (63)	0.17	0.04	0.97	0.34	0.08	0.03
Tools/Instruments/Equipment (7)	0.20	0.04	***		***	
Recreation Equipment (78)	0.13	0.04	***		***	
Water Sports Equipment (786)	*0.06*	*0.03*	***		***	
Vehicles (8)	0.31	0.05	1.39	0.35	0.18	0.04
Highway Vehicles (82)	0.07	0.03	***		***	
Off-Road Vehicles (84)	0.17	0.04	***		***	
All Terrain Vehicle (841)	*0.17*	*0.04*	***		***	
Industrial Vehicles (85)	0.06	0.02	***		***	
Tractors (853)	*0.06*	*0.02*	***		***	
Other and Unknown Sources*	0.35		1.11		0.22	
Total	2.08	0.16	7.91	1.01	1.30	0.12

† Categories based on the Bureau of Labor Statistics Occupational Injury and Illness Coding Structure (OIICS). OIICS codes are provided in parentheses.

* Other and Unknown Sources includes "Chemicals," "Containers," "Furniture and Fixtures," "Machinery," "Other Sources," and "Unknown Sources."

*** Estimate is not reportable or is suppressed because of a non-reportable cell.

Table 4.64 National estimates of **injury rates for all youth** less than 20 years of age on Native American farms by work status and type of injury event, 2000

Type of Injury Event [†]	Total		Working		Non-Working	
	Rate/1000	se	Rate/1000	se	Rate/1000	se
Contact With Objects (0)	**0.61**	**0.08**	**3.19**	**0.60**	**0.30**	**0.06**
Struck Against Object (01)	0.23	0.05	1.60	0.39	0.08	0.03
Against Stationary Object (012)	*0.20*	*0.04*	***		***	
Struck by Object (02)	0.26	0.05	0.99	0.29	0.16	0.04
Struck by Falling Object (021)	*0.06*	*0.02*	***		***	
Struck by Slipping Handheld Object (0232)	*0.06*	*0.02*	***		***	
Caught in Objects (03)	0.09	0.03	***		***	
Caught in Objects n.e.c. (039)*	*0.08*	*0.03*	***		***	
Falls (1)	**0.56**	**0.07**	**2.10**	**0.49**	**0.36**	**0.05**
Fall to Lower Level (11)	0.37	0.06	***		***	
Fall to Lower Level n.e.c. (119)*	*0.33*	*0.06*	***		***	
Fall on Same Level (13)	0.13	0.03	***		***	
Fall to Floor/Walkway/Ground (131)	*0.11*	*0.03*	***		***	
Exposure to Substances/Environments (3)	**0.10**	**0.04**	***		***	
Exposure Caustic/Allergenic Substance (34)	0.06	0.04	***		***	
Transportation Events (4)	**0.30**	**0.05**	**1.01**	**0.30**	**0.20**	**0.04**
Non-highway Events (42)	0.25	0.05	1.01	0.30	0.16	0.04
Fall From Moving Vehicle (4231)	*0.06*	*0.02*	***		***	
Overturn (4233)	*0.10*	*0.03*	***		***	
Loss of Control (4234)	*0.06*	*0.02*	***		***	
Assaults and Violent Acts (6)	**0.18**	**0.04**	***		***	
Assault by Animal (63)	0.18	0.04	***		***	
Assault by Animal n.e.c. (639)*	*0.16*	*0.04*	***		***	
Other and Unknown Events**	**0.34**		**1.18**		**0.20**	
Total	**2.08**	**0.16**	**7.91**	**1.01**	**1.30**	**0.12**

[†] Categories based on the Bureau of Labor Statistics Occupational Injury and Illness Coding Structure (OIICS). OIICS codes are provided in parentheses.

* "n.e.c." is an abbreviation for "not elsewhere classified."

** Other and Unknown Events includes "Bodily Reaction/Exertion," "Fires and Explosions," "Other Events," and "Unknown Events."

*** Estimate is not reportable or is suppressed because of a non-reportable cell.

Table 4.65 National estimates of **injury rates for household youth** less than 20 years of age on Native American farms by sex and age, 2000

Age	Total		Male		Female	
	Rate/1000	se	Rate/1000	se	Rate/1000	se
<10 years	**21.96**	**3.75**	**24.30**	**5.48**	**19.60**	**5.08**
10-15 years	**31.22**	**3.89**	**40.46**	**6.20**	**21.55**	**4.58**
10-11 years	36.80	7.88	44.09	11.82	28.56	10.34
12-13 years	25.06	6.30	35.20	11.02	16.02	6.58
14-15 years	32.03	6.24	41.61	9.72	21.46	7.49
16-19 years	**18.32**	**3.42**	**23.40**	**5.43**	**12.58**	**3.74**
16-17 years	23.90	5.59	***		***	
18-19 years	12.18	3.68	***		***	
Total	**23.98**	**2.24**	**30.20**	**3.47**	**18.34**	**2.67**

*** Estimate is not reportable or is suppressed because of a non-reportable cell.

Table 4.66 National estimates of **injury rates for household youth** less than 20 years of age on Native American farms by work status and age, 2000

Age	Total		Working		Non-Working	
	Rate/1000	se	Rate/1000	se	Rate/1000	se
<10 years	**21.96**	**3.75**	**21.82**	**7.25**	**15.50**	**2.96**
10-15 years	**31.22**	**3.89**	**16.30**	**3.03**	**19.57**	**3.07**
10-11 years	36.80	7.88	***		***	
12-13 years	25.06	6.30	***		***	
14-15 years	32.03	6.24	25.63	6.18	12.76	3.42
16-19 years	**18.32**	**3.42**	**17.97**	**3.95**	**5.22**	**1.79**
16-17 years	23.90	5.59	***		***	
18-19 years	12.18	3.68	***		***	
Total	**23.98**	**2.24**	**17.74**	**2.59**	**13.83**	**1.57**

*** Estimate is not reportable or is suppressed because of a non-reportable cell.

Table 4.67 National estimates of **injury rates for household youth** less than 20 years of age on Native American farms by sex and type of farm, 2000

Type of Farm	Total Rate/1000	se	Male Rate/1000	se	Female Rate/1000	se
All crop	**18.89**	**4.37**	**21.50**	**5.53**	**15.76**	**6.98**
Grain and oil seed	20.83	9.16	***		***	
All other crop*	17.78		***		***	
All livestock	**26.99**	**2.78**	**34.10**	**4.36**	**19.79**	**2.98**
Beef	26.34	3.08	34.45	4.82	17.61	3.09
Equine	35.05	10.54	***		***	
All other livestock**	25.17		***		***	
Total	**23.98**	**2.24**	**30.20**	**3.47**	**18.34**	**2.67**

* All other crop includes "Tobacco," "Cotton," "Vegetable and melon," "Fruit, nut, and berry," "Nursery and floriculture," and "Other crop" farms.
** All other livestock includes "Dairy," "Hog," "Sheep and goat," "Poultry and egg," "Aquaculture," and "Other livestock" farms.
*** Estimate is not reportable or is suppressed because of a non-reportable cell.

Table 4.68 National estimates of **injury rates for household youth** less than 20 years of age on Native American farms by age and type of farm, 2000

Type of Farm	Total Rate/1000	se	<10 years Rate/1000	se	10-15 years Rate/1000	se	16-19 years Rate/1000	se
All crop	**18.89**	**4.37**	***		**34.47**	**8.67**	***	
Grain and oil seed	20.83	9.16	***		***		***	
All other crop*	17.78		***		***		***	
All livestock	**26.99**	**2.78**	***		**31.80**	**4.59**	***	
Beef	26.34	3.08	19.60	4.25	31.07	4.86	28.27	5.74
Equine	35.05	10.54	58.64	24.34	***		***	
All other livestock**	25.17		***		***		***	
Total	**23.98**	**2.24**	**21.96**	**3.75**	**31.22**	**3.89**	**18.32**	**3.42**

* All other crop includes "Tobacco," "Cotton," "Vegetable and melon," "Fruit, nut, and berry," "Nursery and floriculture," and "Other crop" farms.
** All other livestock includes "Dairy," "Hog," "Sheep and goat," "Poultry and egg," "Aquaculture," and "Other livestock" farms.
*** Estimate is not reportable or is suppressed because of a non-reportable cell.

Table 4.69 National estimates of **injury rates for household youth** less than 20 years of age on Native American farms by sex and type of injury, 2000

Type of Injury	Total Rate/1000	se	Male Rate/1000	se	Female Rate/1000	se
Scrape, abrasion	1.65	0.49	***		***	
Bruise, contusion	2.82	0.73	3.09	1.08	2.64	0.88
Sprain, strain	1.38	0.47	***		***	
Broken bone, fracture	7.89	1.25	12.53	2.22	3.29	1.19
Cut, laceration	5.93	0.95	7.48	1.43	4.56	1.34
Multiple injuries	1.57	0.46	***		***	
All other injuries*	1.67		***		***	
Total	23.98	2.24	30.20	3.47	18.34	2.67

* All other injuries includes "Dislocation," "Puncture, stab, jab," "Traumatic rupture," "Crushed," "Amputation," "Nerve injury," "Burn, blister, scald," and "Other injury."

*** Estimate is not reportable or is suppressed because of a non-reportable cell.

Table 4.70 National estimates of **injury rates for household youth** less than 20 years of age on Native American farms by age and type of injury, 2000

Type of Injury	Total Rate/1000	se	<10 years Rate/1000	se	10-15 years Rate/1000	se	16-19 years Rate/1000	se
Scrape, abrasion	1.65	0.49	***		2.46	0.93	***	
Bruise, contusion	2.82	0.73	***		4.21	1.25	***	
Sprain, strain	1.38	0.47	***		***		***	
Broken bone, fracture	7.89	1.25	9.26	2.52	9.57	2.12	4.59	1.84
Cut, laceration	5.93	0.95	6.46	1.84	6.82	1.65	4.59	1.60
Multiple injuries	1.57	0.46	***		3.36	1.11	***	
All other injuries*	1.67		***		***		***	
Total	23.98	2.24	21.96	3.75	31.22	3.89	18.32	3.42

* All other injuries includes "Dislocation," "Puncture, stab, jab," "Traumatic rupture," "Crushed," "Amputation," "Nerve injury," "Burn, blister, scald," and "Other injury."

*** Estimate is not reportable or is suppressed because of a non-reportable cell.

Table 4.71 National estimates of **injury rates for household youth** less than 20 years of age on Native American farms by work status and type of injury, 2000

Type of Injury	Total Rate/1000	se	Working Rate/1000	se	Non-Working Rate/1000	se
Scrape, abrasion	1.65	0.49	***		***	
Bruise, contusion	2.82	0.73	2.11	0.95	1.63	0.47
Sprain, strain	1.38	0.47	***		***	
Broken bone, fracture	7.89	1.25	4.81	1.45	5.13	0.91
Cut, laceration	5.93	0.95	5.45	1.14	2.82	0.71
Multiple injuries	1.57	0.46	***		***	
All other injuries*	1.67		***		***	
Total	23.98	2.24	17.74	2.59	13.83	1.57

* All other injuries includes "Dislocation," "Puncture, stab, jab," "Traumatic rupture," "Crushed," "Amputation," "Nerve injury," "Burn, blister, scald," and "Other injury."
*** Estimate is not reportable or is suppressed because of a non-reportable cell.

Table 4.72 National estimates of **injury rates for household youth** less than 20 years of age on Native American farms by sex and body part injured, 2000

Body Part Injured	Total Rate/1000	se	Male Rate/1000	se	Female Rate/1000	se
Head, skull	2.55	0.67	***		***	
Face	1.37	0.46	***		***	
Shoulder, chest, back	2.09	0.57	***		***	
Arm	5.54	0.99	7.23	1.57	4.00	1.28
Hand, wrist, fingers	4.16	0.83	***		***	
Leg	3.62	0.79	4.55	1.27	2.78	0.94
Foot, ankle, toes	1.34	0.46	***		***	
Multiple body parts	1.54	0.45	***		***	
All other body parts*	1.76		***		***	
Total	23.98	2.24	30.20	3.47	18.34	2.67

* All other body parts includes "Neck," "Abdomen," "Pelvic region," "Internal injury," and "Other body parts."
*** Estimate is not reportable or is suppressed because of a non-reportable cell.

Table 4.73 National estimates of **injury rates for household youth** less than 20 years of age on Native American farms by age and body part injured, 2000

Body Part Injured	Total		<10 years		10-15 years		16-19 years	
	Rate/1000	se	Rate/1000	se	Rate/1000	se	Rate/1000	se
Head, skull	2.55	0.67	***		4.36	1.54	***	
Face	1.37	0.46	3.36	1.32	***		***	
Shoulder, chest, back	2.09	0.57	***		***		3.67	1.41
Arm	5.54	0.99	***		8.68	2.01	***	
Hand, wrist, fingers	4.16	0.83	***		6.89	1.69	***	
Leg	3.62	0.79	***		5.25	1.43	***	
Foot, ankle, toes	1.34	0.46	***		***		***	
Multiple body parts	1.54	0.45	***		2.50	0.93	***	
All other body parts*	1.76		***		***		***	
Total	23.98	2.24	21.96	3.75	31.22	3.89	18.32	3.42

   * All other body parts includes "Neck," "Abdomen," "Pelvic region," "Internal injury," and "Other body parts."
  *** Estimate is not reportable or is suppressed because of a non-reportable cell.

Table 4.74 National estimates of **injury rates for household youth** less than 20 years of age on Native American farms by work status and body part injured, 2000

Body Part Injured	Total		Working		Non-Working	
	Rate/1000	se	Rate/1000	se	Rate/1000	se
Head, skull	2.55	0.67	2.20	0.74	1.29	0.43
Face	1.37	0.46	***		***	
Shoulder, chest, back	2.09	0.57	***		***	
Arm	5.54	0.99	3.29	1.02	3.66	0.75
Hand, wrist, fingers	4.16	0.83	3.06	0.95	2.41	0.64
Leg	3.62	0.79	3.91	1.09	1.40	0.47
Foot, ankle, toes	1.34	0.46	***		***	
Multiple body parts	1.54	0.45	***		***	
All other body parts*	1.76		***		***	
Total	23.98	2.24	17.74	2.59	13.83	1.57

   * All other body parts includes "Neck," "Abdomen," "Pelvic region," "Internal injury," and "Other body parts."
  *** Estimate is not reportable or is suppressed because of a non-reportable cell.

Table 4.75 National estimates of **injury rates for household youth** less than 20 years of age on Native American farms by sex and source of injury, 2000

Source of Injury [†]	Total		Male		Female	
	Rate/1000	se	Rate/1000	se	Rate/1000	se
Parts/Materials (4)	**1.33**	**0.45**	***		***	
Persons/Animals/Plants/Minerals (5)	**3.17**	**0.72**	**3.42**	**1.05**	**3.06**	**1.05**
Animals (51)	3.17	0.72	3.42	1.05	3.06	1.05
Cattle (5152)	*1.54*	*0.54*	***		***	
Horses (5154)	*1.63*	*0.49*	***		***	
Structures and Surfaces (6)	**9.54**	**1.30**	**10.81**	**1.92**	**8.56**	**1.68**
Floors/Walkways/Ground (62)	7.18	1.10	***		***	
Ground (623)	*6.56*	*1.06*	***		***	
Other Structural Elements (63)	1.94	0.61	***		***	
Tools/Instruments/Equipment (7)	**2.10**	**0.60**	***		***	
Recreation Equipment (78)	1.15	0.47	***		***	
Vehicles (8)	**4.02**	**0.78**	***		***	
Highway Vehicles (82)	1.19	0.47	***		***	
Off-Road Vehicles (84)	2.17	0.53	***		***	
All Terrain Vehicle (841)	*2.17*	*0.53*	***		***	
Other and Unknown Sources*	3.81		4.30		3.46	
Total	**23.98**	**2.24**	**30.20**	**3.47**	**18.34**	**2.67**

† Categories based on the Bureau of Labor Statistics Occupational Injury and Illness Coding Structure (OIICS). OIICS codes are provided in parentheses.

* Other and Unknown Sources includes "Chemicals," "Containers," "Furniture and Fixtures," "Machinery," "Other Sources," and "Unknown Sources."

*** Estimate is not reportable or is suppressed because of a non-reportable cell.

Table 4.76 National estimates of **injury rates for household youth** less than 20 years of age on Native American farms by age and source of injury, 2000

Source of Injury †	Total		<10 years		10-15 years		16-19 years	
	Rate/1000	se	Rate/1000	se	Rate/1000	se	Rate/1000	se
Parts/Materials (4)	**1.33**	**0.45**	***		***		***	
Persons/Animals/Plants/Minerals (5)	**3.17**	**0.72**	**3.61**	**1.45**	**2.71**	**1.04**	**3.53**	**1.40**
Animals (51)	3.17	0.72	3.61	1.45	2.71	1.04	3.53	1.40
Cattle (5152)	*1.54*	*0.54*	***		***		***	
Horses (5154)	*1.63*	*0.49*	***		***		***	
Structures and Surfaces (6)	**9.54**	**1.30**	**12.40**	**2.45**	**14.11**	**2.56**	**5.66**	**1.99**
Floors/Walkways/Ground (62)	7.18	1.10	***		9.82	2.16	***	
Ground (623)	*6.56*	*1.06*	***		*8.93*	*2.08*	***	
Other Structural Elements (63)	1.94	0.61	***		4.32	1.33	***	
Tools/Instruments/Equipment (7)	**2.10**	**0.60**	***		**3.96**	**1.43**	***	
Recreation Equipment (78)	1.15	0.47	***		***		***	
Vehicles (8)	**4.02**	**0.78**	***		**7.11**	**1.69**	***	
Highway Vehicles (82)	1.19	0.47	***		***		***	
Off-Road Vehicles (84)	2.17	0.53	***		3.32	1.11	***	
All Terrain Vehicle (841)	*2.17*	*0.53*	***		*3.32*	*1.11*	***	
Other and Unknown Sources*	3.81		5.05		2.54		4.40	
Total	**23.98**	**2.24**	**21.96**	**3.75**	**31.22**	**3.79**	**18.32**	**3.42**

† Categories based on the Bureau of Labor Statistics Occupational Injury and Illness Coding Structure (OIICS). OIICS codes are provided in parentheses.

* Other and Unknown Sources includes "Chemicals," "Containers," "Furniture and Fixtures," "Machinery," "Other Sources," and "Unknown Sources."

*** Estimate is not reportable or is suppressed because of a non-reportable cell.

Table 4.77 National estimates of **injury rates for household youth** less than 20 years of age on Native American farms by work status and source of injury, 2000

Source of Injury †	Total Rate/1000	se	Working Rate/1000	se	Non-Working Rate/1000	se
Parts/Materials (4)	**1.33**	**0.45**	***		***	
Persons/Animals/Plants/Minerals (5)	**3.17**	**0.72**	**2.70**	**0.95**	**1.63**	**0.49**
Animals (51)	3.17	0.72	2.70	0.95	1.63	0.49
Cattle (5152)	*1.54*	*0.54*	***		***	
Horses (5154)	*1.63*	*0.49*	***		***	
Structures and Surfaces (6)	**9.54**	**1.30**	**6.75**	**1.48**	**5.68**	**0.94**
Floors/Walkways/Ground (62)	7.18	1.10	3.91	1.09	4.95	0.86
Ground (623)	*6.56*	*1.06*	*3.91*	*1.09*	*4.32*	*0.80*
Other Structural Elements (63)	1.94	0.61	***		***	
Tools/Instruments/Equipment (7)	**2.10**	**0.60**	***		***	
Recreation Equipment (78)	1.15	0.47	0.00		1.15	0.47
Vehicles (8)	**4.02**	**0.78**	**2.96**	**0.88**	**2.33**	**0.58**
Highway Vehicles (82)	1.19	0.47	***		***	
Off-Road Vehicles (84)	2.17	0.53	1.63	0.62	1.23	0.41
All Terrain Vehicle (841)	*2.17*	*0.53*	*1.63*	*0.62*	*1.23*	*0.41*
Other and Unknown Sources*	**3.81**		**2.68**		**2.28**	
Total	**23.98**	**2.24**	**17.74**	**2.59**	**13.83**	**1.57**

† Categories based on the Bureau of Labor Statistics Occupational Injury and Illness Coding Structure (OIICS). OIICS codes are provided in parentheses.

* Other and Unknown Sources includes "Chemicals," "Containers," "Furniture and Fixtures," "Machinery," "Other Sources," and "Unknown Sources."

*** Estimate is not reportable or is suppressed because of a non-reportable cell.

Table 4.78 National estimates of **injury rates for household youth** less than 20 years of age on Native American farms by sex and type of injury event, 2000

Type of Injury Event [†]	Total		Male		Female	
	Rate/1000	se	Rate/1000	se	Rate/1000	se
Contact With Objects (0)	**7.44**	**1.17**	**10.41**	**1.84**	**4.59**	**1.36**
Struck Against Object (01)	3.33	0.71	4.52	1.13	2.21	0.88
Against Stationary Object (012)	*3.01*	*0.67*	***		***	
Struck by Object (02)	2.71	0.67	***		***	
Struck by Slipping Handheld Object (0232)	*0.96*	*0.37*	*1.91*	*0.73*	*0.00*	
Caught in Objects (03)	0.99	0.39	***		***	
Caught in Objects n.e.c. (039)*	*0.99*	*0.39*	***		***	
Falls (1)	**7.28**	**1.12**	**7.83**	**1.73**	**7.00**	**1.48**
Fall to Lower Level (11)	5.00	0.97	***		***	
Fall to Lower Level n.e.c. (119)*	*4.67*	*0.94*	*5.06*	*1.46*	*4.45*	*1.22*
Fall on Same Level (13)	1.64	0.49	***		***	
Fall to Floor/Walkway/Ground (131)	*1.64*	*0.49*	***		***	
Transportation Events (4)	**3.69**	**0.75**	***		***	
Non-highway Events (42)	2.93	0.65	***		***	
Overturn (4233)	*0.93*	*0.35*	***		***	
Assaults and Violent Acts (6)	**1.76**	**0.53**	***		***	
Assault by Animal (63)	1.76	0.53	***		***	
Assault by Animal n.e.c. (639)*	*1.76*	*0.53*	***		***	
Other and Unknown Events**	**3.81**		**4.30**		**3.46**	
Total	**23.98**	**2.24**	**30.20**	**3.47**	**18.34**	**2.67**

[†] Categories based on the Bureau of Labor Statistics Occupational Injury and Illness Coding Structure (OIICS). OIICS codes are provided in parentheses.

* "n.e.c." is an abbreviation for "not elsewhere classified."

** Other and Unknown Events includes "Bodily Reaction/Exertion," "Exposure to Substances/Environments," "Fires and Explosions," "Other Events," and "Unknown Events."

*** Estimate is not reportable or is suppressed because of a non-reportable cell.

Table 4.79 National estimates of **injury rates for household youth** less than 20 years of age on Native American farms by age and type of injury event, 2000

Type of Injury Event†	Total		<10 years		10-15 years		16-19 years	
	Rate/1000	se	Rate/1000	se	Rate/1000	se	Rate/1000	se
Contact With Objects (0)	**7.44**	**1.17**	**4.67**	**1.62**	**11.50**	**2.23**	**5.66**	**1.99**
Struck Against Object (01)	3.33	0.71	4.67	1.62	***		***	
Against Stationary Object (012)	*3.01*	*0.67*	***		*3.29*	*1.07*	***	
Struck by Object (02)	2.71	0.67	***		5.54	1.58	***	
Struck by Slipping Handheld Object (0232)	*0.96*	*0.37*	***		***		***	
Caught in Objects (03)	0.99	0.39	***		***		***	
Caught in Objects n.e.c. (039)*	*0.99*	*0.39*	***		***		***	
Falls (1)	**7.28**	**1.12**	**9.09**	**2.01**	**8.14**	**2.01**	**4.59**	**1.84**
Fall to Lower Level (11)	5.00	0.97	4.88	1.45	5.68	1.83	4.59	1.84
Fall to Lower Level n.e.c. (119)*	*4.67*	*0.94*	*3.86*	*1.28*	*5.68*	*1.83*	*4.59*	*1.84*
Fall on Same Level (13)	1.64	0.49	4.20	1.41	***		***	
Fall to Floor/Walkway/Ground (131)	*1.64*	*0.49*	*4.20*	*1.41*	***		***	
Transportation Events (4)	**3.69**	**0.75**	***		**6.21**	**1.58**	***	
Non-highway Events (42)	2.93	0.65	***		5.36	1.47	***	
Overturn (4233)	*0.93*	*0.35*	***		***		***	
Assaults and Violent Acts (6)	**1.76**	**0.53**	***		***		***	
Assault by Animal (63)	1.76	0.53	***		***		***	
Assault by Animal n.e.c. (639)*	*1.76*	*0.53*	***		***		***	
Other and Unknown Events**	**3.81**		**4.03**		**3.39**		**4.40**	
Total	**23.98**	**2.24**	**21.96**	**3.75**	**31.22**	**3.79**	**18.32**	**3.42**

† Categories based on the Bureau of Labor Statistics Occupational Injury and Illness Coding Structure (OIICS). OIICS codes are provided in parentheses.

* "n.e.c." is an abbreviation for "not elsewhere classified."

** Other and Unknown Events includes "Bodily Reaction/Exertion," "Exposure to Substances/Environments," "Fires and Explosions," "Other Events," and "Unknown Events."

*** Estimate is not reportable or is suppressed because of a non-reportable cell.

Table 4.80 National estimates of **injury rates for household youth** less than 20 years of age on Native American farms by work status and type of injury event, 2000

Type of Injury Event [†]	Total		Working		Non-Working	
	Rate/1000	se	Rate/1000	se	Rate/1000	se
Contact With Objects (0)	**7.44**	**1.17**	**7.29**	**1.52**	**3.27**	**0.77**
Struck Against Object (01)	3.33	0.71	3.96	1.00	1.07	0.42
Against Stationary Object (012)	*3.01*	*0.67*	***		***	
Struck by Object (02)	2.71	0.67	2.16	0.71	1.48	0.53
Struck by Slipping Handheld Object (0232)	*0.96*	*0.37*	***		***	
Caught in Objects (03)	0.99	0.39	***		***	
*Caught in Objects n.e.c. * (039)*	*0.99*	*0.39*	***		***	
Falls (1)	**7.28**	**1.12**	**4.64**	**1.21**	**4.62**	**0.82**
Fall to Lower Level (11)	5.00	0.97	***		***	
*Fall to Lower Level n.e.c. * (119)*	*4.67*	*0.94*	*3.36*	*1.04*	*2.75*	*0.65*
Fall on Same Level (13)	1.64	0.49	***		***	
Fall to Floor/Walkway/Ground (131)	*1.64*	*0.49*	***		***	
Transportation Events (4)	**3.69**	**0.75**	**2.37**	**0.81**	**2.33**	**0.58**
Non-highway Events (42)	2.93	0.65	2.37	0.81	1.57	0.46
Overturn (4233)	*0.93*	*0.35*	***		***	
Assaults and Violent Acts (6)	**1.76**	**0.53**	***		***	
Assault by Animal (63)	1.76	0.53	***		***	
*Assault by Animal n.e.c. * (639)*	*1.76*	*0.53*	***		***	
Other and Unknown Events**	3.81		2.68		2.28	
Total	23.98	2.24	17.74	2.59	13.83	1.57

† Categories based on the Bureau of Labor Statistics Occupational Injury and Illness Coding Structure (OIICS). OIICS codes are provided in parentheses.

* "n.e.c." is an abbreviation for "not elsewhere classified."

** Other and Unknown Events includes "Bodily Reaction/Exertion," "Exposure to Substances/Environments," "Fires and Explosions," "Other Events," and "Unknown Events."

*** Estimate is not reportable or is suppressed because of a non-reportable cell.

Table 4.81 National estimates of **asthma among household youth** less than 20 years of age on Native American farms by sex, 2000

Sex	Asthma Estimate	se	No Asthma Estimate	se	Unknown Estimate
Male	399	24	3,307	72	12
Female	261	20	3,262	72	5
Unknown	0		4		131
Total [†]	660	33	6,573	114	148

† Estimates may not add to the total because of rounding.

Table 4.82 National estimates of **asthma among household youth** less than 20 years of age on Native American farms by age, 2000

Age	Asthma Estimate	se	No Asthma Estimate	se	Unknown Estimate
< 10 years	**167**	**17**	**2,185**	**62**	**3**
10-15 years	**307**	**20**	**2,488**	**63**	**5**
10-11 years	81	9	729	29	2
12-13 years	108	11	790	30	0
14-15 years	119	12	968	34	2
16-19 years	**186**	**15**	**1,876**	**50**	**7**
16-17 years	84	10	998	35	2
18-19 years	102	11	878	32	5
Unknown	**0**		**25**		**133**
Total [†]	660	33	6,573	114	148

† Estimates may not add to the total because of rounding.

Table 4.83 National estimates of **asthma among household youth** less than 20 years of age on Native American farms by sex and age, 2000

Age	Total [†] Estimate	se	Male Estimate	se	Female Estimate	se
< 10 years	**167**	**17**	**97**	**11**	**69**	**12**
10-15 years	**307**	**20**	**186**	**15**	**122**	**12**
10-11 years	81	9	51	8	30	6
12-13 years	108	11	67	9	41	7
14-15 years	119	12	68	9	51	8
16-19 years	**186**	**15**	**116**	**12**	**70**	**9**
16-17 years	84	10	53	8	31	6
18-19 years	102	11	63	9	39	7
Total [†]	660	33	399	24	261	20

† Estimates may not add to the total because of rounding.

Table 4.84 National estimates of **asthma among household youth** less than 20 years of age on Native American farms by sex and type of farm, 2000

Type of Farm	Total † Estimate	se	Male Estimate	se	Female Estimate	se
All crop	**143**	**16**	**84**	**11**	**60**	**12**
Grain and oil seed	77	12	38	7	39	10
Vegetable and melon	14	7	***		***	
Fruit, nut, and berry	23	5	14	4	9	3
All other crop*	29		***		***	
All livestock	**498**	**29**	**299**	**21**	**199**	**16**
Beef	383	26	238	19	146	14
Dairy	18	6	8	4	9	5
Hog	16	4	***		***	
Sheep and goat	11	3	***		***	
Equine	51	8	25	6	26	6
Poultry and egg	9	3	***		***	
All other livestock**	10		***		***	
Unknown	**19**		**17**		**2**	
Total †	**660**	**33**	**399**	**24**	**261**	**20**

† Estimates may not add to the total because of rounding.
* All other crop includes "Tobacco," "Cotton," "Nursery and floriculture," and "Other crop" farms.
** All other livestock includes "Aquaculture" and "Other livestock" farms.
*** Estimate is not reportable or is suppressed because of a non-reportable cell.

Table 4.85 National estimates of **asthma among household youth** less than 20 years of age on Native American farms by age and type of farm, 2000

Type of Farm	Total † Estimate	se	<10 years Estimate	se	10-15 years Estimate	se	16-19 years Estimate	se
All crop	**143**	**16**	**40**	**10**	**47**	**8**	**57**	**8**
Grain and oil seed	77	12	27	8	26	5	24	6
Vegetable and melon	14	7	***		***		***	
Fruit, nut, and berry	23	5	***		***		14	4
All other crop*	29		***		***		***	
All livestock	**498**	**29**	**124**	**15**	**248**	**18**	**127**	**13**
Beef	383	26	109	13	183	16	92	11
Dairy	18	6	***		11	4	***	
Hog	16	4	***		11	4	***	
Sheep and goat	11	3	***		***		***	
Equine	51	8	8	3	33	6	10	4
Poultry and egg	9	3	***		7	3	***	
All other livestock**	10		***		***		***	
Unknown	**19**		**3**		**13**		**2**	
Total †	**660**	**33**	**167**	**17**	**307**	**20**	**186**	**15**

† Estimates may not add to the total because of rounding.
* All other crop includes "Tobacco," "Cotton," "Nursery and floriculture," and "Other crop" farms.
** All other livestock includes "Aquaculture" and "Other livestock" farms.
*** Estimate is not reportable or is suppressed because of a non-reportable cell.

Table 4.86 National estimates of **asthmatic household youth** less than 20 years of age with 1 or more **asthma attacks while doing farm work** by sex on Native American farms, 2000

Sex	Total [†] Estimate	se	Attack at Work Estimate	se	No Attack at Work Estimate	se	Unknown Estimate
Male	399	24	137	13	151	16	111
Female	261	20	115	14	81	11	65
Total [†]	660	33	252	20	232	22	177

† Estimates may not add to the total because of rounding.

Table 4.87 National estimates of **asthmatic household youth** less than 20 years of age with 1 or more **asthma attacks while doing farm work** by age on Native American farms, 2000

Age	Total [†] Estimate	se	Attack at Work Estimate	se	No Attack at Work Estimate	se	Unknown Estimate
< 10 years	**167**	**17**	**71**	**13**	**44**	**8**	**52**
10-15 years	**307**	**20**	**98**	**11**	**100**	**12**	**110**
10-11 years	81	9	23	5	24	5	34
12-13 years	108	11	28	5	38	7	41
14-15 years	119	12	46	7	37	7	36
16-19 years	**186**	**15**	**84**	**10**	**88**	**11**	**15**
16-17 years	84	10	35	6	37	7	12
18-19 years	102	11	49	7	51	8	0
Total [†]	**660**	**33**	**252**	**20**	**232**	**22**	**177**

† Estimates may not add to the total because of rounding.

Table 4.88 National estimates of **asthmatic household youth** less than 20 years of age with 1 or more **asthma attacks while doing farm work** by type of farm on Native American farms, 2000

Type of Farm	Total [†] Estimate	se	Attack at Work Estimate	se	No Attack at Work Estimate	se	Unknown Estimate
All crop	**143**	**16**	**72**	**12**	**40**	**9**	**31**
Grain and oil seed	77	12	34	9	20	6	24
Vegetable and melon	14	7	***		***		0
Fruit, nut, and berry	23	5	***		***		3
All other crop*	29		15		9		6
All livestock	**498**	**29**	**175**	**16**	**192**	**20**	**132**
Beef	383	26	123	14	159	19	102
Dairy	18	6	***		***		9
Hog	16	4	***		***		7
Sheep and goat	11	3	***		***		0
Equine	51	8	28	6	12	3	11
Poultry and egg	9	3	***		***		3
All other livestock**	10		***		***		0
Unknown	**19**		**5**		**0**		**13**
Total [†]	**660**	**33**	**252**	**20**	**232**	**22**	**177**

† Estimates may not add to the total because of rounding.
* All other crop includes "Tobacco," "Cotton," "Nursery and floriculture," and "Other crop" farms.
** All other livestock includes "Aquaculture" and "Other livestock" farms.
*** Estimate is not reportable or is suppressed because of a non-reportable cell.

Table 4.89 National estimates of **asthmatic household youth** less than 20 years of age with 1 or more **asthma attacks requiring professional medical attention** by sex on Native American farms, 2000

Sex	Total [†] Estimate	se	Medical Attention Estimate	se	No Medical Attention Estimate	se
Male	399	24	100	11	300	21
Female	261	20	41	7	220	19
Total [†]	660	33	140	14	520	29

† Estimates may not add to the total because of rounding.

Table 4.90 National estimates of **asthmatic household youth** less than 20 years of age with 1 or more **asthma attacks requiring professional medical attention** by age on Native American farms, 2000

Age	Total [†] Estimate	se	Medical Attention Estimate	se	No Medical Attention Estimate	se
< 10 years	**167**	**17**	**51**	**8**	**116**	**14**
10-15 years	**307**	**20**	**66**	**9**	**241**	**18**
10-11 years	81	9	16	4	65	9
12-13 years	108	11	31	6	77	10
14-15 years	119	12	20	5	99	11
16-19 years	**186**	**15**	**23**	**5**	**163**	**14**
16-17 years	84	10	10	4	73	9
18-19 years	102	11	21	5	89	10
Total [†]	**660**	**33**	**140**	**14**	**520**	**29**

† Estimates may not add to the total because of rounding.

Table 4.91 National estimates of **asthmatic household youth** less than 20 years of age with 1 or more **asthma attacks requiring professional medical attention** by type of farm on Native American farms, 2000

Type of Farm	Total [†] Estimate	se	Medical Attention Estimate	se	No Medical Attention Estimate	se
All crop	**143**	**16**	**22**	**5**	**121**	**15**
Grain and oil seed	77	12	10	3	67	12
Vegetable and melon	14	7	***		***	
Fruit, nut, and berry	23	5	7	3	16	4
All other crop*	29		***		***	
All livestock	**498**	**29**	**115**	**13**	**383**	**25**
Beef	383	26	100	12	284	22
Dairy	18	6	***		***	
Hog	16	4	***		***	
Sheep and goat	11	3	***		***	
Equine	51	8	***		***	
Poultry and egg	9	3	***		***	
All other livestock**	10		***		***	
Unknown	**19**		**3**		**16**	
Total [†]	**660**	**33**	**140**	**14**	**520**	**29**

† Estimates may not add to the total because of rounding.
* All other crop includes "Tobacco," "Cotton," "Nursery and floriculture," and "Other crop" farms.
** All other livestock includes "Aquaculture" and "Other livestock" farms.
*** Estimate is not reportable or is suppressed because of a non-reportable cell.

Table 4.92 National estimates of **asthma prevalence rates for household youth** less than 20 years of age on Native American farms by sex and age, 2000

Age	Total Rate/1000	se	Male Rate/1000	se	Female Rate/1000	se
<10 years	**70.84**	**7.40**	**82.47**	**10.07**	**59.06**	**10.45**
10-15 years	**109.79**	**7.60**	**129.62**	**11.14**	**89.06**	**9.29**
10-11 years	99.45	12.19	117.66	18.42	78.88	15.81
12-13 years	119.86	13.40	158.04	22.78	85.79	15.37
14-15 years	109.22	11.34	117.89	16.31	99.67	15.82
16-19 years	**89.87**	**7.61**	**105.60**	**11.60**	**72.16**	**9.53**
16-17 years	77.24	9.48	96.86	15.27	57.14	11.33
18-19 years	103.77	11.64	114.30	16.51	90.66	16.12
Total	**89.43**	**4.72**	**107.28**	**6.83**	**74.02**	**5.92**

Table 4.93 National estimates of **asthma prevalence rates for household youth** less than 20 years of age on Native American farms by sex and type of farm, 2000

Type of Farm	Total Rate/1000	se	Male Rate/1000	se	Female Rate/1000	se
All crop	**90.55**	**11.07**	**98.64**	**13.31**	**81.10**	**17.16**
Grain and oil seed	132.81	23.67	125.67	24.97	140.58	38.59
Vegetable and melon	117.94	63.95	***		***	
Fruit, nut, and berry	164.33	39.06	165.89	50.21	161.97	56.64
All other crop*	39.08		***		***	
All livestock	**91.32**	**5.55**	**108.29**	**8.10**	**74.24**	**6.24**
Beef	87.69	6.28	104.89	9.00	69.35	6.76
Dairy	144.14	54.47	154.85	74.18	135.57	76.53
Hog	198.50	64.19	***		***	
Sheep and goat	77.79	25.51	***		***	
Equine	104.73	18.18	120.35	30.78	94.01	21.58
Poultry and egg	76.79	27.85	***		***	
All other livestock**	75.41		***		***	
Total	**89.43**	**4.72**	**107.28**	**6.83**	**74.02**	**5.92**

* All other crop includes "Tobacco," "Cotton," "Nursery and floriculture," and "Other crop" farms.

** All other livestock includes "Aquaculture" and "Other livestock" farms.

*** Estimate is not reportable or is suppressed because of a non-reportable cell.

Table 4.94 National estimates of **asthma prevalence rates for household youth** less than 20 years of age on Native American farms by age and type of farm, 2000

Type of Farm	Total Rate/1000	se	<10 years Rate/1000	se	10-15 years Rate/1000	se	16-19 years Rate/1000	se
All crop	**90.55**	**11.07**	**84.34**	**21.55**	**78.56**	**13.43**	**110.81**	**17.30**
Grain and oil seed	132.81	23.67	146.57	49.32	120.26	25.76	134.08	34.46
Vegetable and melon	117.94	63.95	***		***		***	
Fruit, nut, and berry	164.33	39.06	***		***		261.60	79.35
All other crop*	39.08		***		***		***	
All livestock	**91.32**	**5.55**	**67.88**	**8.23**	**117.45**	**9.15**	**84.73**	**8.75**
Beef	87.69	6.28	73.79	9.09	106.04	9.69	79.60	9.63
Dairy	144.14	54.47	***		233.61	102.68	***	
Hog	198.50	64.19	***		***		***	
Sheep and goat	77.79	25.51	***		***		***	
Equine	104.73	18.18	48.77	19.89	186.79	39.80	68.94	25.62
Poultry and egg	76.79	27.85	***		147.12	64.17	***	
All other livestock**	75.41		***		***		***	
Total	**89.43**	**4.72**	**70.84**	**7.40**	**109.79**	**7.60**	**89.87**	**7.61**

* All other crop includes "Tobacco," "Cotton," "Nursery and floriculture," and "Other crop" farms.
** All other livestock includes "Aquaculture" and "Other livestock" farms.
*** Estimate is not reportable or is suppressed because of a non-reportable cell.

Table 4.95 National estimates of **asthma prevalence rates for household youth** less than 20 years of age with 1 or more **asthma attacks while doing farm work** by sex on Native American farms, 2000

Sex	Total Rate/1000	se
Male	56.04	5.67
Female	64.84	8.24
Total	59.68	5.00

Table 4.96 National estimates of **asthma prevalence rates for household youth** less than 20 years of age with 1 or more **asthma attacks while doing farm work** by age on Native American farms, 2000

Age	Total Rate/1000	se
<10 years	**101.64**	**18.88**
10-15 years	**48.75**	**5.42**
10-11 years	43.45	9.15
12-13 years	43.30	8.46
14-15 years	56.50	9.27
16-19 years	**55.51**	**6.65**
16-17 years	43.66	7.96
18-19 years	68.93	10.80
Total	**59.68**	**5.00**

Table 4.97 National estimates of **asthma prevalence rates for household youth** less than 20 years of age with 1 or more **asthma attacks while doing farm work** by type of farm on Native American farms, 2000

Type of Farm	Total Rate/1000	se
All crop	**85.65**	**15.41**
Grain and oil seed	114.14	32.91
Fruit, nut, and berry	174.88	52.82
All other crop*	52.07	
All livestock	**52.79**	**5.04**
Beef	46.23	5.44
Sheep and goat	106.83	35.21
Equine	100.82	24.09
All other livestock**	46.50	
Total	**59.68**	**5.00**

* All other crop includes "Tobacco," "Cotton," "Vegetable and melon," "Nursery and floriculture," and "Other crop" farms.

** All other livestock includes "Dairy," "Hog," "Poultry and egg," "Aquaculture," and "Other livestock" farms.

Table 4.98 National estimates of **asthma prevalence rates for household youth** less than 20 years of age with 1 or more **asthma attacks requiring professional medical attention** by sex on Native American farms, 2000

Sex	Total Rate/1000	se
Male	26.76	2.96
Female	11.59	1.92
Total	19.02	1.87

Table 4.99 National estimates of **asthma prevalence rates for household youth** less than 20 years of age with 1 or more **asthma attacks requiring professional medical attention** by age on Native American farms, 2000

Age	Total Rate/1000	se
<10 years	**21.49**	**3.45**
10-15 years	**23.72**	**3.23**
10-11 years	19.57	4.50
12-13 years	34.09	6.68
14-15 years	18.27	4.45
16-19 years	**11.31**	**2.63**
16-17 years	9.50	3.24
18-19 years	21.22	5.23
Total	**19.02**	**1.87**

Table 4.100 National estimates of **asthma prevalence rates for household youth** less than 20 years of age with 1 or more **asthma attacks requiring professional medical attention** by type of farm on Native American farms, 2000

Type of Farm	Total Rate/1000	se
All crop	**14.09**	**3.22**
Fruit, nut, and berry	49.16	19.19
All other crop*	10.62	
All livestock	**21.07**	**2.33**
Beef	22.84	2.73
All other livestock**	13.93	
Total	**19.02**	**1.87**

* All other crop includes "Grain and oil seed," "Tobacco," "Cotton," "Vegetable and melon," "Nursery and floriculture," and "Other crop" farms.
** All other livestock includes "Dairy," "Hog," "Sheep and goat," "Equine," "Poultry and egg," "Aquaculture," and "Other livestock" farms.

Section V: National Demographic, Injury, and Asthma Estimates for Youth Less Than 20 Years of Age on Asian Farm Operations

Table 5.1 National estimates of Asian farms from the 1997 Census of Agriculture by business status, 2000

Status	Total [†] Estimate	se
In business	7,547	38
Out of business	1,184	38
Total [†]	8,731	

[†] Estimates may not add to the total because of rounding.

Table 5.2 National estimates of **all youth** less than 20 years of age on Asian farms by relationship to the farm and type of farm, 2000

Type of Farm	Total [†] Estimate	se	Household Youth Estimate	se	Hired Youth Estimate	se	Visiting Youth Estimate	se	Relatives Estimate	se	Non-Relatives Estimate	se
All crop	**32,921**	**2,592**	**4,500**	**112**	**2,011**	**10**	**26,409**	**2,533**	**11,697**	**388**	**14,712**	**2,455**
Grain and oil seed	2,142	356	192	29	34	53	1,915	340	1,097	180	819	193
Vegetable and melon	6,754	504	1,159	68	323	433	5,273	477	2,548	199	2,725	335
Fruit, nut, and berry	11,941	1,050	1,615	64	1,060	33	9,256	939	4,646	224	4,619	889
Nursery and floriculture	7,751	2,258	864	55	222	33	6,665	2,253	***		***	
All other crop*	4,333		669		372		3,300		***		***	
All livestock	**12,998**	**1,417**	**880**	**63**	**100**	**23**	**12,018**	**1,397**	**4,371**	**333**	**7,648**	**1,261**
Beef	5,948	796	375	38	49	17	5,523	785	2,249	213	3,274	650
Hog	667	203	66	16	***		601	191	***		***	
Sheep and goat	691	152	69	14	***		615	114	333	79	283	95
Equine	1,435	584	***		***		***		***		***	
Poultry and egg	2,412	884	221	37	***		***		***		***	
All other livestock**	1,846		***		***		***		***		***	
Unknown	**546**		**319**		**0**		**226**		**168**		**59**	
Total [†]	**46,465**	**2,919**	**5,700**	**127**	**2,111**	**494**	**38,653**	**2,865**	**16,236**	**492**	**22,418**	**2,752**

[†] Estimates may not add to the total because of rounding.
* All other crop includes "Tobacco," "Cotton," and "Other crop" farms.
** All other livestock includes "Dairy," "Aquaculture," and "Other livestock" farms.
*** Estimate is not reportable or is suppressed because of a non-reportable cell.

Table 5.3 National estimates of **all working youth** less than 20 years of age on Asian farms by relationship to the farm and type of farm, 2000

Type of Farm	Total [†]		Working Household Youth		Non-Household Working Youth		Hired Youth		Working Relatives	
	Estimate	se	Estimate	se	Estimate	se	Estimate	se	Estimate	se
All crop	**4,266**	**502**	**1,272**	**56**	**2,994**	**498**	**2,011**	**494**	**982**	**89**
Grain and oil seed	142	31	67	18	75	22	***		***	
Vegetable and melon	930	90	343	31	587	18	323	53	264	54
Fruit, nut, and berry	1,866	439	455	30	1,411	436	1,060	433	352	45
Nursery and floriculture	555	53	190	25	365	43	222	33	143	26
All other crop*	773		217		556		***		***	
All livestock	**975**	**81**	**368**	**38**	**607**	**68**	**100**	**23**	**507**	**63**
Beef	567	64	174	25	393	55	49	17	344	52
Hog	14	4	***		***		***		***	
Sheep and goat	61	19	***		***		***		***	
Equine	97	29	***		***		***		***	
Poultry and egg	139	30	***		***		***		***	
All other livestock**	97		***		***		***		***	
Unknown	**75**		**15**		**60**		**0**		**60**	
Total [†]	**5,315**	**508**	**1,655**	**67**	**3,660**	**502**	**2,111**	**494**	**1,549**	**115**

† Estimates may not add to the total because of rounding.

* All other crop includes "Tobacco," "Cotton," and "Other crop" farms.

** All other livestock includes "Dairy," "Aquaculture," and "Other livestock" farms.

*** Estimate is not reportable or is suppressed because of a non-reportable cell.

Table 5.4 National estimates of **household youth** less than 20 years of age on Asian farms by sex and age, 2000

Age	Total † Estimate	se	Male Estimate	se	Female Estimate	se	Unknown Estimate
<10 years	**1,960**	**68**	**981**	**42**	**980**	**43**	**0**
10-15 years	**2,078**	**65**	**1,172**	**44**	**906**	**39**	**0**
10-11 years	656	30	401	23	256	19	0
12-13 years	751	33	422	25	329	22	0
14-15 years	671	30	350	22	321	21	0
16-19 years	**1,354**	**49**	**767**	**35**	**587**	**29**	**0**
16-17 years	818	35	430	25	388	23	0
18-19 years	536	28	337	22	199	17	0
Unknown	**308**		**16**		**12**		**280**
Total †	**5,700**	**127**	**2,935**	**77**	**2,485**	**71**	**280**

† Estimates may not add to the total because of rounding.

Table 5.5 National estimates of **household youth** less than 20 years of age on Asian farms by sex and type of farm, 2000

Type of Farm	Total † Estimate	se	Male Estimate	se	Female Estimate	se	Unknown Estimate
All crop	**4,500**	**112**	**2,384**	**69**	**2,056**	**64**	**59**
Grain and oil seed	192	29	103	17	89	17	0
Vegetable and melon	1,159	68	613	39	505	34	41
Fruit, nut, and berry	1,615	64	871	39	732	37	13
Nursery and floriculture	864	55	453	35	406	30	5
All other crop*	669		344		325		0
All livestock	**880**	**63**	**496**	**39**	**384**	**33**	**0**
Beef	375	38	210	24	165	21	0
Hog	66	16	28	7	37	11	0
Sheep and goat	69	14	37	8	32	10	0
Poultry and egg	221	37	118	20	103	19	0
All other livestock**	150		103		47		0
Unknown	**319**		**55**		**44**		**220**
Total †	**5,700**	**127**	**2,935**	**77**	**2,485**	**71**	**280**

† Estimates may not add to the total because of rounding.
* All other crop includes "Tobacco," "Cotton," and "Other crop" farms.
** All other livestock includes "Dairy," "Equine," "Aquaculture," and "Other livestock" farms.

Table 5.6   National estimates of **household youth** less than 20 years of age on Asian farms by age and type of farm, 2000

Type of Farm	Total [†] Estimate	se	<10 years Estimate	se	10-15 years Estimate	se	16-19 years Estimate	se	Unknown Estimate
All crop	**4,500**	**112**	**1,603**	**60**	**1,711**	**58**	**1,119**	**42**	**68**
Grain and oil seed	192	29	71	14	84	18	38	9	0
Vegetable and melon	1,159	68	395	33	423	32	296	23	44
Fruit, nut, and berry	1,615	64	520	33	598	33	478	27	19
Nursery and floriculture	864	55	342	30	350	28	167	19	5
All other crop*	669		274		256		140		0
All livestock	**880**	**63**	**321**	**32**	**320**	**30**	**225**	**25**	**14**
Beef	375	38	97	14	161	20	106	19	10
Hog	66	16	35	10	15	5	16	5	0
Sheep and goat	69	14	18	6	31	8	20	8	0
Poultry and egg	221	37	83	16	76	18	59	13	4
All other livestock**	150		89		37		25		0
Unknown	**319**		**36**		**47**		**10**		**226**
Total [†]	**5,700**	**127**	**1,960**	**68**	**2,078**	**65**	**1,354**	**49**	**308**

† Estimates may not add to the total because of rounding.
* All other crop includes "Tobacco," "Cotton," and "Other crop" farms.
** All other livestock includes "Dairy," "Equine," "Aquaculture," and "Other livestock" farms.

Table 5.7   National estimates of **household youth** less than 20 years of age on Asian farms by age, sex, and type of farm, 2000

	<10 years					
Type of Farm	Total [†] Estimate	se	Male Estimate	se	Female Estimate	se
All crop	**1,603**	**60**	**779**	**37**	**823**	**39**
Grain and oil seed	71	14	33	9	38	9
Vegetable and melon	395	33	199	20	196	20
Fruit, nut, and berry	520	33	248	19	273	22
Nursery and floriculture	342	30	164	19	178	18
All other crop*	274		135		139	
All livestock	**321**	**32**	**186**	**20**	**135**	**18**
Beef	97	14	56	9	41	8
Hog	35	10	***		***	
Sheep and goat	18	6	***		***	
Poultry and egg	83	16	37	9	45	12
All other livestock**	89		66		23	
Unknown	**36**		**15**		**21**	
Total [†]	**1,960**	**68**	**981**	**42**	**980**	**43**

Continued

196

Table 5.7 National estimates of **household youth** less than 20 years of age on Asian farms by age, sex, and type of farm, 2000 (Continued)

	10-15 years					
	Total †		Male		Female	
Type of Farm	Estimate	se	Estimate	se	Estimate	se
All crop	**1,711**	**58**	**978**	**40**	**733**	**34**
Grain and oil seed	84	18	49	10	35	12
Vegetable and melon	423	32	241	21	182	17
Fruit, nut, and berry	598	33	366	23	232	18
Nursery and floriculture	350	28	183	18	167	16
All other crop*	256		138		118	
All livestock	**320**	**30**	**165**	**19**	**154**	**19**
Beef	161	20	85	12	76	13
Hog	15	5	***		***	
Sheep and goat	31	8	***		***	
Poultry and egg	76	18	37	11	38	10
All other livestock**	37		20		18	
Unknown	**47**		**29**		**18**	
Total †	**2,078**	**65**	**1,172**	**44**	**906**	**39**

	16-19 years					
	Total †		Male		Female	
Type of Farm	Estimate	se	Estimate	se	Estimate	se
All crop	**1,119**	**42**	**625**	**30**	**493**	**26**
Grain and oil seed	38	9	21	6	17	6
Vegetable and melon	296	23	170	16	127	14
Fruit, nut, and berry	478	27	257	18	221	17
Nursery and floriculture	167	19	106	15	61	9
All other crop*	140		71		68	
All livestock	**225**	**25**	**134**	**18**	**91**	**14**
Beef	106	19	61	13	45	10
Hog	16	5	***		***	
Sheep and goat	20	8	***		***	
Poultry and egg	59	13	39	9	19	6
All other livestock**	24		18		6	
Unknown	**10**		**8**		**3**	
Total †	**1,354**	**49**	**767**	**35**	**587**	**29**

† Estimates may not add to the total because of rounding.
* All other crop includes "Tobacco," "Cotton," and "Other crop" farms.
** All other livestock includes "Dairy," "Equine," "Aquaculture," and "Other livestock" farms.
*** Estimate is not reportable or is suppressed because of a non-reportable cell.

Table 5.8   National estimates of **household youth** less than 20 years of age on Asian farms by work status and sex, 2000

Sex	Total †		Working		Non-Working		Unknown
	Estimate	se	Estimate	se	Estimate	se	Estimate
Male	2,935	77	1,038	47	1,892	61	5
Female	2,485	71	616	36	1,863	61	5
Unknown	280		0		30		250
Total †	5,700	127	1,655	67	3,785	100	260

† Estimates may not add to the total because of rounding.

Table 5.9   National estimates of **household youth** less than 20 years of age on Asian farms by work status and age, 2000

Age	Total †		Working		Non-Working		Unknown
	Estimate	se	Estimate	se	Estimate	se	Estimate
<10 years	**1,960**	**68**	**205**	**20**	**1,752**	**64**	**3**
10-15 years	**2,078**	**65**	**769**	**40**	**1,306**	**50**	**3**
10-11 years	656	30	181	16	473	26	3
12-13 years	751	33	278	22	473	26	0
14-15 years	671	30	311	21	360	22	0
16-19 years	**1,354**	**49**	**674**	**35**	**678**	**33**	**3**
16-17 years	818	35	403	26	413	23	3
18-19 years	536	28	270	20	265	21	0
Unknown	**308**		**7**		**49**		**252**
Total †	5,700	127	1,655	67	3,785	100	260

† Estimates may not add to the total because of rounding.

Table 5.10   National estimates of **household youth** less than 20 years of age on Asian farms by age, work status, and sex, 2000

	<10 years						
	Total [†]		Working		Non-Working		Unknown
Sex	Estimate	se	Estimate	se	Estimate	se	Estimate
Male	981	42	117	13	861	39	3
Female	980	43	88	12	891	41	0
Total [†]	1,960	68	205	20	1,752	64	3

	10-15 years						
	Total [†]		Working		Non-Working		Unknown
Sex	Estimate	se	Estimate	se	Estimate	se	Estimate
Male	1,172	44	474	28	698	34	0
Female	906	39	296	24	608	30	3
Total [†]	2,078	65	769	40	1,306	50	3

	16-19 years						
	Total [†]		Working		Non-Working		Unknown
Sex	Estimate	se	Estimate	se	Estimate	se	Estimate
Male	767	35	444	28	323	21	0
Female	587	29	229	18	355	23	3
Total [†]	1,354	49	674	35	678	33	3

† Estimates may not add to the total because of rounding.

Table 5.11   National estimates of **household youth** less than 20 years of age on Asian farms by whether they rode a horse and sex, 2000

	Total [†]		Rode a Horse: Yes		Rode a Horse: No		Unknown
Sex	Estimate	se	Estimate	se	Estimate	se	Estimate
Male	2,935	77	209	20	2,717	75	10
Female	2,485	71	196	22	2,284	68	5
Unknown	280		0		30		250
Total [†]	5,700	127	405	36	5,030	120	265

† Estimates may not add to the total because of rounding.

Table 5.12 National estimates of **household youth** less than 20 years of age on Asian farms by whether they rode a horse and age, 2000

Age	Total[†] Estimate	se	Rode a Horse: Yes Estimate	se	Rode a Horse: No Estimate	se	Unknown Estimate
<10 years	**1,960**	**68**	**146**	**20**	**1,807**	**65**	**8**
10-15 years	**2,078**	**65**	**167**	**20**	**1,908**	**63**	**3**
10-11 years	656	30	58	11	595	28	3
12-13 years	751	33	59	10	692	32	0
14-15 years	671	30	50	9	620	29	0
16-19 years	**1,354**	**49**	**88**	**11**	**1,263**	**47**	**3**
16-17 years	818	35	62	9	754	34	3
18-19 years	536	28	26	6	509	28	0
Unknown	**308**		**3**		**52**		**252**
Total[†]	**5,700**	**127**	**405**	**36**	**5,030**	**120**	**265**

† Estimates may not add to the total because of rounding.

Table 5.13 National estimates of **household youth** less than 20 years of age on Asian farms by age, whether they rode a horse, and sex, 2000

	<10 years						
Sex	Total[†] Estimate	se	Rode a Horse: Yes Estimate	se	Rode a Horse: No Estimate	se	Unknown Estimate
Male	981	42	70	11	903	40	8
Female	980	43	75	13	904	41	0
Total[†]	1,960	68	146	20	1,807	65	8

	10-15 years						
Sex	Total[†] Estimate	se	Rode a Horse: Yes Estimate	se	Rode a Horse: No Estimate	se	Unknown Estimate
Male	1,172	44	91	13	1,081	43	0
Female	906	39	76	13	827	37	3
Total[†]	2,078	65	167	20	1,908	63	3

	16-19 years						
Sex	Total[†] Estimate	se	Rode a Horse: Yes Estimate	se	Rode a Horse: No Estimate	se	Unknown Estimate
Male	767	35	47	7	720	34	0
Female	587	29	42	8	543	28	3
Total[†]	1,354	49	88	11	1,263	47	3

† Estimates may not add to the total because of rounding.

200

Table 5.14   National estimates of **household youth** less than 20 years of age on Asian farms by whether they drove an all-terrain vehicle (ATV) and sex, 2000

Sex	Total [†] Estimate	se	Drove an ATV: Yes Estimate	se	Drove an ATV: No Estimate	se	Unknown Estimate
Male	2,935	77	484	35	2,143	66	309
Female	2,485	71	224	23	1,981	62	280
Unknown	280		0		0		280
Total [†]	5,700	127	708	48	4,123	106	869

† Estimates may not add to the total because of rounding.

Table 5.15   National estimates of **household youth** less than 20 years of age on Asian farms by whether they drove an all-terrain vehicle (ATV) and age, 2000

Age	Total [†] Estimate	se	Drove an ATV: Yes Estimate	se	Drove an ATV: No Estimate	se	Unknown Estimate
<10 years	**1,960**	**68**	**91**	**13**	**1,316**	**52**	**553**
10-15 years	**2,078**	**65**	**352**	**30**	**1,723**	**58**	**3**
10-11 years	656	30	98	13	556	27	3
12-13 years	751	33	130	16	621	30	0
14-15 years	671	30	124	13	547	27	0
16-19 years	**1,354**	**49**	**265**	**24**	**1,084**	**42**	**5**
16-17 years	818	35	156	17	660	31	3
18-19 years	536	28	109	15	424	25	3
Unknown	**308**		**0**		**0**		**308**
Total [†]	**5,700**	**127**	**708**	**48**	**4,123**	**106**	**869**

† Estimates may not add to the total because of rounding.

Table 5.16 National estimates of **household youth** less than 20 years of age on Asian farms by age, whether they drove an all-terrain vehicle (ATV), and sex, 2000

	<10 years						
	Total [†]		Drove an ATV: Yes		Drove an ATV: No		Unknown
Sex	Estimate	se	Estimate	se	Estimate	se	Estimate
Male	981	42	53	9	637	33	290
Female	980	43	38	8	679	34	263
Total [†]	1,960	68	91	13	1,316	52	553

	10-15 years						
	Total [†]		Drove an ATV: Yes		Drove an ATV: No		Unknown
Sex	Estimate	se	Estimate	se	Estimate	se	Estimate
Male	1,172	44	241	21	931	40	0
Female	906	39	111	16	793	35	3
Total [†]	2,078	65	352	30	1,723	58	3

	16-19 years						
	Total [†]		Drove an ATV: Yes		Drove an ATV: No		Unknown
Sex	Estimate	se	Estimate	se	Estimate	se	Estimate
Male	767	35	190	20	575	29	3
Female	587	29	75	12	509	27	3
Total [†]	1,354	49	265	24	1,084	42	5

† Estimates may not add to the total because of rounding.

Table 5.17 National estimates of **household youth** less than 20 years of age on Asian farms by whether they drove a tractor and sex, 2000

	Total [†]		Drove a Tractor: Yes		Drove a Tractor: No		Unknown
Sex	Estimate	se	Estimate	se	Estimate	se	Estimate
Male	2,935	77	474	32	2,157	65	304
Female	2,485	71	168	17	2,036	63	280
Unknown	280		0		0		280
Total [†]	5,700	127	643	40	4,194	104	864

† Estimates may not add to the total because of rounding.

Table 5.18 National estimates of **household youth** less than 20 years of age on Asian farms by whether they drove a tractor and age, 2000

Age	Total † Estimate	se	Drove a Tractor: Yes Estimate	se	Drove a Tractor: No Estimate	se	Unknown Estimate
<10 years	**1,960**	**68**	**23**	**5**	**1,386**	**53**	**551**
10-15 years	**2,078**	**65**	**260**	**22**	**1,815**	**59**	**3**
10-11 years	656	30	43	8	610	29	3
12-13 years	751	33	96	12	654	31	0
14-15 years	671	30	120	14	551	27	0
16-19 years	**1,354**	**49**	**359**	**26**	**992**	**40**	**3**
16-17 years	818	35	222	20	593	29	3
18-19 years	536	28	137	15	399	24	0
Unknown	**308**		**0**		**0**		**308**
Total †	**5,700**	**127**	**643**	**40**	**4,194**	**104**	**864**

† Estimates may not add to the total because of rounding.

Table 5.19 National estimates of **household youth** less than 20 years of age on Asian farms by age, whether they drove a tractor, and sex, 2000

	<10 years Total † Estimate	se	Drove a Tractor: Yes Estimate	se	Drove a Tractor: No Estimate	se	Unknown Estimate
Sex							
Male	981	42	***		***		288
Female	980	43	***		***		263
Total †	1,960	68	23	5	1,386	53	551

	10-15 years Total † Estimate	se	Drove a Tractor: Yes Estimate	se	Drove a Tractor: No Estimate	se	Unknown Estimate
Sex							
Male	1,172	44	***		***		0
Female	906	39	***		***		3
Total †	2,078	65	260	22	1,815	59	3

	16-19 years Total † Estimate	se	Drove a Tractor: Yes Estimate	se	Drove a Tractor: No Estimate	se	Unknown Estimate
Sex							
Male	767	35	269	22	498	27	0
Female	587	29	90	12	494	27	3
Total †	1,354	49	359	26	992	40	3

† Estimates may not add to the total because of rounding.
*** Estimate is not reportable or is suppressed because of a non-reportable cell.

Table 5.20   National estimates of **injuries to all youth** less than 20 years of age on Asian farms by relationship to the farm, 2000

Relationship to Farm	Total [†] Estimate	se
Household youth	26	6
Hired youth	***	
Visiting youth	***	
Relatives	18	6
Non-relatives	***	
Total [†]	50	9

† Estimates may not add to the total because of rounding.
*** Estimate is not reportable or is suppressed because of a non-reportable cell.

Table 5.21   National estimates of **injuries to all youth** less than 20 years of age on Asian farms by race, 2000

Race	Total [†] Estimate	se
Asian	35	7
All other races*	15	
Total [†]	50	9

† Estimates may not add to the total because of rounding.
* All other races includes "White," "Black," "Native American," and "Other races."

Table 5.22   National estimates of **injuries to all youth** less than 20 years of age on Asian farms by age, 2000

Age	Total [†] Estimate	se
<10 years	10	5
10-15 years	19	5
10-11 years	***	
12-13 years	***	
14-15 years	10	3
16-19 years	21	6
16-17 years	8	3
18-19 years	12	5
Unknown	0	
Total [†]	50	9

† Estimates may not add to the total because of rounding.
*** Estimate is not reportable or is suppressed because of a non-reportable cell.

Table 5.23   National estimates of **injuries to all youth** less than 20 years of age on Asian farms by work status and type of farm, 2000

Type of Farm	Total[†] Estimate	se	Working Estimate	se	Non-Working Estimate	se	Unknown Estimate
All crop	**38**	**8**	**13**	**5**	**23**	**6**	**3**
Vegetable and melon	15	5	***		***		0
Fruit, nut, and berry	8	3	***		***		0
All other crop*	14		***		***		0
All livestock	**12**	**5**	0		12	5	0
Total[†]	**50**	**9**	**13**	**5**	**35**	**7**	**3**

† Estimates may not add to the total because of rounding.
* All other crop includes "Grain and oil seed," "Tobacco," "Cotton," "Nursery and floriculture," and "Other crop" farms.
*** Estimate is not reportable or is suppressed because of a non-reportable cell.

Table 5.24   National estimates of **injuries to all youth** less than 20 years of age on Asian farms by work status and type of injury, 2000

Type of Injury	Total[†] Estimate	se	Working Estimate	se	Non-Working Estimate	se	Unknown Estimate
Broken bone, fracture	12	4	0		12	4	0
Puncture, stab, jab	9	4	***		***		0
All other injuries*	30		***		***		3
Total[†]	**50**	**9**	**13**	**5**	**35**	**7**	**3**

† Estimates may not add to the total because of rounding.
* All other injuries includes "Scrape, abrasion," "Bruise, contusion," "Sprain, strain," "Dislocation," "Cut, laceration," "Traumatic rupture," "Crushed," "Amputation," "Nerve injury," "Burn, blister, scald," "Multiple injuries," and "Other injury."
*** Estimate is not reportable or is suppressed because of a non-reportable cell.

Table 5.25   National estimates of **injuries to all youth** less than 20 years of age on Asian farms by work status and body part injured, 2000

Body Part Injured	Total[†] Estimate	se	Working Estimate	se	Non-Working Estimate	se	Unknown Estimate
Face	8	3	***		***		3
Arm	9	4	0		9	4	0
Hand, wrist, fingers	16	6	***		***		0
All other body parts*	17		***		***		
Total[†]	**50**	**9**	**13**	**5**	**35**	**7**	**3**

† Estimates may not add to the total because of rounding.
* All other body parts includes "Head, skull," "Neck," "Shoulder, chest, back," "Abdomen," "Pelvic region," "Leg," "Foot, ankle, toes," "Internal injury," "Multiple body parts," and "Other body parts."
*** Estimate is not reportable or is suppressed because of a non-reportable cell.

Table 5.26   National estimates of **injuries to all youth** less than 20 years of age on Asian farms by work status and source of injury, 2000

Source of Injury ‡	Total † Estimate	se	Working Estimate	se	Non-Working Estimate	se	Unknown Estimate
Persons/Animals/Plants/Minerals (5)	14	5	0		12	5	3
Animals (51)	9	4	0		9	4	0
Dogs (5153)	*9*	*4*	*0*		*9*	*4*	*0*
Structures and Surfaces (6)	12	5	***		***		0
Floors/Walkways/Ground (62)	12	5	***		***		0
Ground (623)	*12*	*5*	***		***		*0*
Other and Unknown Sources*	24		***		***		0
Total †	50	9	13	5	35	7	3

† Estimates may not add to the total because of rounding.

‡ Categories based on the Bureau of Labor Statistics Occupational Injury and Illness Coding Structure (OIICS). OIICS codes are provided in parentheses.

* Other and Unknown Sources includes "Chemicals," "Containers," "Furniture and Fixtures," "Machinery," "Parts/Materials," "Tools/Instruments/Equipment," "Vehicles," "Other Sources," and "Unknown Sources."

*** Estimate is not reportable or is suppressed because of a non-reportable cell.

Table 5.27   National estimates of **injuries to all youth** less than 20 years of age on Asian farms by work status and type of injury event, 2000

Type of Injury Event ‡	Total † Estimate	se	Working Estimate	se	Non-Working Estimate	se	Unknown Estimate
Contact With Objects (0)	14	4	***		***		0
Struck by Object (02)	14	4	***		***		0
Struck by Falling Object (021)	*11*	*4*	***		***		*0*
Falls (1)	12	5	***		***		0
Assaults and Violent Acts (6)	9	4	0		9	4	0
Assault by Animal (63)	9	4	0		9	4	0
Nonvenomous Bites (631)	*9*	*4*	*0*		*9*	*4*	*0*
Other and Unknown Events*	15		***		***		0
Total †	50	9	13	5	35	7	3

† Estimates may not add to the total because of rounding.

‡ Categories based on the Bureau of Labor Statistics Occupational Injury and Illness Coding Structure (OIICS). OIICS codes are provided in parentheses.

* Other and Unknown Events includes "Bodily Reaction/Exertion," "Exposure to Substances/Environments," "Transportation Events," "Fires and Explosions," "Other Events," and "Unknown Events."

*** Estimate is not reportable or is suppressed because of a non-reportable cell.

Table 5.28   National estimates of **injury rates for all youth** less than 20 years of age on Asian farms by relationship to the farm, 2000

Relationship to Farm	Total Rate/1000	se
Household youth	**4.54**	**1.11**
Hired youth	***	
Visiting youth	***	
Relatives	1.12	0.35
Non-relatives	***	
Total	**1.08**	**0.21**

*** Estimate is not reportable or is suppressed because of a non-reportable cell.

Table 5.29   National estimates of **injury rates for all youth** less than 20 years of age on Asian farms by work status and type of farm, 2000

Type of Farm	Total Rate/1000	se	Working Rate/1000		Non-Working Rate/1000	se
All crop	**1.15**	**0.25**	**3.00**	**1.19**	**0.68**	**0.18**
Vegetable and melon	2.28	0.78	***		***	
Fruit, nut, and berry	0.70	0.29	***		***	
All other crop*	1.00		***		***	
All livestock	**0.95**	**0.38**	**0.00**		**0.95**	**0.38**
Total	**1.08**	**0.21**	**2.41**	**0.94**	**0.75**	**0.17**

* All other crop includes "Grain and oil seed," "Tobacco," "Cotton," "Nursery and floriculture," and "Other crop" farms.
*** Estimate is not reportable or is suppressed because of a non-reportable cell.

Table 5.30   National estimates of **injury rates for all youth** less than 20 years of age on Asian farms by work status and type of injury, 2000

Type of Injury	Total Rate/1000	se	Working Rate/1000	se	Non-Working Rate/1000	se
Broken bone, fracture	0.25	0.09	0.00		0.25	0.09
Puncture, stab, jab	0.20	0.09	***		***	
All other injuries*	0.64		***		***	
Total	1.08	0.21	2.41	0.94	0.75	0.17

* All other injuries includes "Scrape, abrasion," "Bruise, contusion," "Sprain, strain," "Dislocation," "Cut, laceration," "Traumatic rupture," "Crushed," "Amputation," "Nerve injury," "Burn, blister, scald," "Multiple injuries," and "Other injury."
*** Estimate is not reportable or is suppressed because of a non-reportable cell.

Table 5.31 National estimates of **injury rates for all youth** less than 20 years of age on Asian farms by work status and body part injured, 2000

Body Part Injured	Total Rate/1000	se	Working Rate/1000	se	Non-Working Rate/1000	se
Face	0.17	0.06	***		***	
Arm	0.20	0.09	0.00		0.20	0.09
Hand, wrist, fingers	0.35	0.12	***		***	
All other body parts*	0.37		***		***	
Total	1.08	0.21	2.41	0.94	0.75	0.17

* All other body parts includes "Head, skull," "Neck," "Shoulder, chest, back," "Abdomen," "Pelvic region," "Leg," "Foot, ankle, toes," "Internal injury," "Multiple body parts," and "Other body parts."
*** Estimate is not reportable or is suppressed because of a non-reportable cell.

Table 5.32 National estimates of **injury rates for all youth** less than 20 years of age on Asian farms by work status and source of injury, 2000

Source of Injury [†]	Total Rate/1000	se	Working Rate/1000	se	Non-Working Rate/1000	se
Persons/Animals/Plants/Minerals (5)	**0.31**	**0.10**	**0.00**		**0.26**	**0.10**
Animals (51)	0.20	0.09	0.00		0.20	0.09
Dogs (5153)	*0.20*	*0.09*	*0.00*		*0.20*	*0.09*
Structures and Surfaces (6)	**0.26**	**0.10**	***		***	
Floors/Walkways/Ground (62)	0.26	0.10	***		***	
Ground (623)	*0.26*	*0.10*	***		***	
Other and Unknown Sources*	**0.52**		***		***	
Total	**1.08**	**0.21**	**2.41**	**0.94**	**0.75**	**0.17**

† Categories based on the Bureau of Labor Statistics Occupational Injury and Illness Coding Structure (OIICS). OIICS codes are provided in parentheses.
* Other and Unknown Sources includes "Chemicals," "Containers," "Furniture and Fixtures," "Machinery," "Parts/Materials," "Tools/Instruments/Equipment," "Vehicles," "Other Sources," and "Unknown Sources."
*** Estimate is not reportable or is suppressed because of a non-reportable cell.

Table 5.33 National estimates of **injury rates for all youth** less than 20 years of age on Asian farms by work status and type of injury event, 2000

Type of Injury Event [†]	Total Rate/1000	se	Working Rate/1000	se	Non-Working Rate/1000	se
Contact With Objects (0)	**0.30**	**0.10**	***		***	
Struck by Object (02)	0.30	0.10	***		***	
Struck by Falling Object (021)	*0.23*	*0.08*	***		***	
Falls (1)	**0.26**	**0.10**	***		***	
Assaults and Violent Acts (6)	**0.20**	**0.09**	**0.00**		**0.20**	**0.09**
Assault by Animal (63)	0.20	0.09	0.00		0.20	0.09
Nonvenomous Bites (631)	*0.20*	*0.09*	*0.00*		*0.20*	*0.09*
Other and Unknown Events*	**0.32**		***		***	
Total	**1.08**	**0.21**	**2.41**	**0.94**	**0.75**	**0.17**

† Categories based on the Bureau of Labor Statistics Occupational Injury and Illness Coding Structure (OIICS). OIICS codes are provided in parentheses.

* Other and Unknown Events includes "Bodily Reaction/Exertion," "Exposure to Substances/Environments," "Transportation Events," "Fires and Explosions," "Other Events," and "Unknown Events."

*** Estimate is not reportable or is suppressed because of a non-reportable cell.

Table 5.34 National estimates of **asthma among household youth** less than 20 years of age on Asian farms by sex, 2000

Sex	Asthma Estimate	se	No Asthma Estimate	se	Unknown Estimate
Male	298	21	2,615	73	23
Female	171	16	2,309	68	5
Unknown	0		17		263
Total [†]	469	28	4,941	117	291

† Estimates may not add to the total because of rounding.

Table 5.35   National estimates of **asthma among household youth** less than 20 years of age on Asian farms by age, 2000

Age	Asthma Estimate	se	No Asthma Estimate	se	Unknown Estimate
<10 years	**139**	**15**	**1,811**	**65**	**10**
10-15 years	**211**	**17**	**1,861**	**62**	**6**
10-11 years	81	10	573	28	3
12-13 years	69	9	679	32	3
14-15 years	62	9	609	29	0
16-19 years	**115**	**13**	**1,234**	**46**	**5**
16-17 years	81	10	732	33	5
18-19 years	34	7	502	28	0
Unknown	**3**		**35**		**269**
Total [†]	**469**	**28**	**4,941**	**117**	**291**

[†] Estimates may not add to the total because of rounding.

Table 5.36   National estimates of **asthma among household youth** less than 20 years of age on Asian farms by sex and age, 2000

Age	Total [†] Estimate	se	Male Estimate	se	Female Estimate	se
<10 years	**139**	**15**	**82**	**11**	**58**	**9**
10-15 years	**211**	**17**	**148**	**14**	**63**	**9**
10-11 years	81	10	63	9	18	5
12-13 years	69	9	45	7	24	6
14-15 years	62	9	41	8	21	5
16-19 years	**115**	**13**	**68**	**10**	**47**	**8**
16-17 years	81	10	***		***	
18-19 years	34	7	***		***	
Unknown	**3**		**0**		**3**	
Total [†]	**469**	**28**	**298**	**21**	**171**	**16**

[†] Estimates may not add to the total because of rounding.
*** Estimate is not reportable or is suppressed because of a non-reportable cell.

Table 5.37 National estimates of **asthma among household youth** less than 20 years of age on Asian farms by sex and type of farm, 2000

Type of Farm	Total† Estimate	se	Male Estimate	se	Female Estimate	se
All crop	**395**	**25**	**254**	**20**	**141**	**14**
Grain and oil seed	21	7	***		***	
Vegetable and melon	63	10	32	6	32	7
Fruit, nut, and berry	141	14	90	11	51	8
Nursery and floriculture	82	12	64	11	18	5
All other crop*	88		***		***	
All livestock	**71**	**11**	**41**	**7**	**30**	**7**
Beef	41	8	19	5	22	6
Hog	13	6	***		***	
All other livestock**	17		***		***	
Unknown	**3**		**3**		**0**	
Total†	**469**	**28**	**298**	**21**	**171**	**16**

† Estimates may not add to the total because of rounding.
* All other crop includes "Tobacco," "Cotton," and "Other crop" farms.
** All other livestock includes "Dairy," "Sheep and goat," "Equine," "Poultry and egg," "Aquaculture," and "Other livestock" farms.
*** Estimate is not reportable or is suppressed because of a non-reportable cell.

Table 5.38 National estimates of **asthma among household youth** less than 20 years of age on Asian farms by age and type of farm, 2000

Type of Farm	Total† Estimate	se	<10 years Estimate	se	10-15 years Estimate	se	16-19 years Estimate	se	Estimate Unknown
All crop	**395**	**25**	**119**	**14**	**184**	**15**	**93**	**11**	**0**
Grain and oil seed	21	7	***		11	4	***		0
Vegetable and melon	63	10	8	4	36	7	19	5	0
Fruit, nut, and berry	141	14	49	8	64	9	28	6	0
Nursery and floriculture	82	12	21	5	39	7	23	6	0
All other crop*	88		***		33		***		0
All livestock	**71**	**11**	**21**	**6**	**25**	**6**	**22**	**6**	**3**
Beef	41	8	16	5	11	4	11	4	3
Hog	13	6	***		8	4	***		0
All other livestock**	17		***		6		***		0
Unknown	**3**		**0**		**3**		**0**		**0**
Total†	**469**	**28**	**139**	**15**	**211**	**17**	**115**	**13**	**3**

† Estimates may not add to the total because of rounding.
* All other crop includes "Tobacco," "Cotton," and "Other crop" farms.
** All other livestock includes "Dairy," "Sheep and goat," "Equine," "Poultry and egg," "Aquaculture," and "Other livestock" farms.
*** Estimate is not reportable or is suppressed because of a non-reportable cell.

Table 5.39 National estimates of **asthmatic household youth** less than 20 years of age with 1 or more **asthma attacks while doing farm work** by sex on Asian farms, 2000

Sex	Total [†] Estimate	se	Attack at Work Estimate	se	No Attack at Work Estimate	se	Unknown Estimate
Male	298	21	110	13	127	14	61
Female	171	16	57	9	57	9	57
Total [†]	469	28	167	17	184	17	118

† Estimates may not add to the total because of rounding.

Table 5.40 National estimates of **asthmatic household youth** less than 20 years of age with 1 or more **asthma attacks while doing farm work** by age on Asian farms, 2000

Age	Total [†] Estimate	se	Attack at Work Estimate	se	No Attack at Work Estimate	se	Unknown Estimate
<10 years	**139**	**15**	**49**	**10**	**41**	**7**	**49**
10-15 years	**211**	**17**	**70**	**10**	**91**	**11**	**50**
10-11 years	81	10	21	5	37	7	23
12-13 years	69	9	27	9	23	5	19
14-15 years	62	9	23	7	31	6	8
16-19 years	**115**	**13**	**48**	**8**	**51**	**9**	**15**
16-17 years	81	10	30	6	36	7	15
18-19 years	34	7	19	5	15	6	0
Unknown	**3**		**0**		**0**		**3**
Total [†]	**469**	**28**	**167**	**17**	**184**	**17**	**118**

† Estimates may not add to the total because of rounding.

212

Table 5.41   National estimates of **asthmatic household youth** less than 20 years of age with 1 or more **asthma attacks while doing farm work** by type of farm on Asian farms, 2000

Type of Farm	Total [†] Estimate	se	Attack at Work Estimate	se	No Attack at Work Estimate	se	Unknown Estimate
All crop	**395**	**25**	**132**	**15**	**159**	**16**	**104**
Grain and oil seed	21	7	***		***		16
Vegetable and melon	63	10	22	5	21	6	21
Fruit, nut, and berry	141	14	34	7	74	11	34
Nursery and floriculture	82	12	39	8	38	9	5
All other crop*	88		***		***		29
All livestock	**71**	**11**	**35**	**8**	**22**	**6**	**14**
Beef	41	8	14	5	16	5	11
Hog	13	6	13	6	0		0
All other livestock**	17		9		6		0
Unknown	**3**		**0**		**3**		**0**
Total [†]	**469**	**28**	**167**	**17**	**184**	**17**	**118**

† Estimates may not add to the total because of rounding.
* All other crop includes " Tobacco," "Cotton," and "Other crop" farms.
** All other livestock includes "Dairy," "Sheep and goat," "Equine," "Poultry and egg," "Aquaculture," and "Other livestock" farms.
*** Estimate is not reportable or is suppressed because of a non-reportable cell.

Table 5.42   National estimates of **asthmatic household youth** less than 20 years of age with 1 or more **asthma attacks requiring professional medical attention** by sex on Asian farms, 2000

Sex	Total [†] Estimate	se	Medical Attention Estimate	se	No Medical Attention Estimate	se
Male	298	21	34	7	264	20
Female	171	16	18	5	153	15
Total [†]	469	28	52	8	416	26

† Estimates may not add to the total because of rounding.

Table 5.43 National estimates of **asthmatic household youth** less than 20 years of age with 1 or more **asthma attacks requiring professional medical attention** by age on Asian farms, 2000

Age	Total [†] Estimate	se	Medical Attention Estimate	se	No Medical Attention Estimate	se
<10 years	**139**	**15**	***		***	
10-15 years	**211**	**17**	23	5	188	16
10-11 years	81	10	13	4	68	9
12-13 years	69	9	10	3	58	9
14-15 years	62	9	0		62	9
16-19 years	**115**	**13**	***		***	
16-17 years	81	10	***		***	
18-19 years	34	7	***		***	
Unknown	**3**		0		3	
Total [†]	**469**	**28**	**52**	**8**	**416**	**26**

† Estimates may not add to the total because of rounding.
*** Estimate is not reportable or is suppressed because of a non-reportable cell.

Table 5.44 National estimates of **asthmatic household youth** less than 20 years of age with 1 or more **asthma attacks requiring professional medical attention** by type of farm on Asian farms, 2000

Type of Farm	Total [†] Estimate	se	Medical Attention Estimate	se	No Medical Attention Estimate	se
All crop	**395**	**25**	***		***	
Grain and oil seed	21	7	***		***	
Vegetable and melon	63	10	10	4	53	9
Fruit, nut, and berry	141	14	21	5	121	14
Nursery and floriculture	82	12	8	3	75	12
All other crop*	88		***		***	
All livestock	**71**	**11**	***		***	
Beef	41	8	***		***	
Hog	13	6	***		***	
All other livestock**	17		***		***	
Unknown	**3**		0		3	
Total [†]	**469**	**28**	**52**	**8**	**416**	**26**

† Estimates may not add to the total because of rounding.
* All other crop includes "Tobacco," "Cotton," and "Other crop" farms.
** All other livestock includes "Dairy," "Sheep and goat," "Equine," "Poultry and egg," "Aquaculture," and "Other livestock" farms.
*** Estimate is not reportable or is suppressed because of a non-reportable cell.

Table 5.45   National estimates of **asthma prevalence rates for household youth** less than 20 years of age on Asian farms by sex and age, 2000

Age	Total Rate/1000	se	Male Rate/1000	se	Female Rate/1000	se
<10 years	**71.07**	**8.13**	**83.22**	**11.28**	**58.90**	**9.54**
10-15 years	**101.50**	**8.64**	**126.45**	**12.70**	**69.22**	**10.26**
10-11 years	122.98	16.27	156.27	23.24	70.41	20.61
12-13 years	91.51	12.92	105.56	18.39	73.22	17.42
14-15 years	91.67	14.61	117.20	23.22	63.86	15.51
16-19 years	**85.07**	**9.79**	**88.78**	**13.27**	**80.23**	**14.36**
16-17 years	99.23	13.28	***		***	
18-19 years	63.45	14.22	***		***	
Total	**82.23**	**5.18**	**101.52**	**7.57**	**68.74**	**6.54**

*** Estimate is not reportable or is suppressed because of a non-reportable cell.

Table 5.46   National estimates of **asthma prevalence rates for household youth** less than 20 years of age on Asian farms by sex and type of farm, 2000

Type of Farm	Total Rate/1000	se	Male Rate/1000	se	Female Rate/1000	se
All crop	**87.84**	**6.05**	**106.69**	**8.73**	**68.52**	**7.13**
Grain and oil seed	108.65	38.99	***		***	
Vegetable and melon	54.36	9.11	51.42	10.64	62.38	13.74
Fruit, nut, and berry	87.34	9.57	103.57	13.66	69.57	12.01
Nursery and floriculture	95.25	15.57	141.61	25.98	44.38	11.57
All other crop*	131.46		***		***	
All livestock	**80.41**	**13.77**	**82.46**	**16.27**	**77.78**	**18.66**
Beef	109.15	24.32	89.64	25.56	133.95	37.31
Hog	195.90	98.86	***		***	
All other livestock**	38.65		***		***	
Total	**82.23**	**5.18**	**101.52**	**7.57**	**68.74**	**6.54**

* All other crop includes "Tobacco," "Cotton," and "Other crop" farms.
** All other livestock includes "Dairy," "Sheep and goat," "Equine," "Poultry and egg," "Aquaculture," and "Other livestock" farms.
*** Estimate is not reportable or is suppressed because of a non-reportable cell.

Table 5.47   National estimates of **asthma prevalence rates for household youth** less than 20 years of age on Asian farms by age and type of farm, 2000

Type of Farm	Total Rate/1000	se	<10 years Rate/1000	se	10-15 years Rate/1000	se	16-19 years Rate/1000	se
All crop	**87.84**	**6.05**	**74.01**	**9.17**	**107.32**	**9.75**	**83.21**	**10.64**
Grain and oil seed	108.65	38.99	***		134.18	55.19	***	
Vegetable and melon	54.36	9.11	19.47	9.75	85.26	17.44	64.82	17.82
Fruit, nut, and berry	87.34	9.57	94.15	16.11	107.74	16.02	57.98	13.47
Nursery and floriculture	95.25	15.57	60.21	16.63	110.51	22.03	137.61	40.47
All other crop*	131.54		***		129.40		***	
All livestock	**80.41**	**13.77**	**64.08**	**19.44**	**77.29**	**20.94**	**98.28**	**26.91**
Beef	109.15	24.32	159.36	60.32	***		***	
Hog	195.90	98.86	***		***		***	
All other livestock**	38.65		***		41.18		***	
Total	**82.23**	**5.18**	**71.07**	**8.13**	**101.50**	**8.66**	**85.09**	**9.81**

* All other crop includes "Tobacco," "Cotton," and "Other crop" farms.
** All other livestock includes "Dairy," "Sheep and goat," "Equine," "Poultry and egg," "Aquaculture," and "Other livestock" farms.
*** Estimate is not reportable or is suppressed because of a non-reportable cell.

Table 5.48   National estimates of **asthma prevalence rates for household youth** less than 20 years of age with 1 or more **asthma attacks while doing farm work** by sex on Asian farms, 2000

Sex	Total Rate/1000	se
Male	106.03	13.59
Female	92.97	15.88
Total	101.16	11.23

Table 5.49   National estimates of **asthma prevalence rates for household youth** less than 20 years of age with 1 or more **asthma attacks while doing farm work** by age on Asian farms, 2000

Age	Total Rate/1000	se
<10 years	**238.83**	**51.69**
10-15 years	**91.11**	**14.22**
10-11 years	113.75	31.38
12-13 years	95.43	32.22
14-15 years	74.06	22.15
16-19 years	**71.71**	**12.30**
16-17 years	73.18	15.84
18-19 years	69.53	18.83
Total	**101.16**	**11.23**

Table 5.50   National estimates of **asthma prevalence rates for household youth** less than 20 years of age with 1 or more **asthma attacks while doing farm work** by type of farm on Asian farms, 2000

Type of Farm	Total Rate/1000	se
All crop	**104.11**	**12.81**
Vegetable and melon	63.59	16.80
Fruit, nut, and berry	73.64	16.36
Nursery and floriculture	203.90	50.65
All other crop*	177.12	
All livestock	**95.11**	**24.60**
Beef	77.98	30.22
All other livestock**	110.54	
Total	**101.16**	**11.23**

* All other crop includes "Grain and oil seed," "Tobacco," "Cotton," and "Other crop" farms.

** All other livestock includes "Dairy," "Hog," "Sheep and goat," "Equine," "Poultry and egg," "Aquaculture," and "Other livestock" farms.

Table 5.51   National estimates of **asthma prevalence rates for household youth** less than 20 years of age with 1 or more **asthma attacks requiring professional medical attention** by sex on Asian farms, 2000

Sex	Total Rate/1000	se
Male	11.69	2.24
Female	7.24	2.06
Total	9.18	1.47

Table 5.52   National estimates of **asthma prevalence rates for household youth** less than 20 years of age with 1 or more **asthma attacks requiring professional medical attention** by age on Asian farms, 2000

Age	Total Rate/1000	se
<10 years	***	
10-15 years	**11.17**	**2.48**
10-11 years	19.66	5.86
12-13 years	13.72	4.57
14-15 years	0.00	
16-19 years	***	
Total	**9.18**	**1.47**

*** Estimate is not reportable or is suppressed because of a non-reportable cell.

Section VI: National Demographic, Injury, and Asthma Estimates for Youth Less Than 20 Years of Age on "Other Race" Farm Operations

Table 6.1 National estimates of "other race" farms from the 1997 Census of Agriculture by business status, 2000

Status	Total† Estimate	se
In business	8,668	39
Out of business	1,171	39
Total†	9,838	

† Estimates may not add to the total because of rounding.

Table 6.2 National estimates of **all youth** less than 20 years of age on "other race" farms by relationship to the farm and type of farm, 2000

Type of Farm	Total† Estimate	se	Household Youth Estimate	se	Hired Youth Estimate	se	Visiting Youth Estimate	se	Relatives Estimate	se	Non-Relatives Estimate	se
All crop	40,098	1,933	3,730	106	1,066	198	35,301	1,890	17,547	628	17,754	1,633
All livestock	50,805	2,152	3,633	107	487	49	46,686	2,124	24,645	733	22,041	1,844
Unknown	3,201		445		16		2,739		1,832		907	
Total†	94,103	2,792	7,808	142	1,569	202	84,726	2,761	44,024	912	40,702	2,440

† Estimates may not add to the total because of rounding.

Table 6.3 National estimates of **all working youth** less than 20 years of age on "other race" farms by relationship to the farm and type of farm, 2000

Type of Farm	Total† Estimate	se	Working Household Youth Estimate	se	Hired Youth Estimate	se	Non-Household Working Youth Estimate	se	Working Relatives Estimate	se
All crop	3,270	233	1,139	54	1,066	198	2,131	218	1,065	91
All livestock	4,702	204	1,786	72	487	49	2,916	180	2,430	165
Unknown	186		86		16		100		84	
Total†	8,158	302	3,012	88	1,569	202	5,147	279	3,578	188

† Estimates may not add to the total because of rounding.

Table 6.4 National estimates of **household youth** less than 20 years of age on "other race" farms by sex and age, 2000

Age	Total † Estimate	se	Male Estimate	se	Female Estimate	se	Unknown Estimate
<10 years	2,672	80	1,432	53	1,237	50	3
10-15 years	2,818	74	1,502	51	1,315	47	0
16-19 years	2,108	60	1,132	43	976	39	0
Unknown	211		21		9		182
Total †	7,808	142	4,086	93	3,537	86	185

† Estimates may not add to the total because of rounding.

Table 6.5 National estimates of **household youth** less than 20 years of age on "other race" farms by sex and type of farm, 2000

Type of Farm	Total † Estimate	se	Male Estimate	se	Female Estimate	se	Unknown Estimate
All crop	3,730	106	1,970	68	1,723	62	38
All livestock	3,633	107	1,968	69	1,659	63	6
Unknown	445		149		155		141
Total †	7,808	142	4,086	93	3,537	86	185

† Estimates may not add to the total because of rounding.

Table 6.6 National estimates of **household youth** less than 20 years of age on "other race" farms by age and type of farm, 2000

Type of Farm	Total † Estimate	se	<10 years Estimate	se	10-15 years Estimate	se	16-19 years Estimate	se	Unknown Estimate
All crop	3,730	106	1,364	58	1,352	52	970	41	44
All livestock	3,633	107	1,198	57	1,361	56	1,060	45	15
Unknown	445		110		105		78		152
Total †	7,808	142	2,672	80	2,818	74	2,108	60	211

† Estimates may not add to the total because of rounding.

Table 6.7 National estimates of **household youth** less than 20 years of age on "other race" farms by age, sex, and type of farm, 2000

	<10 years						
	Total [†]		Male		Female		Unknown
Type of Farm	Estimate	se	Estimate	se	Estimate	se	Estimate
All crop	1,364	58	748	38	613	35	3
All livestock	1,198	57	636	37	562	36	0
Unknown	110		48		62		0
Total [†]	2,672	80	1,432	53	1,237	50	3

	10-15 years						
	Total [†]		Male		Female		Unknown
Type of Farm	Estimate	se	Estimate	se	Estimate	se	Estimate
All crop	1,352	52	726	35	626	32	0
All livestock	1,361	56	724	38	637	35	0
Unknown	105		53		52		0
Total [†]	2,818	74	1,502	51	1,315	47	0

	16-19 years						
	Total [†]		Male		Female		Unknown
Type of Farm	Estimate	se	Estimate	se	Estimate	se	Estimate
All crop	970	41	487	29	483	27	0
All livestock	1,060	45	605	33	455	29	0
Unknown	78		39		38		0
Total [†]	2,108	60	1,132	43	976	39	0

† Estimates may not add to the total because of rounding.

Table 6.8 National estimates of **household youth** less than 20 years of age on "other race" farms by work status and sex, 2000

	Total [†]		Working		Non-Working		Unknown
Sex	Estimate	se	Estimate	se	Estimate	se	Estimate
Male	4,086	93	1,903	63	2,163	68	21
Female	3,537	86	1,109	48	2,418	71	11
Unknown	185		0		22		163
Total [†]	7,808	142	3,012	88	4,602	109	195

† Estimates may not add to the total because of rounding.

Table 6.9 National estimates of **household youth** less than 20 years of age on "other race" farms by work status and age, 2000

Age	Total [†] Estimate	se	Working Estimate	se	Non-Working Estimate	se	Unknown Estimate
<10 years	2,672	80	428	30	2,239	73	6
10-15 years	2,818	74	1,456	24	1,358	51	3
16-19 years	2,108	60	1,116	44	978	41	14
Unknown	211		12		28		171
Total [†]	7,808	142	3,012	88	4,602	109	195

[†] Estimates may not add to the total because of rounding.

Table 6.10 National estimates of **household youth** less than 20 years of age on "other race" farms by age, work status, and sex, 2000

Sex	Total [†] Estimate	se	Working Estimate	se	Non-Working Estimate	se	Unknown Estimate
<10 years							
Male	1,432	53	251	22	1,178	49	3
Female	1,237	50	177	18	1,058	16	3
Unknown	3		0		3		0
Total [†]	2,672	80	428	30	2,239	73	6
10-15 years							
Male	1,502	51	895	40	604	32	3
Female	1,315	47	561	31	754	36	0
Total [†]	2,818	74	1,456	54	1,358	51	3
16-19 years							
Male	1,132	43	745	35	378	26	9
Female	976	39	371	25	600	31	5
Total [†]	2,108	60	1,116	44	978	41	14

[†] Estimates may not add to the total because of rounding.

Table 6.11 National estimates of **household youth** less than 20 years of age on "other race" farms by whether they rode a horse and sex, 2000

Sex	Total [†] Estimate	se	Rode a Horse: Yes Estimate	se	Rode a Horse: No Estimate	se	Unknown Estimate
Male	4,086	93	1,069	49	2,999	82	18
Female	3,537	86	944	44	2,583	74	11
Unknown	185		0		3		182
Total [†]	7,808	142	2,012	74	5,585	125	211

† Estimates may not add to the total because of rounding.

Table 6.12 National estimates of **household youth** less than 20 years of age on "other race" farms by whether they rode a horse and age, 2000

Age	Total [†] Estimate	se	Rode a Horse: Yes Estimate	se	Rode a Horse: No Estimate	se	Unknown Estimate
<10 years	2,672	80	547	36	2,120	71	6
10-15 years	2,818	74	889	43	1,923	62	6
16-19 years	2,108	60	577	32	1,522	52	8
Unknown	211		0		21		190
Total [†]	7,808	142	2,012	74	5,585	125	211

† Estimates may not add to the total because of rounding.

Table 6.13 National estimates of **household youth** less than 20 years of age on "other race" farms by age, whether they rode a horse, and sex, 2000

	<10 years						
	Total [†]		Rode a Horse: Yes		Rode a Horse: No		Unknown
Sex	Estimate	se	Estimate	se	Estimate	se	Estimate
Male	1,432	53	282	23	1,146	49	3
Female	1,237	50	264	22	970	44	3
Unknown	3		0		3		0
Total [†]	2,672	80	547	36	2,120	71	6

	10-15 years						
	Total [†]		Rode a Horse: Yes		Rode a Horse: No		Unknown
Sex	Estimate	se	Estimate	se	Estimate	se	Estimate
Male	1,502	51	458	30	1,038	42	6
Female	1,315	47	431	27	885	39	0
Total [†]	2,818	74	889	43	1,923	62	6

	16-19 years						
	Total [†]		Rode a Horse: Yes		Rode a Horse: No		Unknown
Sex	Estimate	se	Estimate	se	Estimate	se	Estimate
Male	1,132	43	329	24	800	37	3
Female	976	39	249	20	722	34	5
Total [†]	2,108	60	577	32	1,522	52	8

[†] Estimates may not add to the total because of rounding.

Table 6.14 National estimates of **household youth** less than 20 years of age on "other race" farms by whether they drove an all-terrain vehicle (ATV) and sex, 2000

	Total [†]		Drove an ATV: Yes		Drove an ATV: No		Unknown
Sex	Estimate	se	Estimate	se	Estimate	se	Estimate
Male	4,086	93	1,065	45	2,575	75	447
Female	3,537	86	543	32	2,621	73	373
Unknown	185		0		3		182
Total [†]	7,808	142	1,608	62	5,199	117	1,001

[†] Estimates may not add to the total because of rounding.

Table 6.15 National estimates of **household youth** less than 20 years of age on "other race" farms by whether they drove an all-terrain vehicle (ATV) and age, 2000

Age	Total † Estimate	se	Drove an ATV: Yes Estimate	se	Drove an ATV: No Estimate	se	Unknown Estimate
<10 years	2,672	80	215	21	1,685	58	773
10-15 years	2,818	74	732	38	2,076	65	9
16-19 years	2,108	60	661	34	1,439	50	8
Unknown	211		0		0		211
Total †	7,808	142	1,608	62	5,199	117	1,001

† Estimates may not add to the total because of rounding.

Table 6.16 National estimates of **household youth** less than 20 years of age on "other race" farms by age, whether they drove an all-terrain vehicle (ATV), and sex, 2000

<10 years							
Sex	Total † Estimate	se	Drove an ATV: Yes Estimate	se	Drove an ATV: No Estimate	se	Unknown Estimate
Male	1,432	53	131	15	884	40	417
Female	1,237	50	84	12	797	38	356
Unknown	3		0		3		0
Total †	2,672	80	215	21	1,685	58	773

10-15 years							
Sex	Total † Estimate	se	Drove an ATV: Yes Estimate	se	Drove an ATV: No Estimate	se	Unknown Estimate
Male	1,502	51	462	28	1,034	43	6
Female	1,315	47	270	22	1,042	42	3
Total †	2,818	74	732	38	2,076	65	9

16-19 years							
Sex	Total † Estimate	se	Drove an ATV: Yes Estimate	se	Drove an ATV: No Estimate	se	Unknown Estimate
Male	1,132	43	472	28	657	34	3
Female	976	39	189	17	782	36	5
Total †	2,108	60	661	34	1,439	50	8

† Estimates may not add to the total because of rounding.

Table 6.17 National estimates of **household youth** less than 20 years of age on "other race" farms by whether they drove a tractor and sex, 2000

Sex	Total [†] Estimate	se	Drove a Tractor: Yes Estimate	se	Drove a Tractor: No Estimate	se	Unknown Estimate
Male	4,086	93	1,163	46	2,477	72	447
Female	3,537	86	389	27	2,775	75	373
Unknown	185		0		3		182
Total [†]	7,808	142	1,552	57	5,254	115	1,001

† Estimates may not add to the total because of rounding.

Table 6.18 National estimates of **household youth** less than 20 years of age on "other race" farms by whether they drove a tractor and age, 2000

Age	Total [†] Estimate	se	Drove a Tractor: Yes Estimate	se	Drove a Tractor: No Estimate	se	Unknown Estimate
<10 years	2,672	80	85	12	1,814	60	773
10-15 years	2,818	74	669	35	2,139	64	9
16-19 years	2,108	60	799	37	1,301	48	8
Unknown	211		0		0		211
Total [†]	7,808	142	1,552	57	5,254	115	1,001

† Estimates may not add to the total because of rounding.

Table 6.19 National estimates of **household youth** less than 20 years of age on "other race" farms by age, whether they drove a tractor, and sex, 2000

<10 Years

Sex	Total [†] Estimate	se	Drove a Tractor: Yes Estimate	se	Drove a Tractor: No Estimate	se	Unknown Estimate
Male	1,432	53	65	11	950	41	417
Female	1,237	50	20	5	862	40	356
Unknown	3		0		3		0
Total [†]	2,672	80	85	12	1,814	60	773

10-15 years

Sex	Total [†] Estimate	se	Drove a Tractor: Yes Estimate	se	Drove a Tractor: No Estimate	se	Unknown Estimate
Male	1,502	51	487	28	1,009	42	6
Female	1,315	47	182	17	1,130	44	3
Total [†]	2,818	74	669	35	2,139	64	9

16-19 years

Sex	Total [†] Estimate	se	Drove a Tractor: Yes Estimate	se	Drove a Tractor: No Estimate	se	Unknown Estimate
Male	1,132	43	611	32	518	30	3
Female	976	39	188	17	783	36	5
Total [†]	2,108	60	799	37	1,301	48	8

† Estimates may not add to the total because of rounding.

Table 6.20 National estimates of **injuries to all youth** less than 20 years of age on "other race" farms by relationship to the farm, 2000

Relationship to Farm	Total [†] Estimate	se
Household youth	**96**	**15**
Hired youth	***	
Visiting youth	***	
Relatives	11	4
Non-relatives	***	
Total [†]	**112**	**16**

† Estimates may not add to the total because of rounding.
*** Estimate is not reportable or is suppressed because of a non-reportable cell.

Table 6.21 National estimates of **injuries to all youth** less than 20 years of age on "other race" farms by race, 2000

Race	Total [†] Estimate	se
Other race	96	15
All other races*	11	
Unknown	5	
Total [†]	112	16

† Estimates may not add to the total because of rounding.
* All other races includes "White," "Black," "Native American," and "Asian."

Table 6.22 National estimates of **injuries to all youth** less than 20 years of age on "other race" farms by work status and age, 2000

Age	Total [†] Estimate	se	Working Estimate	se	Non-Working Estimate	se
< 10 years	42	10	***		***	
10-15 years	39	8	20	5	19	5
16-19 years	29	7	***		***	
Unknown	3		0		3	
Total [†]	112	16	46	9	66	12

† Estimates may not add to the total because of rounding.
*** Estimate is not reportable or is suppressed because of a non-reportable cell.

Table 6.23 National estimates of **injuries to all youth** less than 20 years of age on "other race" farms by work status and type of farm, 2000

Type of Farm	Total [†]		Working		Non-Working	
	Estimate	se	Estimate	se	Estimate	se
All crop	41	9	11	4	31	7
All livestock	71	13	35	8	36	9
Total [†]	112	16	46	9	66	12

† Estimates may not add to the total because of rounding.

Table 6.24 National estimates of **injuries to all youth** less than 20 years of age on "other race" farms by work status and type of injury, 2000

Type of Injury	Total [†]		Working		Non-Working	
	Estimate	se	Estimate	se	Estimate	se
Scrape, abrasion	8	3	0		8	3
Bruise, contusion	18	5	***		***	
Broken bone, fracture	11	4	***		***	
Cut, laceration	36	8	11	4	25	7
Puncture, stab, jab	15	5	***		***	
Multiple injuries	11	4	***		***	
All other injuries*	14		***		***	
Total [†]	112	16	46	9	66	12

† Estimates may not add to the total because of rounding.

* All other injuries includes "Sprain, strain," "Dislocation," "Traumatic rupture," "Crushed," "Amputation," "Nerve injury," "Burn, blister, scald," and "Other injury."

*** Estimate is not reportable or is suppressed because of a non-reportable cell.

Table 6.25 National estimates of **injuries to all youth** less than 20 years of age on "other race" farms by work status and body part injured, 2000

Body Part Injured	Total [†]		Working		Non-Working	
	Estimate	se	Estimate	se	Estimate	se
Head, skull	22	6	8	3	14	5
Face	13	5	***		***	
Shoulder, chest, back	9	4	***		***	
Leg	14	5	***		***	
Foot, ankle, toes	23	6	14	5	9	4
Multiple body parts	8	3	***		***	
All other body parts*	20		***		***	
Unknown	3		0		3	
Total [†]	112	16	46	9	66	12

† Estimates may not add to the total because of rounding.

* All other body parts includes "Neck," "Abdomen," "Pelvic region," " Arm," "Hand, wrist, fingers," "Internal injury," and "Other body parts."

*** Estimate is not reportable or is suppressed because of a non-reportable cell.

Table 6.26 National estimates of **injuries to all youth** less than 20 years of age on "other race" farms by work status and source of injury, 2000

Source of Injury ‡	Total †		Working		Non-Working	
	Estimate	se	Estimate	se	Estimate	se
Containers (1)	8	3	***		***	
Parts/Materials (4)	16	5	***		***	
Structures and Surfaces (6)	30	8	0		30	8
Tools/Instruments/Equipment (7)	11	4	***		***	
Vehicles (8)	16	5	***		***	
Other and Unknown Sources*	31		15		16	
Total †	112	16	46	9	66	12

† Estimates may not add to the total because of rounding.

‡ Categories based on the Bureau of Labor Statistics Occupational Injury and Illness Coding Structure (OIICS). OIICS codes are provided in parentheses.

* Other and Unknown Sources includes "Chemicals," "Furniture and Fixtures," "Machinery," "Persons/Animals/Plants/Minerals," "Other Sources," and "Unknown Sources."

*** Estimate is not reportable or is suppressed because of a non-reportable cell.

Table 6.27 National estimates of **injuries to all youth** less than 20 years of age on "other race" farms by work status and type of injury event, 2000

Type of Injury Event ‡	Total †		Working		Non-Working	
	Estimate	se	Estimate	se	Estimate	se
Contact With Objects (0)	38	8	28	7	9	4
Falls (1)	33	8	0		33	8
Other and Unknown Events*	42		18		14	
Total †	112	16	46	9	66	12

† Estimates may not add to the total because of rounding.

‡ Categories based on the Bureau of Labor Statistics Occupational Injury and Illness Coding Structure (OIICS). OIICS codes are provided in parentheses.

* Other and Unknown Events includes "Bodily Reaction/Exertion," "Exposure to Substances/Environments," "Transportation Events," "Fires and Explosions," "Assaults and Violent Acts," "Other Events," and "Unknown Events."

Table 6.28 National estimates of **injury rates for all youth** less than 20 years of age on "other race" farms by relationship to the farm, 2000

Relationship to Farm	Total Rate/1000	se
Household youth	**12.33**	**1.87**
Hired youth	***	
Visiting youth	***	
Relatives	0.25	0.09
Non-relatives	***	
Total	**1.19**	**0.17**

*** Estimate is not reportable or is suppressed because of a non-reportable cell.

Table 6.29 National estimates of **injury rates for all youth** less than 20 years of age on "other race" farms by work status and type of farm, 2000

Type of Farm	Total Rate/1000	se	Working Rate/1000	se	Non-Working Rate/1000	se
All crop	1.03	0.23	3.27	1.16	0.76	0.18
All livestock	1.40	0.26	7.53	1.65	0.71	0.19
Total	1.19	0.17	5.65	1.06	0.70	0.13

Table 6.30 National estimates of **injury rates for all youth** less than 20 years of age on "other race" farms by work status and type of injury, 2000

Type of Injury	Total Rate/1000	se	Working Rate/1000	se	Non-Working Rate/1000	se
Scrape, abrasion	0.09	0.03	0.00		0.09	0.03
Bruise, contusion	0.19	0.06	***		***	
Broken bone, fracture	0.12	0.04	***		***	
Cut, laceration	0.38	0.09	1.35	0.48	0.26	0.08
Puncture, stab, jab	0.16	0.05	***		***	
Multiple injuries	0.12	0.04	***		***	
All other injuries*	0.15		***		***	
Total	1.19	0.17	5.65	1.06	0.70	0.13

* All other injuries includes "Sprain, strain," "Dislocation," "Traumatic rupture," "Crushed," "Amputation," "Nerve injury," "Burn, blister, scald," and "Other injury."

*** Estimate is not reportable or is suppressed because of a non-reportable cell.

Table 6.31 National estimates of **injury rates for all youth** less than 20 years of age on "other race" farms by work status and body part injured, 2000

Body Part Injured	Total		Working		Non-Working	
	Rate/1000	se	Rate/1000	se	Rate/1000	se
Head, skull	0.24	0.06	0.99	0.41	0.15	0.05
Face	0.14	0.05	***		***	
Shoulder, chest, back	0.10	0.04	***		***	
Leg	0.15	0.05	***		***	
Foot, ankle, toes	0.25	0.07	1.77	0.58	0.10	0.04
Multiple body parts	0.09	0.04	***		***	
All other body parts*	0.21		***		***	
Total	1.19	0.17	5.65	1.06	0.70	0.13

* All other body parts includes "Neck," "Abdomen," "Pelvic region," " Arm," "Hand, wrist, fingers," "Internal injury," and "Other body parts."

*** Estimate is not reportable or is suppressed because of a non-reportable cell.

Table 6.32 National estimates of **injury rates for all youth** less than 20 years of age on "other race" farms by work status and source of injury, 2000

Source of Injury [†]	Total		Working		Non-Working	
	Rate/1000	se	Rate/1000	se	Rate/1000	se
Containers (1)	0.09	0.04	***		***	
Parts/Materials (4)	0.17	0.06	***		***	
Structures and Surfaces (6)	0.32	0.08	0.00		0.32	0.08
Tools/Instruments/Equipment (7)	0.12	0.04	***		***	
Vehicles (8)	0.17	0.06	***		***	
Other and Unknown Sources*	0.33		1.84		0.17	
Total	1.19	0.17	5.65	1.06	0.70	0.13

† Categories based on the Bureau of Labor Statistics Occupational Injury and Illness Coding Structure (OIICS). OIICS codes are provided in parentheses.

* Other and Unknown Sources includes "Chemicals," "Furniture and Fixtures," "Machinery," "Persons/Animals/ Plants/Minerals," "Other Sources," and "Unknown Sources."

*** Estimate is not reportable or is suppressed because of a non-reportable cell.

Table 6.33 National estimates of **injury rates for all youth** less than 20 years of age on "other race" farms by work status and type of injury event, 2000

Type of Injury Event [†]	Total		Working		Non-Working	
	Rate/1000	se	Rate/1000	se	Rate/1000	se
Contact With Objects (0)	0.40	0.09	3.48	0.81	0.10	0.04
Falls (1)	0.35	0.09	0.00		0.35	0.09
Other and Unknown Events*	0.45		2.21		0.15	
Total	1.19	0.17	5.65	1.06	0.70	0.13

[†] Categories based on the Bureau of Labor Statistics Occupational Injury and Illness Coding Structure (OIICS). OIICS codes are provided in parentheses.

* Other and Unknown Events includes "Bodily Reaction/Exertion," "Exposure to Substances/Environments," "Transportation Events," "Fires and Explosions," "Assaults and Violent Acts," "Other Events," and "Unknown Events."

Table 6.34 National estimates of **asthma among household youth** less than 20 years of age on "other race" farms by sex, 2000

Sex	Asthma		No Asthma		Unknown
	Estimate	se	Estimate	se	Estimate
Male	413	27	3,649	87	24
Female	218	18	3,305	82	14
Unknown	0		3		182
Total [†]	632	34	6,957	134	219

[†] Estimates may not add to the total because of rounding.

Table 6.35 National estimates of **asthma among household youth** less than 20 years of age on "other race" farms by age, 2000

Age	Asthma		No Asthma		Unknown
	Estimate	se	Estimate	se	Estimate
<10 years	168	17	2,499	77	6
10-15 years	248	20	2,557	70	12
16-19 years	216	18	1,881	57	11
Unknown	0		21		190
Total [†]	632	34	6,957	134	219

[†] Estimates may not add to the total because of rounding.

Table 6.36 National estimates of **asthma among household youth** less than 20 years of age on "other race" farms by sex and age, 2000

Age	Total [†] Estimate	se	Male Estimate	se	Female Estimate	se
<10 years	168	17	114	14	53	9
10-15 years	248	20	163	16	85	11
16-19 years	216	18	136	14	80	11
Total [†]	632	34	413	27	218	18

† Estimates may not add to the total because of rounding.

Table 6.37 National estimates of **asthma among household youth** less than 20 years of age on "other race" farms by sex and type of farm, 2000

Type of Farm	Total [†] Estimate	se	Male Estimate	se	Female Estimate	se
All crop	312	25	192	19	120	13
All livestock	290	23	197	18	93	12
Unknown	30		25		5	
Total [†]	632	34	413	27	218	18

† Estimates may not add to the total because of rounding.

Table 6.38 National estimates of **asthma among household youth** less than 20 years of age on "other race" farms by age and type of farm, 2000

Type of Farm	Total [†] Estimate	se	<10 years Estimate	se	10-15 years Estimate	se	16-19 years Estimate	se
All crop	312	25	74	11	114	14	123	13
All livestock	290	23	85	13	118	14	87	12
Unknown	30		8		16		5	
Total [†]	632	34	168	17	248	20	216	18

† Estimates may not add to the total because of rounding.

Table 6.39 National estimates of **asthmatic household youth** less than 20 years of age with 1 or more **asthma attacks while doing farm work** by sex on "other race" farms, 2000

Sex	Total [†] Estimate	se	Attack at Work Estimate	se	No Attack at Work Estimate	se	Unknown Estimate
Male	413	27	99	14	210	20	105
Female	218	18	67	10	106	13	46
Total [†]	632	34	165	17	316	26	151

† Estimates may not add to the total because of rounding.

Table 6.40 National estimates of **asthmatic household youth** less than 20 years of age with 1 or more **asthma attacks while doing farm work** by age on "other race" farms, 2000

Age	Total [†] Estimate	se	Attack at Work Estimate	se	No Attack at Work Estimate	se	Unknown Estimate
<10 years	168	17	26	7	74	13	68
10-15 years	248	20	64	10	121	14	63
16-19 years	216	18	76	10	121	14	20
Total [†]	632	34	165	17	316	26	151

† Estimates may not add to the total because of rounding.

Table 6.41 National estimates of **asthmatic household youth** less than 20 years of age with 1 or more **asthma attacks while doing farm work** by type of farm on "other race" farms, 2000

Type of Farm	Total [†] Estimate	se	Attack at Work Estimate	se	No Attack at Work Estimate	se	Unknown Estimate
All crop	312	25	80	12	177	20	55
All livestock	290	23	75	12	128	16	88
Unknown	30		11		11		8
Total [†]	632	34	165	17	316	26	151

† Estimates may not add to the total because of rounding.

Table 6.42 National estimates of **asthmatic household youth** less than 20 years of age with 1 or more **asthma attacks requiring professional medical attention** by sex on "other race" farms, 2000

Sex	Total [†] Estimate	se	Medical Attention Estimate	se	No Medical Attention Estimate	se	Unknown Estimate
Male	413	27	61	10	352	25	0
Female	218	18	51	9	165	16	3
Total [†]	632	34	112	13	517	31	3

† Estimates may not add to the total because of rounding.

Table 6.43 National estimates of **asthmatic household youth** less than 20 years of age with 1 or more **asthma attacks requiring professional medical attention** by age on "other race" farms, 2000

Age	Total [†] Estimate	se	Medical Attention Estimate	se	No Medical Attention Estimate	se	Unknown Estimate
<10 years	168	17	51	9	117	14	0
10-15 years	248	20	42	8	207	19	0
16-19 years	216	18	19	5	194	17	3
Total [†]	632	34	112	13	517	31	3

† Estimates may not add to the total because of rounding.

Table 6.44 National estimates of **asthma prevalence rates for household youth** less than 20 years of age on "other race" farms by sex and age, 2000

Age	Total Rate/1000	se	Male Rate/1000	se	Female Rate/1000	se
<10 years	62.68	6.77	79.63	10.01	43.16	7.32
10-15 years	88.09	7.50	108.56	11.34	64.71	8.90
16-19 years	102.39	8.98	120.28	13.36	81.75	11.45
Total	80.88	4.64	101.12	7.02	61.71	5.28

Table 6.45 National estimates of **asthma prevalence rates for household youth** less than 20 years of age on "other race" farms by sex and type of farm, 2000

Type of Farm	Total Rate/1000	se	Male Rate/1000	se	Female Rate/1000	se
All crop	83.59	7.06	97.32	10.31	69.72	8.00
All livestock	79.80	6.86	100.17	9.99	55.92	7.53
Total	80.88	4.64	101.12	7.02	61.71	5.28

Table 6.46 National estimates of **asthma prevalence rates for household youth** less than 20 years of age on "other race" farms by age and type of farm, 2000

Type of Farm	Total Rate/1000	se	<10 years Rate/1000	se	10-15 years Rate/1000	se	16-19 years Rate/1000	se
All crop	83.59	7.06	54.47	8.10	84.39	10.49	127.18	14.72
All livestock	79.80	6.86	70.80	11.69	86.71	11.09	82.20	11.59
Total	80.88	4.64	62.68	6.77	88.09	7.50	102.39	8.98

Table 6.47 National estimates of **asthma prevalence rates for household youth** less than 20 years of age with 1 or more **asthma attacks while doing farm work** by sex on "other race" farms, 2000

Sex	Total Rate/1000	se
Male	51.77	7.35
Female	60.24	9.22
Total	54.89	5.96

Table 6.48 National estimates of **asthma prevalence rates for household youth** less than 20 years of age with 1 or more **asthma attacks while doing farm work** by age on "other race" farms, 2000

Age	Total Rate/1000	se
<10 years	60.10	17.14
10-15 years	44.01	6.84
16-19 years	67.67	9.69
Total	54.89	5.96

Table 6.49 National estimates of **asthma prevalence rates for household youth** less than 20 years of age with 1 or more **asthma attacks while doing farm work** by type of farm on "other race" farms, 2000

Type of Farm	Total Rate/1000	se
All crop	70.12	11.29
All livestock	41.82	6.66
Total	54.89	5.96

Table 6.50 National estimates of **asthma prevalence rates for household youth** less than 20 years of age with 1 or more **asthma attacks requiring professional medical attention** by sex on "other race" farms, 2000

Sex	Total Rate/1000	se
Male	14.90	2.40
Female	14.36	2.46
Total	14.31	1.72

Table 6.51 National estimates of **asthma prevalence rates for household youth** less than 20 years of age with 1 or more **asthma attacks requiring professional medical attention** by age on "other race" farms, 2000

Age	Total Rate/1000	se
<10 years	19.01	3.53
10-15 years	14.73	2.90
16-19 years	9.20	2.48
Total	14.31	1.72

Appendix A: Bibliography of NIOSH Childhood Agricultural Injury Articles and Documents

Journal and Conference Articles

Adekoya N, Castillo DN, Myers JR [1998]. Youth agricultural work-related injuries treated in emergency departments--United States, October 1995-September 1997. MMWR, 47(35):733-737.

Castillo DN, Hard DL, Myers JR, Pizatella T, Stout NA [1998]. A national childhood agricultural injury prevention initiative. J Agric Saf Health, Special Issue (1): 183-191.

Castillo DN, Adekoya N, Myers JR [1999]. Fatal work-related injuries in the agricultural production and services sectors among youth in the United States, 1992-1996. J Agromedicine, 6(3):27-41.

Goldcamp EM, Hendricks KJ, Myers JR [2002]. Farm fatalities to youth 1995-1997: a comparison by age groups. National Institute for Farm Safety 2002 Annual Meeting, June 23-27, 2002, Ponte Vedra Beach, FL. Columbia, MO: National Institute for Farm Safety.

Goldcamp EM, Myers JR, Hendricks KJ, Layne LA [2003]. Non-fatal injuries: an overview of injuries to youth on racial minority operated farms in the United States, 2000. National Institute for Farm Safety 2003 Annual Meeting, June 22-26, 2003, Windsor, Ontario, Canada. Columbia, MO: National Institute for Farm Safety.

Goldcamp EM, Myers JR, Hendricks KJ, Layne LA [2004]. Nonfatal all-terrain vehicle injuries to youth on farms in the U.S., 2001. National Institute for Farm Safety 2004 Annual Meeting, June 20-24, 2004, Keystone, CO. Columbia, MO: National Institute for Farm Safety.

Goldcamp EM, Hendricks KJ, Myers JR [2004]. Farm fatalities to youth 1995-2000: a comparison by age groups. J Saf Research 35(2):151-157.

Hard DL, Myers JR [2005]. Fatal work-related injuries in the agricultural production sector among youth in the United States, 1992-2002. National Institute for Farm Safety 2005 Annual Meeting, June 19-23, 2005, Wintergreen, VA. Columbia, MO: National Institute for Farm Safety.

Hendricks KJ, Adekoya N [2001]. Non-fatal animal-related injuries to youth occurring on farms in the United States- 1998. National Institute for Farm Safety Annual Meeting, June 24-27, 2001, Pittsburgh, PA. Columbia, MO: National Institute for Farm Safety.

Hendricks KJ, Adekoya N [2001]. Non-fatal animal related injuries to youth occurring on farms in the United States, 1998. Injury Prevention 7(4):307-311.

Hendricks KJ, Goldcamp EM, Myers JR [2002]. Fatal and non-fatal falls in United States agricultural production for youth less than 20 years old. National Institute for Farm Safety 2002 Annual Meeting, June 23-27, 2002, Ponte Vedra Beach, FL. Columbia, MO: National Institute for Farm Safety.

Hendricks KJ, Myers JR, Goldcamp EM, Layne LA . [2003]. Farm hazards to household youth on minority operated farms in the United States, 2000: exposures and injuries from work, horses, ATVs and tractors. National Institute for Farm Safety 2003 Annual Meeting, June 22-26, 2003, Windsor, Ontario, Canada. Columbia, MO: National Institute for Farm Safety.

Hendricks KJ, Goldcamp EM, Myers JR . [2004]. On-farm falls among youth less than 20-years old in the U.S. J Agric Saf Health, 10(1):27-38.

Hendricks KJ, Layne LA, Goldcamp EM, Myers JR [2004]. Injuries among youth on farms in the United States, 2001. National Institute for Farm Safety 2004 Annual Meeting, June 20-24, 2004, Keystone, CO. Columbia, MO: National Institute for Farm Safety.

Hendricks KJ, Myers JR, Layne LA, Goldcamp EM . [2005]. Household youth on minority operated farms in the United States, 2000: exposures to and injuries from work, horses, ATVs and tractors. J Saf Research 36(2):149-157.

Layne LA, Myers JR, Hendricks KJ, Goldcamp EM [2003]. Demographics and non-fatal injury patterns of youth less than 20 years of age on Hispanic operated farms in the United States, 2000. National Institute for Farm Safety 2003 Annual Meeting, June 22-26, 2003, Windsor, Ontario, Canada. Columbia, MO: National Institute for Farm Safety.

Myers JR, Adekoya N [2001]. Fatal on-farm injuries among youth 16 to 19 years of age: 1982-1994. J Agric Saf Health, 7(2):101-112.

Parker DL, Wahl GL, Higgins D [1999]. Childhood work-related agricultural fatalities -- Minnesota, 1994-1997. 1999. MMWR, 48(16):332-335.

Pollack SH, Struttmann TW, Zwerling C, Lundell J, Johnson W, Etre L, Hanrahan LP, Tierney J, Higgins D [1999]. Deaths among children aged less than or equal to 5 years from farm machinery runovers -- Iowa, Kentucky, and Wisconsin, 1995-1998, and United States, 1990-1995. MMWR, 48(28):605-608.

NIOSH and USDA Numbered Documents

Adekoya N, Pratt SG [2001]. Fatal unintentional farm injuries among persons less than 20 years of age in the United States: Geographic profiles. Cincinnati, OH: U.S. Department of Health and Human Services, Public Health Service, Centers for Disease Control and Prevention, National Institute for Occupational Safety and Health, DHHS (NIOSH) Publication No. 2001-131.

Myers JR [1998]. Injuries among farm workers in the United States--1994. Cincinnati, OH: U.S. Department of Health and Human Services, Public Health Service, Centers for Disease Control and Prevention, National Institute for Occupational Safety and Health, DHHS (NIOSH) Publication No. 98-153.

Myers JR [2001]. Injuries among farm workers in the United States, 1995. Cincinnati, OH: U.S. Department of Health and Human Services, Public Health Service, Centers for Disease Control and Prevention, National Institute for Occupational Safety and Health, DHHS (NIOSH) Publication No. 2001-153.

Myers JR, Hendricks KJ [2001]. Injuries among youth on farms in the United States, 1998. Cincinnati, OH: U.S. Department of Health and Human Services, Public Health Service, Centers for Disease Control and Prevention, National Institute for Occupational Safety and Health, DHHS (NIOSH) Publication No. 2001-154.

NIOSH [2004]. Injuries to youth on minority farm operations. Cincinnati, OH: U.S. Department of Health and Human Services, Public Health Service, Centers for Disease Control and Prevention, National Institute for Occupational Safety and Health, DHHS (NIOSH) Publication No. 2004-117.

NIOSH [2004]. Asthma among household youth on minority farm operations. Cincinnati, OH: U.S. Department of Health and Human Services, Public Health Service, Centers for Disease Control and Prevention, National Institute for Occupational Safety and Health, DHHS (NIOSH) Publication No. 2004-118.

NIOSH [2004]. Worker health chartbook, 2004. Cincinnati, OH: U.S. Department of Health and Human Services, Public Health Service, Centers for Disease Control and Prevention, National Institute for Occupational Safety and Health, DHHS (NIOSH) Pub. No. 2004-146.

NIOSH [2004]. Injuries to youth on Hispanic farm operations. Cincinnati, OH: U.S. Department of Health and Human Services, Public Health Service, Centers for Disease Control and Prevention, National Institute for Occupational Safety and Health, DHHS (NIOSH) Publication No. 2004-157.

NIOSH [2004]. Asthma among household youth on Hispanic farm operations. Cincinnati, OH: U.S. Department of Health and Human Services, Public Health Service, Centers for Disease Control and Prevention, National Institute for Occupational Safety and Health, DHHS (NIOSH) Publication No. 2004-158.

NIOSH. [2004]. Injuries among youth on farms, 2001. Cincinnati, OH: U.S. Department of Health and Human Services, Public Health Service, Centers for Disease Control and Prevention, National Institute for Occupational Safety and Health, DHHS (NIOSH) Pub. No. 2004-172.

USDA [1999]. 1998 Childhood agricultural injuries. Washington, DC: US Department of Agriculture, National Agricultural Statistics Service, Sp Cr 8 (10-99).

USDA [2002]. 2000 Childhood agricultural injuries on minority-operated farms. Washington, DC: US Department of Agriculture, National Agricultural Statistics Service, Sp Cr 9 (02).

USDA [2004]. 2001 Childhood agricultural-related injuries. Washington, DC: US Department of Agriculture, National Agricultural Statistics Service, Sp Cr 9 (1-04).

NIOSH Fatality Assessment and Control Evaluation (FACE) Reports

NIOSH [1989]. Five family members die after entering manure waste pit on dairy farm. Morgantown, WV: U.S. Department of Health and Human Services, Public Health Service, Centers for Disease Control and Prevention, National Institute for Occupational Safety and Health, FACE Report No. 89-46.

NIOSH [1998]. 9-year-old child helping with blueberry harvest dies after being run over by cargo truck on field road. Morgantown, WV: U.S. Department of Health and Human Services, Public Health Service, Centers for Disease Control and Prevention, National Institute for Occupational Safety and Health, FACE Report No. 98-15.

NIOSH [2000]. Sixteen-year-old farmworker dies in a cotton packing machine after being covered with a load of cotton--Georgia. Morgantown, WV: U.S. Department of Health and Human Services, Public Health Service, Centers for Disease Control and Prevention, National Institute for Occupational Safety and Health, FACE Report No. 2000-06.

NIOSH [2000]. A 15-year-old male farm laborer dies after the tractor he was operating overturned into a manure pit--Pennsylvania. Morgantown, WV: U.S. Department of Health and Human Services, Public Health Service, Centers for Disease Control and Prevention, National Institute for Occupational Safety and Health, FACE Report No. 2000-18.

NIOSH [2002]. Youth farm worker dies after falling into operating feed grinder/mixer--Ohio. Morgantown, WV: U.S. Department of Health and Human Services, Public Health Service, Centers for Disease Control and Prevention, National Institute for Occupational Safety and Health, FACE Report No. 2002-10.

State Fatality Assessment and Control Evaluation (FACE) Reports

The University of Iowa [1995]. 12 year old boy dies from a tractor rollover in a roadside ditch. Iowa City, IA: The University of Iowa, Iowa Fatality Assessment and Control Evaluation Program, FACE Investigation No. 95IA009.

The University of Iowa [1999]. Youth farm worker is killed when he becomes entangled in PTO driveline of an old grinder-mixer. Iowa City, IA: The University of Iowa, Iowa Fatality Assessment and Control Evaluation Program, FACE Investigation No. 99IA003.

Kentucky Injury Prevention and Research Center [2001]. Youth riding as passenger on tractor killed by overturn. Lexington, KY: Kentucky Injury Prevention and Research Center, Kentucky Fatality Assessment and Control Evaluation Program, FACE Investigation No. 01KY062.

Michigan State University [2003]. Farm youth died when he became entangled in an unguarded PTO shaft. East Lansing, MI: Michigan State University, Michigan Fatality Assessment and Control Evaluation Program, FACE Investigation No. 03MI052.

Minnesota Department of Health [1994]. Farm youth dies after being crushed by a "run away" chopper wagon. Minneapolis, MN: Minnesota Department of Health, Minnesota Fatality Assessment and Control Evaluation Program, FACE Investigation No. 94MN030.

Minnesota Department of Health [1994]. Farm youth dies after tractor he was driving rolled over on him. Minneapolis, MN: Minnesota Department of Health, Minnesota Fatality Assessment and Control Evaluation Program, FACE Investigation No. 94MN039.

Minnesota Department of Health [1994]. Farm youth dies after tractor he was driving rolled over on him. Minneapolis, MN: Minnesota Department of Health, Minnesota Fatality Assessment and Control Evaluation Program, FACE Investigation No. 94MN041.

Minnesota Department of Health [1995]. Farm youth dies after being engulfed in corn inside a steel grain bin. Minneapolis, MN: Minnesota Department of Health, Minnesota Fatality Assessment and Control Evaluation Program, FACE Investigation No. 95MN045.

Minnesota Department of Health [1995]. Farmer youth dies after being struck by a loader bucket. Minneapolis, MN: Minnesota Department of Health, Minnesota Fatality Assessment and Control Evaluation Program, FACE Investigation No. 95MN046.

Minnesota Department of Health [1997]. Farmer youth dies after being run over by a grass seeder. Minneapolis, MN: Minnesota Department of Health, Minnesota Fatality Assessment and Control Evaluation Program, FACE Investigation No. 97MN038.

Minnesota Department of Health [2000]. Farm youth dies after falling from and being run over by tractor in Minnesota. Minneapolis, MN: Minnesota Department of Health, Minnesota Fatality Assessment and Control Evaluation Program, FACE Investigation No. 00MN029.

Missouri Department of Health [1999]. Eleven-year-old farm-boy dies following tractor accident. Jefferson City, MO: Missouri Department of Health, Missouri Fatality Assessment and Control Evaluation Program, FACE Investigation No. 99MO022.

Nebraska Department of Labor [1998]. Tractor overturn kills temporary worker. Lincoln, NE: Nebraska Department of Labor, Nebraska Workforce Development, Nebraska Fatality Assessment and Control Evaluation Program, FACE Investigation No. 98NE029.

Nebraska Department of Labor [1999]. Farm youth suffocated in corn bin. Lincoln, NE: Nebraska Department of Labor, Nebraska Workforce Development, Nebraska Fatality Assessment and Control Evaluation Program, FACE Investigation No. 99NE028.

Oklahoma State Department of Health [1998]. Farm worker dies of burn-related injuries while trapped in a burning hay baler--Oklahoma. Oklahoma City, OK: Oklahoma State Department of Health, Oklahoma Fatality Assessment and Control Evaluation Program, FACE Investigation No. 98OK025.

Oklahoma State Department of Health [2000]. A 17-year old on a hay hauling crew died from injuries received when he fell from a moving hay truck and was apparently run over by the vehicle's tire in Oklahoma. Oklahoma City, OK: Oklahoma State Department of Health, Oklahoma Fatality Assessment and Control Evaluation Program, FACE Investigation No. 00OK045.

Washington State Department of Labor and Industries [1999]. Tractor overturn kills 16-year-old farm worker in Washington State. Olympia, WA: Washington State Department of Labor and Industries, Washington Fatality Assessment and Control Evaluation Program, FACE Investigation No. 99WA056.

Wisconsin Division of Health [2000]. Youth farm worker pinned under overturned horse-drawn manure sled. Madison, WI: Wisconsin Division of Health, Wisconsin Fatality Assessment and Control Evaluation Program, FACE Investigation 00WI025.

Wyoming Department of Health [1992]. Sheepherder struck by lightning in Wyoming. Laramie, WY: Wyoming Department of Health, Wyoming Fatality Assessment and Control Evaluation Program, FACE Investigation 92WY013.

Appendix B: Minority Farm Operator Childhood Agricultural Injury Survey Questionnaire

2000 Minority Farm Operator Childhood Agricultural Injury Questionnaire

Hello, my name is _____ and I am working with the National Agricultural Statistics Service on behalf of the Centers for Disease Control and Prevention. We are interested in learning more about injuries that occur on farms operated by minorities. We are asking farm/ranch families for information about their farming operations, as well as information on injuries that occurred on the farm/ranch in the past year. This will take about ___ minutes.

The information you provide will be strictly CONFIDENTIAL. Your Cooperation is VOLUNTARY, and you may refuse to answer any question. This information will be combined with others' to help identify common patterns of injuries on farms and to develop injury prevention and health promotion programs nationwide. Would you help us by answering these questions?

> 01 YES [Continue on INT 2]
> 03 NO [Refuse]

I assure you that everything you tell us will be kept CONFIDENTIAL.

Your answers are very important even if you did not have a youth on your farm, or did not have an injury on your farm in the past year. This project will be used to identify how often injuries occur on farms, and what the common patterns are for these injuries. This information will help identify programs for preventing these injuries in the future. Your cooperation will benefit all minority farm/ranch families. Would you please consider helping us?

> 01 YES [Continue on INT 2]
> 03 NO [Refused]
> 04 Says not a farm [Continue on Int 1a]
> 05 Does not speak English

Int 1a:

1. Please answer the following question(s) for the total acres you (Name on Label) operate.

a. Did you grow any crops or cut hay in 2000   Yes - [Go to Int 2.]   No -[Continue]

b. Is any of the land in this operation cropland?   Yes - [Go to Int 2.]   No -[Continue]
   (Including idle cropland and cropland government programs
   such as CRP, etc

c. In 2000 did you have any whole grains, oilseeds, or hay stored on
   this operation?   Yes - [Go to Int 2.]   No -[Continue]

d. Do you have facilities for storing whole grains or oilseeds?   Yes - [Go to Int 2.]   No -[Continue]

e. Do you own or raise any livestock or poultry?   Yes - [Go to Int 2.]   No -[Go to conclusion]

Int 2

1. Hello, may I please speak with the adult female of the household?

     01 YES
     03 NOT AVAILABLE. WHEN WOULD BE A GOOD TIME TO CALL BACK?

          Time to call back: _____

     04 SPOUSE WILL GIVE INFORMATION
     05 NO FEMALE HEAD OF HOUSEHOLD

2. Please verify name and mailing address of this operation. Make corrections (Including the correct operation name) on the label and continue.

          Check box if name and address are verified. ▢

3. I would like to know how many people live in your household,
          (INCLUDING yourself, and EXCLUDING temporary visitors)?

          Number of People _____

4. How many of the people living in your household are under the age of 20?

          Number Under Age of 20_____

(If 0 Skip to HOUSEHOLD SUMMARY, Page 3, Question 1)

5. Where do the youth in your household most often go when they need medical attention?   Do they go to a doctor's office, a clinic, an emergency room, an urgent care center, or to some other place?

     01 Doctor's office
     02 Clinic
     03 Emergency Room
     04 Urgent Care Center
     05 Some other place
     77 Don't know
     99 Refused

6. What kind of health practitioner do the youth in your household usually see, a doctor, a nurse, a nurse practitioner (CNP), a physician's assistant (PA), or someone else?

     01 Doctor
     02 Nurse
     03 Certified Nurse Practioner
     04 Physician Assistant
     05 Someone else
     77 Don't know
     99 Refused

7. The last time any youth (under 20 years of age) in your household received professional medical attention, who paid the majority of the cost? Was it...

    01 Paid out of pocket
    02 Medicare/Medicaid
    03 Public Clinic/No charge
    04 Employer paid health plan
    05 Individual health plan (self/family)
    06 Billed, did not pay
    07 Workers' Compensation
    08 Other (Specify _____)
    77 Don't know
    99 Refused

HOUSEHOLD SUMMARY

1. ENUM: Respondent's gender?

    01 Male
    03 Female

2. What was your age on your last birthday?

    Age _____

3. How many years of schooling have you completed?

    Years of Schooling Completed _____

4. What is the highest education level you have achieved? (Check ONLY ONE)

    01 Less than High School
    02 High School Diploma
    03 Associates, two-year Junior College degree
    04 Vocational/Technical School
    05 Bachelors Degree
    06 Masters Degree
    07 Doctorate
    08 Professional - MD, JD, DDS, etc.
    09 Other (Specify _____)
    77 Don't know
    99 Refused

5. Are you of Spanish, Hispanic or Latino origin or background such as Mexican, Cuban, or Puerto Rican, regardless of race?

    01 Yes   77 Don't know
    03 No   99 Refused

6. What is your Race? (Mark one or more of the following.)

    01 White
    02 Black or African American
    03 American Indian or Alaska Native (Specify tribe_____)
    04 Native Hawaiian or Other Pacific Islander
    05 Asian
    77 Don't know
    99 Refused

7. What is your marital status? (Please check ONLY ONE.)

01 Married	05 Married, but apart
02 Widowed	06 Single, never married
03 Divorced	77 Don't know
04 Separated	99 Refused

ENUM: Ask Questions 8 - 13 if married in Question 7.

8. ENUM: Respondent spouse's gender?

    01 Male
    02 Female

9. What was your spouse's age on their last birthday?

    Age _____

10. How many years of schooling has your spouse completed?

    Years of Schooling Completed_____

11. What is the highest level of education your spouse has achieved?   (Please check ONLY ONE.)

    01 Less than High School
    02 High School Diploma
    03 Associates, two-year Junior College degree
    04 Vocational/Technical School
    05 Bachelors Degree
    06 Masters Degree
    07 Doctorate
    08 Professional - MD, JD, DDS, etc.
    09 Other (Specify: _____)
    77 Don't know
    99 Refused

12. Is your spouse of Spanish, Hispanic or Latino origin or background such as Mexican, Cuban, or Puerto Rican, regardless of race?

01 Yes	77 Don't know
03 No	99 Refused

13. What is the Race of your spouse? (Mark one or more of the following.)

    01 White
    02 Black or African American
    03 American Indian or Alaska Native (Specify tribe_____)
    04 Native Hawaiian or Other Pacific Islander
    05 Asian
    77 Don't know
    99 Refused

ENUM: If no youth under 20, live in the household, (Int 2 Item 4=0), then go to Operation Summary, Page 7, Question 1.

ENUM: Ask the following questions for each person under the age of 20 living in your household. Should match the number reported in Int 2 Item 4.

Now, I would like to ask you some questions about each of the people living in your household who are under the age of 20.

Starting with the oldest child:

A. What is his/her gender?

    01 Male
    02 Female

B. What was (his/her) age on (his/her) last birthday?

    Age: _____

C. How many years of schooling has (he/she) completed?

    Years of Schooling Completed : _____

D. Is (he/she) of Spanish, Hispanic or Latino origin or background such as Mexican, Cuban, or Puerto Rican, regardless of race?

    01 Yes   77 Don't know
    03 No   99 Refused

E. What is (his/her) race? (Mark one or more of the following.)

    01 White
    02 Black or African American
    03 American Indian or Alaska Native (Specify tribe_____)
    04 Native Hawaiian or Other Pacific Islander
    05 Asian
    77 Don't know
    99 Refused

F. Has (he/she) worked on this farm in the last year?

     01 Yes   77 Don't know
     03 No   99 Refused

G. Has (he/she) ridden a horse for work or for recreation in the last year on this farm?

     01 Yes   77 Don't know
     03 No   99 Refused

H. Has (he/she) driven an all-terrain vehicle on this farm, either for work or for recreation in the last year?

     01 Yes   77 Don't know
     03 No   99 Refused

I. Has (he/she) operated a tractor on this farm in the last year?

     01 Yes   77 Don't know
     03 No   99 Refused

J. Has (he/she) been diagnosed as having asthma by a health professional?

     01 Yes   77 Don't know
     03 No   99 Refused

K. Has (he/she) had a serious asthma attack that required an emergency room visit, hospitalization, or other professional medical attention in the last year?

     01 Yes   77 Don't know
     03 No   99 Refused

L. Has (he/she) had an asthma attack requiring the use of an inhaler, or other medical treatment in the last year while doing farm work?

     01 Yes   77 Don't know
     03 No   99 Refused

ENUM: Repeat A through L for each person under the age of 20 living within the household. (Use supplement worksheet for children 2 - 10. Maximum of 10 youth per household).

OPERATION SUMMARY

Next, I have a few questions about your farm or ranch operation.

Considering:
Sales of all crops, livestock, poultry, and livestock products (milk, eggs, etc.) sold in 2000;
The value of product removed for all crops, livestock, and poultry produced under contract in 2000;
Sales of all miscellaneous agricultural products in 2000;
All government agricultural payments received in 2000;
Landlord's share of government payment and crops sold in 2000;

1. Was the Gross Value of Sales and the value of all crops, livestock, and poultry still on hand for this farm or ranch in 2000: (Please check ONLY ONE.)

    01 Less than $1,000
    02 $1,000 or more

2. Of the farm or ranch income reported, which of these categories represents the largest proportion of the gross income from the operation?

    01 Grains and Oil Seeds (Corn, sorghum, small grains, rice, soybeans, dry beans, dry peas, sunflowers, flaxseed, popcorn, grain silage and forage, grains and oil seeds for seed)
    02 Tobacco
    03 Cotton
    04 Vegetables and Melons (Potatoes, sweet potatoes, beets, cabbage, cantaloupes, pumpkins, sweet corn, tomatoes, watermelons, vegetable seed and others)
    05 Fruit, Tree Nuts and Berries (Apples, blueberries, cherries, cranberries, grapes, oranges, kiwi fruit, peaches, pears, strawberries, almonds, hazelnuts, pecans, walnuts and others)
    06 Nursery, Greenhouse and Floriculture (Cut flowers, potted plants, bedding plants, foliage plants, sod, mushrooms, Christmas trees, bulbs, nursery stock, shrubbery, flower seed and others)
    07 Other Crops (Hay, peanuts, sugar beets, sugarcane, mint, hops, grass seed, maple syrup, CRP)
    08 Beef Cattle (Beef cattle for breeding stock, fed cattle, stockers and feeders, veal calves)
    09 Dairy (milk and other dairy products, sales of dairy animals)
    10 Hogs
    11 Sheep, Goats, Wool and Mohair
    12 Equine (Horses, ponies, mules, donkeys, burros)
    13 Poultry and Eggs (Chickens, broilers, eggs, turkeys, ducks, geese, pheasants, poultry products, hatcheries)
    14 Aquaculture (Catfish, trout and other finfish, and shellfish)
    15 Other Animals (Fur-bearing animals, bees, honey, rabbits, and other animal specialties)

3. How many acres are included in this operation?

    01 Less than 101
    02 101-300
    03 301-500
    04 501-700
    05 701-999
    06 More than 1000
    07 Don't know
    09 Refused

4. Is this a full-time operation (A full-time operation is a farm that contributes more than 50% towards family living expenses) or a part-time operation?

      01 Full-time   77 Don't know
      02 Part-time   99 Refused

5. When hiring farm workers, do you require them to have any type of formal training (e.g., tractor or machinery operator certification, pesticide application certification, commercial driver's license?

      01 Yes   77 Don't know
      03 No   99 Refused

6. Do you provide safety training for workers on your farm, excluding, unsupervised on-the-job training (i.e., training on the proper operation of tools, equipment, or machinery; pesticide safety training, training of proper lifting techniques, training on safe work practices?)

      01 Yes (Specify: _____)   77 Don't know
      03 No   99 Refused

7. During 2000, approximately how many people under the age of 20 were hired to work on the farm (excluding youth previously reported in your household, and contract laborers)? Number of workers: _____

Enumerator: If there are no hired workers under the age of 20, the go to Item 15.

8. For each of these workers, please tell me their age, gender, whether or not they are of Spanish, Hispanic, or Latino origin, their race, and whether or not they operated a tractor, an ATV, or rode a horse on the farm or ranch <u>as part of their job</u>. (Maximum of 20 workers)

WORKER:		
Age:	_____	
Gender:	01 Male 03 Female	
Race:	01 White	
	02 Black or African American	
	03 American Indian or Alaska Native	
	04 Native Hawaiian or other Pacific Islander	
	05 Asian	
	77 Don't know	
	99 Refused	
	MARK ONE OR MORE	
Operate a tractor on this farm?	01 Yes	77 Don't know
	03 No	99 Refused
Operate an ATV on this farm?	01 Yes	77 Don't know
	03 No	99 Refused
Rode a horse on this farm?	01 Yes	77 Don't know
	03 No	99 Refused

We've already discussed household youth and youth hired to work on your farm. Next, we'd like to ask you about other visitors to your farm and whether or not they may have helped out with work on the farm.

9. How many relatives under the age of 20 visited the farm during 2000, excluding those reported as hired or part of the household? (If none, skip to 11)
   Number: _____

10. How many of these relatives performed work on your farm during 2000 (either paid or unpaid)?
    Number: _____

11. Excluding hired workers, relatives, or household members, how many other people under the age of 20 visited the farm during 2000, for example, friends of your children?
    Number: _____

YOUTH INJURY SUMMARY

Next, I am going to ask you some questions about any injuries to children or adolescents under the age of 20 that occurred on this farm during 2000.

12. During 2000, did anyone on this farm under the age of 20 experience any injuries which required professional medical attention or required at least 4 hours of restricted activity? These injuries include those resulting from farm work, chores, or recreation on the farm/ranch or in the home.

    01 Yes   77 Don't know (Go to conclusion)
    03 No (Go to conclusion)   99 Refused (Go to conclusion)

13. During 2000, how many injuries occurred on this farm to anyone under the age of 20 which required professional medical attention or required at least 4 hours of restricted activity? These injuries include those resulting from farm work, chores, or recreation on the farm/ranch or in the home.

    Number of injuries during 2000: ____

Now we would like to get some information on each of these injuries, starting with the most recent injury to anyone under the age of twenty. If the same youth had more than one injury during 2000, please provide information on all injury events.

Enumerator Note: If respondent does not want to provide the name of the injured person, please assign a unique identifier (such as "Child A") which will also be used when completing the narrative).

14. Starting with the most recent child/adolescent injury, what is the first name of the injured person?

    Name: _____

15. What was the age of this injured person at the time of the injury?

    Age: _____

16. What is the gender of this person?

    01 Male
    02 Female

259

17. What is the injured person's relationship to farm family?

01 Self
02 Child/Step-Child
03 Spouse
04 Other relative

05 Worker
06 Boarder
10 Other (Specify :_____)
      (E.g. friend, visiting school youth)

18. Is the injured person of Spanish, Hispanic or Latino origin or background such as Mexican, Cuban, or Puerto Rican, regardless of race?

01 Yes
03 No

77 Don't know
99 Refused

19. What is the injured person's Race? (Mark one or more of the following.)

01 White
02 Black or African American
03 American Indian or Alaska Native (Specify tribe_____)
04 Native Hawaiian or Other Pacific Islander
05 Asian
77 Don't know
99 Refused

20. In what month did the injury occur?

01 January
02 February
03 March
04 April
05 May
06 June
07 July
08 August
09 September
10 October
11 November
12 December

Enumerator: If over 16 and the person resides in this household, ask to speak to that person. If injured person is not part of this household, is not available, or is under 16 continue interviewing respondent.

Enumerator: *If you are talking to the youth please put a 1 in the box:*
                    If you are talking to the original respondent put a 2 in the box:

21. Did the injured person live on the farm?

01 Yes (Go to Question 23)
03 No

77 Don't know
99 Refused

22. Was the injured person visiting the farm at the time of the injury?

01 Yes
03 No

77 Don't know
99 Refused

23. Did this injury occur while completing work or doing chores on the farm?

    01 Yes   77 Don't know
    03 No (Go to Question 27)   99 Refused

24. At the time of the injury, how many hours per week did (you/the injured person) typically work on the farm?

    01 0-10
    02 11-20
    03 21-30
    04 31-40
    05 More than 40
    77 Don't know
    99 Refused

25. Was (your/the injured person's) supervisor in the immediate area at the time of the injury?

    01 Yes   77 Don't know
    03 No   99 Refused

26. How much experience did (you/the injured person) have in performing the task being completed at the time of the injury?

    01 None
    02 Less than 4 hours
    03 4 hours to 1 day
    04 More than 1 day to 7 days
    05 More than 1 week to 4 weeks
    06 More than 1 month to 12 months
    07 More than 1 year
    77 Don't know
    99 Refused

27. Where on the farm did the injury occur?

    01 Crop field, orchard, nursery   77 Don't know
    02 Pasture   99 Refused
    03 In the farm yard/barn yard
    04 Grain storage/silo
    05 Farm outbuilding
    06 Barn
    07 Farm roadway
    08 Public roadway
    09 In the home
    10 Garage
    11 House yard
    12 Driveway/sidewalk
    13 Outdoors, general
    14 Other: Specify: _____

28. Now I would like you to describe how the injury occurred. Include where the injury occurred, what tasks were being completed, what equipment was being used or materials being handled, and any other factors you think might be important. **[ENUM: PROBE FOR DETAIL]**

Enumerator Note: If injury resulted in a fatality, you may terminate the interview unless the respondent wishes to continue.

_____
_____
_____
_____
_____
_____
_____

Interviewer Checklist: ___Location (Barn, field, house, etc.) ___Specific Activity ___Equipment & Tools (Powered On/Off, Using/Cleaning) ___Materials Handled (Ag, Chemicals, Fertilizer, etc.)

NIOSH USE ONLY: Source_____ 2nd Source_____Event_____E-code_____

29. What part of the body was injured? (Please check ALL that apply.)

> 01 Head/Skull
> 02 Face
> 03 Neck
> 04 Shoulder/Chest/Back
> 05 Abdomen
> 06 Pelvic Region
> 07 Arm
> 08 Hand/Wrist/Fingers
> 09 Leg
> 10 Foot/Ankle/Toes
> 11 Internal Injuries
> 12 Other: (Specify: _____)
> 77 Don't know
> 99 Refused

30. What type of injury occurred to the _____ (Specify Body Part)? (Please check ALL that apply.)

> 01 Scrape/Abrasion
> 02 Bruise/Contusion
> 03 Sprain/Strain/Torn Ligament
> 04 Broken Bone/Fracture
> 05 Dislocation
> 06 Cut/Laceration
> 07 Puncture/Stab/Jab
> 08 Traumatic Rupture
> 09 Crushed/Mangled
> 10 Loss of Body Part/Amputation
> 11 Nerve Injury
> 12 Burn/Blister/Scald
> 13 Other (Specify: _____)
> 77 Don't know
> 99 Refused

31. How long were/was (your/the injured person's) normal activities restricted as a result of this injury?

       01 No restrictions
       02 Less than one day
       03 1 day to less than 7 days
       04 7 days to less than 14 days
       05 14 days to less than 1 month
       06 1 month to less than 3 months
       07 3 months or more
       77 Don't know
       99 Refused

32. Did the injury result in permanent disability?

       01 Yes   77 Don't know
       03 No   99 Refused

33. How would you rate the overall seriousness of this injury? (Read List)

       01 Minor
       02 Moderate
       03 Serious
       04 Severe
       05 Life-threatening
       06 Fatal (*ENUM: If respondent does not wish to continue, Leave note and terminate interview*)
       77 Don't know
       99 Refused

34. Did this injury require medical attention?

       01 Yes   77 Don't know
       03 No (Go to conclusion)   99 Refused

35. Where did (you/the injured person) initially receive treatment for this injury?

       01 Doctor's office or Clinic
       02 Hospital Emergency Department
       03 Non-emergency Clinic at Hospital
       04 Public Clinic
       05 Dentist
       06 Chiropractor
       07 Urgent Care Center
       08 At the scene
       13 Other (Specify: _____)
       77 Don't know
       99 Refused

36. Did this injury require admission to the hospital?

       01 Yes   77 Don't know (Go to conclusion)
       03 No (Go to conclusion)   99 Refused (Go to conclusion)

37. How long was the hospitalization?

Total Days: _____

CONCLUSION

ENUM: If more than one injury was reported in question 13, return to question 14 to collect information for the next most recent injury event (record information for up to four injury events). If no more injury events, then end with the following:

That is all the questions I have for you today. Thank you very much for your time. We hope this information will help us learn more about how to prevent injuries on farms and ranches.

Appendix C: Definitions Used for the Racial Minority Farm Operator Childhood Agricultural Injury Survey

Asthma

> A positive asthmatic status for a youth that has been diagnosed by a health professional.

Asthma attack at work

> An asthma attack that occurred while doing farm work that required the use of an inhaler, or other medical treatment.

Asthma attack requiring professional medical treatment

> An asthma attack that required an emergency room visit, hospitalization, or other professional medical attention beyond the use of an inhaler.

Farm

> Any operations with $1,000 or more of gross agricultural production within a calendar year, including both crop and livestock operations.

Hired youth

> Youth who were hired directly by the farm operator to work on a farm. These exclude working household youth or contract laborers.

Household youth

> All youth who resided on a farm.

Injury

> Any condition that resulted in 4 hours or more of restricted activity, or a condition that required professional medical treatment.

NASS

> National Agricultural Statistics Service - the primary statistical agency of the U.S. Department of Agriculture.

Non-household youth

> All youth who did not reside on the farm. This is the combination of hired youth, relatives, and non-relative visiting youth.

Non-household working youth

> Youth who worked on the farm, but were not part of the farm household. This is the combination of hired youth and working relatives.

Non-relatives

> Youth who were visiting the farm, but not related to the farm family.

Non-work injury

> Any injury that occurred on the farm that was not due to farm work, even if the injury occurred in a work area of the farm, or where farm work was ongoing.

Other race
Individuals native to or of ancestry from Mexico, the Caribbean, Central America, or South America.

Racial minority
Any person who is Black, Native American, Asian, or who identified themselves as of "Other" race, excluding white.

Relatives
Youth who were visiting the farm and related to the farm family.

Visiting youth
Other youth who were on the farm, but were not household members or hired workers.

Work

Any activity performed by the youth that has a direct impact on the farming operation as a business, regardless of whether the activity is performed for pay. In general, if the activity is such that the farmer would pay an individual to do this task, or would have to do this task themselves as part of the farming business, then the activity is work-related.

Working household youth
Household youth who worked on the farm.

Working relatives
Relatives who did non-paid work on the farm. Relatives who were hired to work on the farm were classified as hired youth.

Work-related injury
Any injury that occurred while performing work for the farm business.

Youth
Any person under the age of 20 years.

Appendix D: Sampling Estimators Used for the Racial Minority Farm Operator Childhood Agricultural Injury Survey

1. Equations to derive the non-benchmarked estimates, y, and variances, $v(y)$, for injury, asthma, or youth for racial minority farms.

$$y = \sum_{g=1}^{9} \sum_{h=1}^{4} \left[\sum_{i=1}^{n_{gh}} \frac{N_{gh}}{n_{gh}} y_{ghi} \right] = \sum_{g=1}^{9} \sum_{h=1}^{4} y_{gh} \tag{D.1}$$

$$v(y) = \sum_{g=1}^{9} \sum_{h=1}^{4} \left[\frac{N_{gh} - n_{gh}}{N_{gh}} \sum_{i=1}^{n_{gh}} \frac{\left(N_{gh} y_{ghi} - y_{gh}\right)^2}{n_{gh}(n_{gh}-1)} \right] = \sum_{g=1}^{9} \sum_{h=1}^{4} v(y_{gh}) \tag{D.2}$$

where:

g = regional strata used in post-stratification;

h = racial strata used in post stratification;

N_{gh} = number of farms of race h in region g from the NASS sampling list;

n_{gh} = number of respondents of race h in region g from the survey;

y_{ghi} = value of the variable of interest (i.e., injury, asthma, youth) on farm i of race h in region g from the survey;

y_{gh} = estimate of variable of interest (i.e., injury, asthma, youth) for race h in region g;

$v(y_{gh})$ = sampling variance for the variable of interest (i.e., injury, asthma, youth) for race h in region g.

2. Equations to derive the benchmarked national estimates, $y_{(bm)}$, and variances, $v(y_{(bm)})$, for injury, asthma, or youth for racial minority farms.

$$y_{(bm)} = \sum_{g=1}^{9} \sum_{h=1}^{4} \left[\frac{N_{(bm)gh}}{N_{gh}} y_{gh} \right] \tag{D.3}$$

$$v(y_{(bm)}) = \sum_{g=1}^{9} \sum_{h=1}^{4} \left[\left(\frac{N_{(bm)gh}}{N_{gh}} \right)^2 v(y_{gh}) \right] \tag{D.4}$$

where non-benchmarked values are as previously defined in D.1 and D.2, and:

$N_{(bm)gh}$ = number of farms of race h in region g from the published 1997 Census of Agriculture.

Note: Summing equations D.3 and D.4 over the four racial strata, h, within a specific region, g, provides the benchmarked estimate for the variable of interest and its corresponding variance for all racial minority farms in region g.

Summing equations D.3 and D.4 over the nine geographic strata, g, for a specific racial group, h, provides the benchmarked national estimate for the variable of interest and its corresponding variance for racial group h.

3. Equations to derive the benchmarked national injury incidence or asthma prevalence rate estimates, R, and variances, $v(R)$, for racial minority farms.

$$R = 1000 \left(\frac{y_{(bm)}}{x_{(bm)}} \right) \tag{D.5}$$

$$v(R) = \frac{1000^2}{n} \left(\frac{1}{\overline{x}_{(bm)}} \right)^2 \left[v(y_{(bm)}) + R^2 v(x_{(bm)}) - 2R \operatorname{cov}(y_{(bm)}, x_{(bm)}) \right] \tag{D.6}$$

where:

$y_{(bm)}$ = benchmarked national estimate for injury or asthma from the survey;

$x_{(bm)}$ = benchmarked national estimate for youth at risk from the survey;

$\overline{x}_{(bm)}$ = benchmarked national average of youth at risk per farm from the survey;

$v(y_{(bm)})$ = benchmarked variance for the national injury or asthma estimate from the survey;

$v(x_{(bm)})$ = benchmarked variance for the national estimate of youth at risk from the survey;

$\operatorname{cov}(y_{(bm)}, x_{(bm)})$ = covariance between the benchmarked injury or asthma estimate and the benchmarked estimate of youth at risk from the survey;

n = the number of farms from the NASS sampling frame used to derive the covariance between $y_{(bm)}$ and $x_{(bm)}$.

Alternatively, the variance for R can be determined by:

$$v(R) = 1000^2 R^2 \left[\left(\frac{\sqrt{v(y_{(bm)})}}{y_{(bm)}} \right)^2 + \left(\frac{\sqrt{v(x_{(bm)})}}{x_{(bm)}} \right)^2 - 2 \left(\frac{\operatorname{cov}(y_{(bm)}, x_{(bm)})}{\overline{y}_{(bm)} \overline{x}_{(bm)} n} \right) \right] \tag{D.6.1}$$

where:

$$\frac{\sqrt{v(y_{(bm)})}}{y_{(bm)}} = \text{relative standard error for } y_{(bm)} \text{ (i.e., injury or asthma);}$$

$$\frac{\sqrt{v(x_{(bm)})}}{x_{(bm)}} = \text{relative standard error for } x_{(bm)} \text{ (i.e., youth at risk);}$$

$$\frac{\text{cov}(y_{(bm)}, x_{(bm)})}{\overline{y}_{(bm)} \overline{x}_{(bm)} n} = \text{relative covariance between } y_{(bm)} \text{ and } x_{(bm)};$$

$\overline{y}_{(bm)}$ = benchmarked national average for injury or asthma per farm from the survey;

n = the number of farms from the NASS sampling frame used to derive the covariance between $y_{(bm)}$ and $x_{(bm)}$.

Because the relative covariance between the estimated number of injury or asthma cases and the number of youth at risk is typically negligible, the estimate $v(R)$ may be approximated as:

$$v(R) = 1000^2 R^2 \left[\left(\frac{\sqrt{v(y_{(bm)})}}{y_{(bm)}} \right)^2 + \left(\frac{\sqrt{v(x_{(bm)})}}{x_{(bm)}} \right)^2 \right] \qquad \text{(D.6.2)}$$

Equation D.6.2 was the method used to derive the standard errors for all rates in this document.